Brigadier General Henry Lewis Benning

BENNING'S BRIGADE

Volume 1

A History and Roster
of the
Fifteenth Georgia

J. David Dameron

HERITAGE BOOKS
2007

HERITAGE BOOKS
AN IMPRINT OF HERITAGE BOOKS, INC.

Books, CDs, and more—Worldwide

For our listing of thousands of titles see our website
at
www.HeritageBooks.com

Published 2007 by
HERITAGE BOOKS, INC.
Publishing Division
100 Railroad Ave. #104
Westminster, Maryland 21157

Copyright © 1997 J. David Dameron

Other books by the author:

Benning's Brigade: Volume 2, A History and Roster of the Second, Seventeenth, and Twentieth Georgia Volunteer Infantry Regiments

General Henry Lewis Benning: "This was a man," A Biography of Georgia's Supreme Court Justice and Confederate General

Women Airforce Service Pilots of World War II: The WASP

All rights reserved. No part of this book may be reproduced or transmitted in any form or by any means, electronic or mechanical, including photocopying, recording or by any information storage and retrieval system without written permission from the author, except for the inclusion of brief quotations in a review.

International Standard Book Number: 978-0-7884-2445-8

To
Harold E. Brown

In Memoriam
February 24, 1932—September 19, 1996

Contents

Acknowledgments ix
Introduction xi

CHAPTER 1 1
From the Heart of Georgia, to the Field of Battle
January 1861—January 1862
(The Fifteenth Georgia is formed)

CHAPTER 2 9
"Move Forward and Feel the Enemy"
February 1862—August 1862
(Yorktown Campaign/Bull Run)

CHAPTER 3 21
Fighting the Enemy at Burnside's Bridge
September 1862
(Maryland Campaign)

CHAPTER 4 31
"The Heroes Are Welcomed with Fair Ladies Waving Handkerchiefs"
September 1862—June 1863
(Fredericksburg/Suffolk Campaign)

CHAPTER 5 41
With Benning's Brigade in the "Devil's Den"
June 1863—August 1863
(Gettysburg Campaign)

CHAPTER 6 55
"I Then Marched upon Them and Attacked Them"
September 1863—October 1863
(Chickamauga/Tennessee Campaign)

CHAPTER 7 69
The Union Lines Were "Rolled Up like a Wet Blanket"
November 1863—June 1864
Tennessee Campaign/Richmond Campaign)

CHAPTER 8 77
"The 15th Georgia Captured 433 Prisoners and Buried 119 Enemy, Up Close to Ft. Gilmer"
June 1864—September 1864
(Siege of Richmond and Petersburg)

CHAPTER 9 87
"O . . . How long must it continue!"
September 1864—April 1865
(The Fall of Richmond and Petersburg/ Appomattox Campaign)

Photos of Unit Members 95

Unit Statistics and Charts 103

APPENDIX A 109
Roster of Parolees at Appomattox, 15th Georgia

APPENDIX B 115
Roster of the 15th Georgia Infantry Regiment

End Notes 185

Bibliography 193

Index 195

Acknowledgments

Numerous people have assisted me in the development of this book and I am indebted for their time, contributions, and encouragement. For me, the best part of exploring the past is meeting, working, and sharing it with the caretakers of our American heritage. From the National Archives in Washington, D.C., to the local county archives of northeast Georgia, I have been assisted by many generous people with professional expertise and a genuine love of the past. I hereby express my sincere appreciation to them all.

I especially enjoyed the hospitable assistance rendered by the staffs of the Virginia Historical Society, the Virginia State Library and Archives, as well as the Museum of the Confederacy, which are all located in Richmond; the United States Military Institute in Carlisle, Pennsylvania; and the United Daughters of the Confederacy, Arlington, Virginia.

I am especially grateful to Dr. Richard Shrader and his archival staff at UNC, Chapel Hill, Wilson Library, for guiding me through the Southern Historical Collection. This tremendous collection contains the notes and manuscripts of E. P. Alexander, the papers of Henry L. Benning, and the diary of Thomas L. Ware, which are literary treasures of the Civil War.

Dorothy Olson of the Georgia State Capitol, Secretary of State's Office, graciously led me to the regimental colors of the Fifteenth Georgia, and she generously provided an official photo of the flag for this book. The Georgia State Capitol Collection contains twenty-seven Confederate battle flags and twenty other military flags of the Civil War period. Georgia's Secretary of State has recently published an informative and splendid full-color book of their collection.

Robert Krick, chief historian of the Richmond National Battlefield Park, provided me with battlefield maps and deep insight into the fighting around Richmond, Virginia. His vast knowledge of the Battles of Fort Gilmer and Fort Harrison were especially helpful in piecing together the actions of Benning's Brigade during their desperate defense of Richmond.

For a genuine, pleasant reminder of southern hospitality, photographs, and a historic tour of the beautiful town of Washington, Georgia, I extend a hearty "Thank ya, ma'am," to Betty Slaton, curator of the Washington

Museum. Washington's artifacts, archives, and architecture provide a wonderful adventure in Georgia's past.

For researching the Hancock County, Georgia, cemeteries for Confederate veterans of the Fifteenth Georgia, and providing other information about Hancock County during the Civil War, I sincerely appreciate the endeavors of Mr. and Mrs. Rick Joslyn.

For providing information and making suggestions I am beholden to Mr. J. W. Hyde of the Elbert County (Georgia) Historical Society and Mr. George M. Rooks, Jr., of the Hart County (Georgia) Historical Society.

For researching photographic archives and providing photos, I extend my appreciation to Gail Miller DeLoach, Photo Archivist, Georgia Department of Archives and History, Atlanta, Georgia; Mary Ellen Brooks, Hargrett Rare Book and Manuscript Library, University of Georgia Library, Athens, Georgia; and Corrine Hudgins, photo curator, Museum of the Confederacy, Richmond, Virginia.

For providing me with a deeper understanding of the human psyche and the methods of waging a war of rebellion, I also thank the staff of the Marquatt Library, John F. Kennedy Special Warfare Center and School, Fort Bragg, North Carolina; Dr. Glenn Sheffield, professor of history, Campbell University, and analyst, First Psychological Operations Group, Fort Bragg, North Carolina, the "Quiet Professionals," officers and NCOs of the Seventh Special Forces Group, Fort Bragg, North Carolina, whom I served with in El Salvador and Colombia (to name a few) on numerous counter-insurgency, trainer and advisory missions in the modern wars of rebellion; and I am especially indebted to Chief Warrant Officer Timothy "Chief" Peters, my friend, brother-in-arms, and mentor. "Lo que sea, Cuando sea, Donde sea."

For their professional expertise and guidance through the myriad procedures of editing and publication, I thank Tom Smith, Monnie Cannon, and all of the staff at the Reprint Company, Publishers, of Spartanburg, South Carolina.

For instilling in me a deep appreciation of history and the pleasure of books, I thank also my parents, Mr. and Mrs. Jerry Dameron. I am forever indebted to my children, Kevin and Christina, for their understanding, genuine inspiration, and humerously candid appraisals of my work. Finally, any written expression inadequately describes the gratitude and affection for my wife, Pamela, whose love, patience, amiable prodding, and gentle criticism keeps me going!

Introduction

On the afternoon of April 2, 1865, as ordered, General Henry Lewis Benning slowly withdrew his men from position to position under a heavy barrage of advancing Union artillery fire. For the last several days, Grant's superior Union forces had finally cracked the Confederate defense line around Petersburg, Virginia. The long siege of Richmond and Petersburg was finally ending. As General Grant began his full-scale assault upon the Southern right flank, Benning's Brigade and the rest of Field's Division were selected to hold the line while the remainder of the Army of Northern Virginia began its retreat to the west.

When the artillery fire ended, General Benning ran to the top of a hill to view the situation. In the distance, Fort Gregg, one of the last Southern bastions, had fallen to the Union, and their massive blue lines of infantry were advancing. Benning returned to his troops and fell back to yet another defensive position as the hail of Union artillery resumed. Meanwhile, General Longstreet himself appeared with reinforcements, which entrenched themselves to the left and right of Benning's position. Upon seeing the reinforced, entrenched line, the advancing Union forces halted. It was now late in the evening, and the Army of Northern Virginia would survive to fight another day. Around midnight, Benning's Brigade stealthily slipped out of its entrenchments and joined the exodus from the field, last in the line of retreat.[1]

During the retreat, Field's Division took turns as the rear-guard (now the front line) as Grant relentlessly pursued Lee's army. Six days later, the Army of Northern Virginia was now in desperate straits. Exhausted, starving, and trapped by Custer's Union cavalry, Lee halted near Appomattox Court House, Virginia. Field's Division of only four thousand men formed its final line of battle facing two corps of Union forces with a combined strength of twenty-four thousand men.

According to General Benning, his brigade was still perfectly organized and not at all demoralized. On April 9, 1865, upon hearing that General Lee had surrendered, the majority of Benning's men wanted to cut through the Union lines and escape. After the war, General Benning wrote that:

"They only waited for the word from me; but I would not give it. On the contrary, I urged them to acquiesce."[2]

General Benning had officially commanded his Georgia Brigade since March 1863, when Brigadier General Robert Toombs resigned his commission; however, since August 1862, Benning had commanded the brigade, because of the absence of Toombs prior to the Battle of Second Manassas, and during the Battle of Sharpsburg because Toombs had assumed command of their Division. Toombs was then wounded, furloughed, and upon his return to the brigade, he resigned.[3] Toombs had been a good commander, but because of old political rivalries and frequent outspoken conflicts with the Confederate heirarchy, he reluctantly chose to return to Georgia.

Under General Toombs, the brigade had fared well and honorably under fire, especially during the Battle of Second Manassas. Under the direction of Colonel Benning, Toombs's brigade charged the Union line on Henry Hill with a massive rebel yell. Their punishing frontal assault cracked the Union left wing, which retreated the next day. Again, at the Battle of Sharpsburg, Benning in conjunction with Toombs not only held the Confederate right wing at "Burnside's Bridge" but flanked the attacking Union corps with a counter-charge. Assisted by troops of General A.P. Hill, they managed to push the Union troops back across the river, thus saving the day.[4]

After Toombs resigned and Benning officially took command of the brigade, they earned a reputation similar to their sister unit, the gallant "Texas Brigade." As a member of Lee's Army of Northern Virginia, assigned to Longstreet's First Corps, and Hood's Division, General Benning led his men and the intermingled members of the "Texas Brigade" into the "Devil's Den" during the Battle of Gettysburg. Benning was the only Southern commander to break through the Union lines at Gettysburg, capturing Union forces and several pieces of artillery. (Perhaps the only artillery captured on Union soil.) Furthermore, he held this terrain until ordered to retreat the following day. When Longstreet's Corps was dispatched to join General Bragg in the western theater, Benning's Brigade again engaged in a frontal assault which not only helped to sever the Union line but sent it running in a mad retreat. During the Battle of Chickamauga, Benning's Brigade captured the Eighth Indiana Battery along with "eight beautiful Napoleon guns."[5]

Benning's Brigade distinguished itself throughout the war, but as the strength of the Confederacy slowly declined, the level of misery and deprivations escalated. During the winter of 1863-64, Longstreet's Corps was isolated in east Tennessee. Many of the Georgians walked barefoot across the frozen soil until they were able to cut and sew rawhide with which to cover their bloodied feet. Upon rejoining General Lee in the spring, they again distinguished themselves with a frontal assault during the Battle of the Wilderness. At the Wilderness, Benning was severely wounded and Colonel Dudley M. DuBose of the Fifteenth Georgia Regiment commanded the brigade.[6]

From then until the end of the war in April 1865, Benning's Brigade and the rest of the Army of Northern Virginia were engaged in a continuous defense of their capital and its environs.

During this time the brigade gained an enviable reputation and took the affectionate and proud nickname of their commander General "Rock" Benning—thus they were often referred to as Benning's "Rock" Brigade. In September 1865, Colonel DuBose led Benning's Brigade in a dramatic defense of Richmond as it was attacked by several Union corps in a massive assault directed by General Grant. DuBose and his Fifteenth Georgia Regiment were credited with the capture of 433 prisoners and 119 enemy killed in action.[7] Even though General Gregg gave the glory to the Fifteenth Georgia, they would not have survived the ordeal without the assistance of her sister units, the Second, Seventeenth and Twentieth regiments. As usual, the valiant "Texas Brigade" was also there.[8]

Benning's Brigade was comprised of an interesting array of strong, dedicated southern warriors. The brigade's composition consisted primarily of farmers who voluntarily served the Confederacy as foot soldiers, and elected officers who were highly respected members of the community. Many of the officers were formerly lawyers and politicians. For example, Robert Toombs had served the state of Georgia as a congressman, a senator, and, for a brief period, the Confederate secretary of state. Henry Benning had served Georgia as an associate justice of the state supreme court. They were men that honored pride, determination, tradition, chivalry, and independence. But, these same virtues coupled with a dogmatic spirit and fervent emotions, trapped them in a torrent of violent events which quickly raged beyond their control. These men represented the life blood of Georgia and they were determined to defend her sovereignty.

Benning's Brigade is a shining example of the stalwart Confederate Army of Northern Virginia. As an integral member of General Robert E. Lee's forces, the experiences of the brigade reflect those of many men. J.B. Polley's "Hood's Texas Brigade" provides a valuable first hand account of the civil war as experienced by the Confederate army, however, an individual's state of origin was a key factor in morale. Several variables greatly affected the fighting spirit of both Georgians and Texans, but in different ways. Primarily, the Texans' social and geographic conditions best illustrate this point. Most of the Texans spent the entire four years of the war painfully separated from their families. Consequently, they were highly motivated warriors with a Spartan spirit; however, their geographic distance from home also provided them with some peace of mind. The Texans never faced the terror of General Sherman's murderous destruction of their home state. Sherman once said that war is "all hell," and he certainly delivered it to Georgia. The mental anguish endured by the Georgian soldiers during the winter of 1864-65 is painfully evident in their letters and journals. It is within their personal thoughts and emotions, and expressed in their own words, that events and human drama transcend the barriers of time. The reader of these personal narratives gains an appreciation of the writer's experiences and a tremendous insight into history.

Benning's Brigade is a history and roster of the individual regiments which comprised the unit. The purpose of the book is twofold. First and primarily, the book is intended to accurately reflect the composition, strength, and disposition of the brigade, chronologically, throughout the civil war, from its inception to its ultimate demobilization. Secondly, the narrative is filled with excerpts from diaries, journals, correspondence, and reports from the officers and men that wrote them. These personal reflections are intended to provide the reader with an intimate and uniquely southern perspective of the American Civil War. From a historical view, it is important to note that civil wars are the ugliest and bloodiest forms of warfare. By nature, racial and ethnic hatred brings forth in man a demonic ability to wage incomprehensible violence. Militarily, an infantryman's job is to close with and destroy his enemy. Benning's Brigade was dedicated, reliable, and efficient in its performance of duty. A detailed analysis of the brigade at the regimental and company level provides the most accurate graphic and historical representation.

Benning's Brigade: Volume 1, A History and Roster of the Fifteenth Georgia, highlights a regiment of volunteer Confederate soldiers from the pastoral farmlands of northeast Georgia. Their chronicle begins in a beautiful region filled with small ante-bellum towns. For example, the picturesque town of Washington is the home of Robert Toombs and Dudley DuBose. Their stately, pillared mansions stand today, representatives of a bygone era. Nearby is the city of Athens. This progressive communications hub is also the home of the University of Georgia, then Franklin College. Most of the prominent men of Georgia were graduates of this school, including Henry L. Benning. The regiment's first commander was the renowned judge, Thomas W. Thomas, and his deputy commander, Linton Stephens, was the half brother of Vice President (C.S.A.) Alexander Stephens. As illustrated, when the regiment was initially formed there were plenty of politicians to go around; however, once the reality of war set in, the politicians disappeared and the real leaders emerged. Tragically, a series of brave commanders died while leading the regiment in frontal assaults, which provided Colonel Dudley DuBose the opportunity to command. In spite of being the son-in-law of General Robert Toombs, DuBose survived and excelled as a gallant leader of the "Fighting Fifteenth." When General Benning was wounded at the Battle of the Wilderness, Colonel DuBose took charge, and successfully led the "Rock" Brigade through the next several months as the Union army pressed closer towards Richmond. DuBose's ability to command was noted with a promotion to the rank of Brigadier General. Yet, the real heroes of the regiment are the common foot soldiers. It is their endurance, personal sacrifice, accomplishments, and fighting spirit that won battles and brought respect to the term "rebel."

The roster of the regiment highlights each soldier individually. The list was compiled from the Official Records of the National Archives. These files contain Union and Confederate documents concerning individual personnel data, such as: rank; promotions; prisoner/exchange data (if captured); wounds or disabilities (hospitilization data); and either their cause of death and burial data; or parole information. In several cases, physical features are provided: height; color of eyes; hair; and complexion, as well as their next of kin. These files were then placed in an electronic data base, from which statistics were extracted and charts created. The result is an accurate and graphic depiction of the "Fifteenth Georgia." Their story is one of courage and dogged determination amidst a life of violence and misery. More than half of the regiment did not survive the war; however, their legacy survived and they are forever an integral part of our American heritage.

Battle Flag of the Fifteenth Georgia ("Office of Secretary of State, Georgia State Capitol")

CHAPTER

1

FROM THE HEART OF GEORGIA, TO THE FIELD OF BATTLE

The State of Georgia joined her sister states in secession on January 19, 1861. Preparations for the defense of her sovereignty were immediately initiated. Commands were organized and Georgians eagerly answered her call to arms. Within one week of secession the federal arsenal in Augusta, Fort Jackson, and the Oglethorpe Barracks in Savannah were all seized by state troops. In February the Confederate States of America was formed and Georgia was requested to provide troops. In April the First Volunteer Regiment was organized and placed into service at Pensacola, Florida. As the pace of national events increased, so did the call for more troops. With great passion, men voluntarily enlisted in anticipation of war. Regiments were hurriedly organized lest they miss the impending fray. On April 12, 1861, the South initiated hostilities at Fort Sumter, South Carolina, and the Civil War began.

The Fifteenth Regiment, Georgia Volunteer Infantry, was comprised of ten separate companies which were organized in seven northeast counties on the thirteenth, fourteenth, and fifteenth of July 1861.[1] The Regiment was formed in the following manner: Company A, Wilkes County; Company B, Franklin County; Company C, Elbert County; Company D, Taliaferro County; Company E, Hancock County; Company F, Elbert County; Company G, Lincoln County; Company H, Hart County; Company I, Elbert County; Company K, Hancock County.[2]

These companies were formed from the heart of Georgia and the men in them were all firm believers in the southern cause and the sovereignty of states' rights. Several prominent Georgians would later command this unit, including Dudley M. DuBose, Henry L. Benning, and Robert Toombs.[3]

All the companies made their way to Atlanta, where they pitched tents and encamped. On July 17, the regimental command and staff officers were elected by popular vote. The first officers were: regimental commander, Colonel Thomas W. Thomas; deputy commander, Lt. Col. Linton Stephens; Major William M. Mcintosh; chaplain, Atticus G. Haygood; surgeon, E.

1

W. Alfriend; adjutant, B. H. Lofton. The first company commanders were Captains Drury B. Cade (A), William T. Millican (B), Luther H. Martin (C), Sylvester J. Farmer (D), Theophilus J. Smith (E), John C. Burch (F), LaFayette Lamar (G), William R. Pool (H), Joseph T. Smith (I), and Thomas H. Latimer (K).[4]

With all the excitement and adventure of conquest and glory, several families accompanied the young soldiers to Atlanta. The sights and sounds of an emerging military machine coupled with the impending action of battle provided entertainment on a grand scale. Georgia was proudly eager to send her sons to defend her honor. All too soon, they said their farewells, and the soldiers were on their way. They were certainly on a rendezvous with an unknown destiny. The general mood was one of optimism and the assumption that the Yankees would be beaten in short order. The men would surely be gone for only a few months!

On July 20 the regiment was issued arms and equipment, packed up, and loaded in the trains. They were being deployed to join General Beauregard and the Confederate Army, which were now poised in an ominous stillness near Manassas, Virginia. President Davis had dispatched them as a response to Beauregard's urgent request for more troops.

Several men in the regiment recorded the events of their first adventure as soldiers—Privates Samuel H. Wiley of Company E and Thomas L. Ware of Company G. Their observations reflect not only factual data concerning their journey, but also their feelings and personal responses to the events as they occurred. They both recorded the dates and times of their journey, the route taken, and most importantly, the conditions. Although it was summer, rain was their constant companion throughout the first few days of their long and arduous journey.

The weather had a tremendous impact upon the daily lives of the common foot soldiers. For the men of the Fifteenth Georgia, it became the first lesson of their training. As civilians, the men were used to exercising their own free will. For example, riding in an alternate car might be more comfortable than the one to which you were assigned; however, as soldiers, they were required to sit where they were told. The privilege of decision making would no longer be afforded them. Although riding a train was certainly more comfortable than marching, the rain put an effective damper on their travel. The trains followed the line northwest through Dalton, Georgia, and entered Tennessee, passing through Chattanooga and stopping in Knoxville. At Knoxville the men got a badly needed rest from their cramped train cars. Many of the men slept in town, at boarding houses or hotels. Via telegraph, the news arrived that the Confederacy had driven the Yankees from the battlefield at Manassas, Virginia. It was a glorious victory for the South. For the Fifteenth Georgia, it was another day back on the trains, with continued rainfall. Ware recorded in his diary:

> Raining this morning. Everything is damp. 8:00 A.M., still raining, all on board and away we go. All are glad to leave the place. Very poorly fixed in the cars, raining in on us. Arrived at Morris Creek Station at 11:00 A.M. Here the road was washed up and delayed us *8 hours*. Still raining, all wet. While repairing the road, we have taken possession of a house. Soon had a hot fire and all are well dried. We left at 5:00 P.M. and traveled all night in a car filled with water and mud, arrived at Greenville, Tenn. at sunrise.

They traveled on to Morristown and arrived about 10:30 P.M. at Bristol, on the border of Virginia and Tennessee, where the troops got another reprieve from the trains. The men were tightly packed within the railcars, however; the nervous excitement of the adventure somewhat quelled their discomfort. Ironically, the fortunate survivors of their early campaigns would return to East Tennessee, where they would spend an agonizing winter similar to Washington's at Valley Forge. The trains departed at 07:00 A.M. heading northeast, traveling through the beautiful Shenandoah Valley. This was Virginia's bread basket and soon to be the sight of numerous battles.

While traveling en route to join their command, they stopped on July 27 in Charlottesville, where the Fifteenth Regiment was dismayed at the sight of the wounded and dying soldiers that had been brought to the University from the battlefield in Manassas. They boarded the trains for the final leg of the journey and arrived at Manassas Gap early on Sunday morning, the twenty-eighth. Here they disembarked, unloaded their cargo, carried it several hundred yards, and began putting up camp. All too soon they were feeling the ill effects of life as a soldier. Hungry, dirty, and tired, they began their newly chosen lifestyles.

On August 2, 1861, the men of the Fifteenth Regiment were officially mustered into Confederate service. The regiment was assigned to "Toombs Brigade," D. R. Jones Division, Army of the Potomac (CSA). This brigade was formed by the Fifteenth, Seventeenth, Second, First, and Twentieth Georgia regiments. Although several companies were unhappy being led by Colonel Thomas, the men settled into a very confident unit. They eagerly anticipated the excitement of combat and the opportunity to express their manhood upon the field of battle.[5]

The regiment remained in several temporary camps throughout the fall of 1861, near Centreville and Manassas, drilling by day and performing picket duty at night. In August they cleared their first drilling ground and named their campsite Camp Walker.

In September they were moved to an area near Fairfax Courthouse, Virginia. The soldiers dubbed this location Camp Pine Creek. It was here that Private Ware recorded: "Here I saw several nice young ladies, the first I have seen in four months." Although he often misspelled words and abbreviated sentences, he had a writer's flair for conveying emotion.

Thomas had been born on September 9, 1838, and so in the fall of 1861 he was twenty-three years old, healthy, single, a Methodist, and a proud son of the South. He was one of the many young men swept up by the call to arms, the fervent emotions of manhood, and the zealous desire to set things right.[6]

Thomas had a younger brother, Robert Ware, who had joined the southern cause also. So together, brothers, cousins, fathers, uncles, nephews, and friends formed the Fifteenth Georgia. Mostly poor farmers from the counties of northeast Georgia, they were now slowly being transformed into soldiers. Anxious for the experience of combat and the opportunity to prove themselves, they were hit hard by the drudgery of camp life and picket duty. They discovered that the opposite pole of the fevered pitch of battle was sheer boredom. Several of the higher ranking officers could afford to send for their wives to be near them. This was another luxury the common foot soldier could not enjoy. For many men, the lifestyle of a soldier was becoming increasingly distasteful. On October 7, 1861, Ware recorded in his diary the events of a typical evening. Just like the warriors of today, "They sat up late at night, around the campfire, reflecting about their loved ones and incidents back home." When they weren't writing or reflecting about home, they were either on guard duty or drilling in camp. In E Company, Private Sam Wiley and his cousin, W. Edgeworth Bird, a first lieutenant, were busy writing to their loved ones. Their letters reflected the same sadness of separation and longing for home as was expressed in Ware's diary. Additionally, Lieutenant. Bird mentioned the many soldiers who had been suffering from illness and the numerous deaths caused by these diseases.[7]

As winter approached during November and December, men continued to succumb to the ever-present and mysterious ailment known to soldiers as camp fever—both the physical illness and the longing for home. Due to the nasty, cramped, damp, and cold living conditions, coupled with the widespread potential for the spread of germs, the men of the Fifteenth Regiment met their first enemy, disease. It proved to be their deadliest foe. With illness always present and with inadequate health care, numerous men had to be transported to the typhoid hospitals in Richmond for care. Many, never returned. From 1861 to 1865 the Fifteenth Georgia lost approximately 225 men to disease, chiefly pneumonia and typhoid.[8]

Smallpox and the measles were ever present as well. Also, during this time, the weak and older men faced the reality of their advanced ages and inability to perform the duties required of a soldier. More than 300 men resigned, were discharged, or were relieved of duty because of disabilities.[9]

In January 1862 the men of the Fifteenth completed their permanent winter quarters, made of tent material, logs, lumber, mud, and stone. This place was named Camp Georgia, and it was located in the vicinity of their first campsite, near Manassas.[10] Very gleefully, the soldiers occupied their new lodgings. Once again they concentrated on survival, wrote letters to their loved ones, carried out their duties, honed their new skills, and contemplated their future in the military. Although life seemed harsh to them, they at least had good uniforms, shoes, pay, and provisions. All too rapidly these items would soon become articles of luxury.[11]

Meanwhile, both the North and South concentrated their efforts on beefing up their armies in anticipation of the coming spring. Strategy, contingencies, and recruitment were the orders of the day. In the North, General McClellan replaced General Scott, while in the South, Jefferson Davis was officially elected to a six-year term as president. The men of the Fifteenth Georgia thought of home, gathered firewood, and stayed warm. Unbeknown to these future southern warriors, they would see plenty of action all too soon. Most of them would never see home again and would fall on the battlefields of Garnett's Farm, Malvern Hill, Thoroughfare Gap, Manassas, Sharpsburg, Fredericksburg, Gettysburg, Chickamauga, Lookout Valley, Knoxville, Wilderness, Spotsylvania, Hanover Junction, Cold Harbor, New Market Heights, Fort Gilmer, Richmond, Petersburg, or Farmville. Only the fortunate ones would survive the pestilence of disease, the pain of separation from home, the agony of nearly six thousand miles of travel, and the inexplicable horrors of war. Four long years of hardship lay ahead.

When the regiment was initially formed, on July 17, 1861, it consisted of approximately 1,074 officers and men; however, by April 9, 1865, the Fifteenth Regiment would be comprised of only 258 members present in the field.[12]

Battle sword of Robert Toombs
(from Toombso House, Washington, Georgia, state museum)

1865

January "Sunday" 1st. We are gratified for yesterday's triumph of man. The time being no familiar to the citizens. Our camp stirs for news. Elijah of Thomas Co. of Va. came to see us. He came on furlough yest. All last at our old triumphant quarters. To sleep on the prairie ground - a pleasant day since I wrote the other. Yesterday I went to get logs to any. I saw Sal treating a lot of young Jennie Thornt. All find cheers on hands. Everything transpiring to make us think that I am

1865

January "Monday" 2nd. Warlike 3 Loan of Warlike legs. All airmen, Coff. I show. Clarbea scattered around. Furnished all to our city. Finished taking off 2 rooms. or commenced the 3 & 4th Col. around his happy home. This house is not crowded by us. We are doing but little —

Cota & Clancy.

Jan. 3rd Tuesday —
Myself, Capt. Lanter Enloe & Oakes, Sergt. Sal & Gulan, & Elja & Haines had a large egg nog at our breakfast. All gratified.

CHAPTER
2
"Move Forward, and Feel the Enemy!"

On March 8, 1862, as the winter slowly surrendered to spring, the men of the Fifteenth Georgia gave up their winter quarters. They packed up their meager belongings and began the first of many foot marches behind the flag of the Confederacy. The army moved slowly south by way of the Rappahannock River to Orange Court House in a giant ribbon of men and wagons eighteen miles long. On April 11 the Fifteenth loaded on trains and rode the rails to Richmond. The Union forces under General McClellan had begun the Peninsula Campaign by moving twelve divisions of the Army of the Potomac (U.S.) via boats to Virginia. After winning naval control over the Confederacy and maintaining a portion of the Tidewater region of Virginia, the Union was free to threaten Richmond from the east.[1]

On April 13 the Fifteenth Georgia was shuttled down the Peninsula towards Yorktown on the steamship ferry "West Point." They disembarked and marched past the Lebanon Church en route to their section of the defensive line near Dam No. 1 in the entrenchments defending Yorktown from the marauding and overwhelming Union forces. The Army of the Potomac (C.S.A.) under Gen. Joseph Johnston established an eight-mile-long line of defense near Yorktown, as the massive Union Army laid siege to it. The Fifteenth Regiment, as a member of "Toombs Brigade," was assigned the task of occupying a section of the trench line.

Their sector was two miles below the city of Yorktown within six hundred yards of the enemy line. The unit was required to occupy these positions for a twenty-four-hour period every other day. They were relieved by their sister brigades and then moved several hundred yards behind the line for rest and recuperation. The regiment had settled into a routine schedule, after several weeks of alternating turns in the trenches. Occasionally there were artillery duels and some sporadic sniper fire. The trenches were very muddy and the men dreaded their turn in them. As McClellan's forces increased in strength, so did their fire.[2]

On April 20, 1862, Private Ware wrote:

> Sun rose quite clear this morning. All were very hungry but our rations have not yet come. All are very hungry. We lie in the pit all day in the water and mud, but the sun shone part the day, in the evening it again rained, the firing of the pickets continued all day, we had none wounded. A few of our company had the chance to try their guns at the enemy, the balls would *whiz* occasionally over our heads. We lie in the pit all day, and at *Eve* our breakfast, dinner and supper came. We were very hungry. Each one drew his piece of bread and meat, though quite fat some still relished it well, and a few crackers to the man. It put me in mind of negroes as all the meat and bread were cut up and put in a pan and brought to us, and so eager were we for it we crowded around the pan like negroes. (*War* is a rough life but healthy to some.)

The stage was now set and the inevitable first battle casualty for the Fifteenth Georgia occurred. Pvt. Jonathan B. Cone of Company E carelessly exposed himself to the Union sharpshooters, who immediately provided Cone with a mortal wound. A well-aimed large-caliber bullet ripped through his chest, lacerating his left lung. In disbelief, his comrades hauled his body out of the trenches and evacuated him to Richmond, where he died an agonizingly painful death. Meanwhile, the following day a cannon round exploded above the trench line in Company E's sector. This resulted in severe shrapnel wounds for three members of the company. The Fifteenth Regiment was in actuality quite lucky, as casualties were higher in several of their sister units. Shortly after these incidents the Confederates evacuated the defense line at Yorktown.

The total Confederate forces numbered fewer than twenty thousand in front of Yorktown, while the Union forces employed more than one hundred thousand. With such overwhelming force opposing them, the Confederates wisely fell back towards Richmond. The Union forces immediately occupied Yorktown and shipped in even more troops. Norfolk, Portsmouth, and Suffolk were soon lost to the Union. Slowly the Union forces began their move towards Richmond, setting the stage for the first major engagement of 1862.

Having evacuated their portion of the defense works on the third of May, the Fifteenth Georgia marched down the Williamsburg Road toward Richmond. The Union forces pursued the retreating Confederates and fought them again at Williamsburg and West Point, Virginia.[3] Here, on May 7,

Private Ware was astounded at the enormity of the conflict. He recorded in his diary the sight of "*30,000* in lines as far as the eye could see was soldiers and could see the glistening of bayonets." The men faced sharpened steel, with its sole purpose being the laceration of the southern cause. The spring rains muddied the roads. The retreating march and rear-guard battle were very hard on the men, but the regiment finally arrived just outside of Richmond on the seventeenth. The unit changed positions several times, along with the rest of the Confederate forces, as the massive Yankee hoard inched ever closer towards their beloved capital city. The Confederate units were being manipulated back and forth in an elaborate game of defensive strategy in order to protect their threatened capital.[4]

On May 25, 1862, the regiment observed a Union reconnaissance balloon. General Toombs, their brigade commander, commented that "the Yankees were afraid to show themselves." The forced march from Yorktown to Richmond caused the deaths of several of the elderly soldiers, and on May 30 the eldest soldiers were discharged to avoid future occurrences. In an attempt to maintain the Union forces' distance from the capital, the Confederates lashed out at the Union forces at the Battle of Seven Pines/ Fair Oaks. This action accomplished very little and General Johnston was wounded.

President Davis named General Robert E. Lee as commander of the Army of Northern Virginia. On June 1 the Fifteenth Georgia was ordered to the vicinity of the Battle of Seven Pines, but arrived too late to take part in the action. On June 9 the regiment took up picket duty on the defensive line by a little house owned by a farmer named James Garnett. The farm was described by Pvt. Thomas Ware as a "nice house with orchards and a garden." While the unit was on picket duty near the Garnett house, seventeen-year-old Pvt. W.T. Fluker of Company D wrote of an unfortunate incident that occurred there.[5] His comrade, Pvt. John McClesky, accidentally discharged his musket and killed his mess-mate, Pvt. Jesse M. Hackney. Overcome with grief McClesky pleaded with Colonel McIntosh to have him shot. Naturally the Colonel refused his request. Ironically, one week later at the Battle of Garnett's Farm, on June 27, 1862, Private McClesky was killed by the enemy within several yards of the place where he had shot his friend. Fluker described McCleskey as a typical Irishman with a very jolly nature, full of Irish song and wit. No one ever saw him smile after the accident. When McClesky was killed, he fell on top of Private Fluker and never spoke again. Lt. John Tilley pulled Hackney off Fluker and was himself killed by the enemy while doing so.[6]

Meanwhile, Gen. Thomas (Stonewall) Jackson arrived from the Shenandoah Valley with his unit and greatly reinforced the Confederate Army. The Confederate Cavalry, led by J.E.B. Stuart, accomplished a daring reconnaissance, riding completely around McClellan's forces. This intimidating and bold maneuver provided Lee with valuable information and a much-needed boost to the troops' morale. In order to end the threat to Richmond, Lee initiated the Seven Days Campaign on June 25. The South succeeded in breaking through the Union lines at Oak Grove and Gaines Mill. On June 27 the Fifteenth Georgia eagerly responded to an order to move forward and "feel the enemy."[7] The regimental commander, Col. Thomas W. Thomas, had found army life too difficult to endure. He had resigned on March 29, 1862. The men of the Fifteenth then elected Col. William M. McIntosh to the post and Lt. Col. William T. Millican of Company B as his deputy. Therefore, the duty of writing the unit's official report upon completion of the Seven Days Campaign fell upon the latter. Colonel Millican wrote:

> SIR: I have the honor to submit through you to the Brigadier General Commanding, the following official report of the operations of this regiment in the recent actions before Richmond: On 26 June the regiment (Col. William M. McIntosh in command), by order of Brigadier General Toombs, occupied the entrenchments on the north side of the Nine-mile road, near Price's house and remained in that position until 6 p.m. of June 27, when, by order of General Toombs, the regiment moved to the front near three-quarters of a mile; took position at the edge of a field some 200 yards to the left of a brick house, known as James Garnett's house; sent two companies, (Captain John C. Burch, Company F, and Captain Stephen Z. Hearnsberger, Company G) as skirmishers to support the pickets of the 2nd Georgia and feel the enemy. In a few minutes the firing on both sides became brisk. Soon the enemy's line was re-enforced, and General Toombs ordered Col. McIntosh with the balance of this command to the support of the skirmishers. We crossed the field at double-quick under a most galling fire from the opposite side of a deep ravine, just beyond which our skirmishers were engaged; crossed the ravine by the right flank and formed line of battle and moved rapidly to the front. The engagement now became general and intensely fierce all along the line and raged till after dark, when the enemy retired and the firing ceased.

Colonel McIntosh, who was at the front and on the most exposed part of the line, gallantly cheering the men on, fell mortally wounded early in the engagement and was borne from the field. The command then devolved upon me as Lt. Col., and after the dead and wounded (a detailed list of which has already been furnished) were carried from the field. The regiment, by order of General Toombs, retired to the rear and rested till daylight on the morning of the 28th, and then moved back to the same point where the previous evening's engagement had taken place, to the support of the Seventh and Eight Georgia Regiments.

The engagement ended with but few casualties in this regiment, which have already been reported in the list of casualties furnished. We bivouacked on the field, and at 3 a.m., June 29, by order of General Toombs, formed line of battle with the entire brigade, and at an early hour entered the enemy's works without much resistance, and moved with the brigade in pursuit of the retreating foe until a late hour at night; bivouacked in the open air.

Early next morning, June 30, took up the line of march and reached the battlefield at Frazier's farm about 11p.m. and remained on the field until dawn, July 1; then advanced in line of battle, Captain George A. Pace's company (B) being thrown forward as skirmishers. The advance continued until after 12 p.m. when I became completely exhausted from fatigue, loss of sleep, and physical weakness, having been in feeble health for several weeks, and was compelled to leave the command of the regiment for a short time to Major T. J. Smith, who was also very feeble from illness, who led the regiment into the engagement at Malvern Hill. He soon became exhausted and was borne from the field. Captain Stephen S. Z. Hearnsberger, the senior captain, assumed the command till the close of the engagement. The list of casualties during this engagement has also been furnished.[8]

> Respectfully, submitted,
> W. T. Millican,
> Colonel Fifteenth Regiment Georgia Volunteers

The following list depicts the casualties suffered by the Fifteenth Georgia during the Peninsula Campaign:

Killed	Wounded	Captured
29	45	1

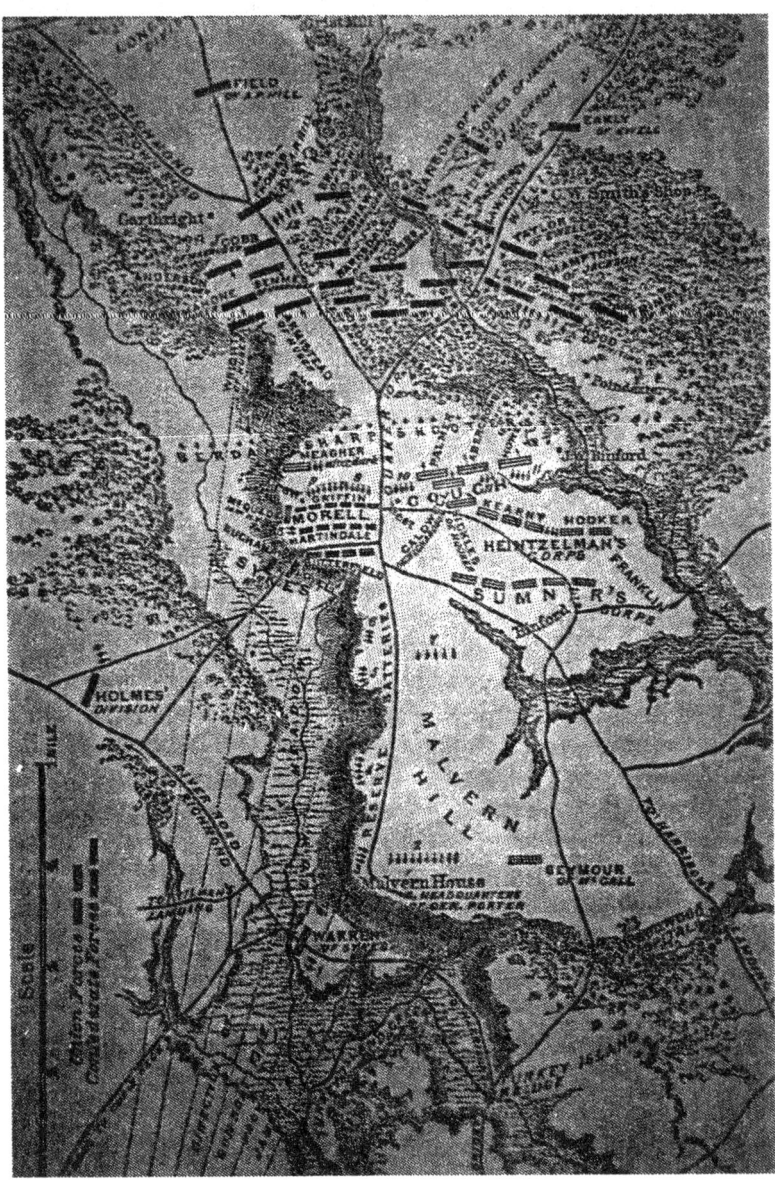

Battle of Malvern Hill (Official Record Atlas, Library of Congress)

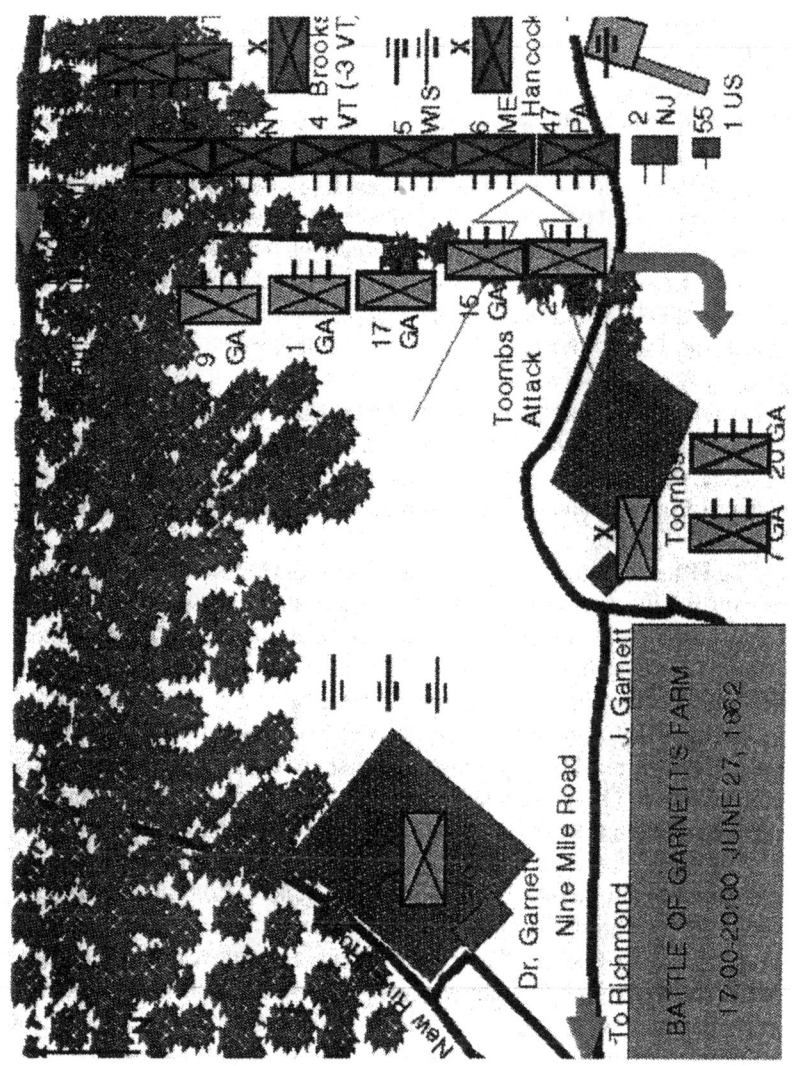

The fighting during the Peninsula Campaign bolstered the morale of the southern populace, but the troops had now experienced the combat that they had so eagerly anticipated. After the battle of Frazier's Farm and Malvern Hill, on the thirtieth of June and the first of July, Private Ware and his fellow Georgians received the gruesome task of collecting the dead for burial. Although their unit had suffered casualties, they had luckily charged Malvern Hill behind several other Confederate units. The frontal ranks absorbed the bulk of the affects of the deadly direct, point-blank artillery fire.

As the Confederate troops charged the Union positions they were literally cut into chunks of human flesh and blasted upon their comrades behind them. Private Ware and his fellow Georgians were repulsed at the grisly duty of collecting and disposing of the remains of their comrades.[9]

In numbers the losses of the Army of Northern Virginia exceeded twenty thousand casualties. The Union forces suffered nearly sixteen thousand; however, the overwhelming Yankee forces were successfully driven a safer distance from Richmond. The Union Army emplaced its headquarters at Harrison's Landing.

The Fifteenth Georgia and the rest of her brigade were now, and would remain for the duration of the war, a subordinate element of General Longstreet's corps. General Lee, with his newly named and restructured Army of Northern Virginia, now set forth on an offensive campaign. It was designed to carry the war north and threaten the enemy's capital.

In August 1862 the Army of Northern Virginia began its Maryland campaign. Jackson and his corps moved out first and engaged the Union forces at the Battle of Cedar Mountain. On August 13 the Fifteenth Georgia, as a member of Longstreet's Corps, moved by rail to Gordonsville, Virginia.[10]

The Army of Northern Virginia halted just south of the Rapidan River, and here an unfortunate incident occurred. General Longstreet issued an order for the Toombs Brigade to post pickets and guard Racoon Ford, a crossing on the Rapidan River. This order was immediately carried out. While this took place, Toombs was away visiting a close friend. Longstreet described him as "an old Congressional friend." Upon his return to camp he discovered that several of his regiments had been dispatched on picket duty on orders from someone other than himself. Infuriated, Toombs impulsively countermanded the order and the pickets were withdrawn. This was a tremendous mistake on Toombs's part. That night the Union cavalry crossed the Rapidan and raided General J.E.B. Stuart's cavalry, capturing important documents and nearly General Stuart himself. Because of his impetuous and insubordinate behavior, Longstreet had Toombs arrested.

The command of the Toombs Brigade then devolved upon Col. Henry L. Benning, the commander of the Seventeenth Georgia.[11]

The regiment then marched north, crossing the Rapidan River on the eighteenth and the Rappahannock River on the twenty-sixth. Longstreet's Corps continued behind Jackson's Corps, turning right to the east, and entered Thoroughfare Gap. This location was a frequently used natural passage in the Bull Run Mountains. These mountains are a beautiful part of the Blue Ridge chain near Manassas, Virginia.[12]

Thoroughfare Gap was reached by the Fifteenth Regiment about 4:00 P.M. on the afternoon of the twenty-eighth, after a very exhausting march. As Longstreet's Corps passed through the gap, it was attacked by Federal troops of General Rickett's Division of General Pope's Army of Virginia (U.S.). This unit was responsible for defending the area west of Manassas.

Just as the Fifteenth and Seventeenth regiments passed through the gap, following the Manassas rail line to the east, they were ambushed from both sides of the gap. The two regiments immediately sought cover and concealment. Then they returned fire on the enemy. Benning's Brigade was ordered to charge up the high ground on their right, Pond Mountain, and flank the Yankees. Benning dispatched two regiments who quickly scaled the heights and drove back the Union forces. At the same time, Anderson's Brigade did the same on the opposite side of the gap, and as darkness fell, the enemy withdrew. Longstreet's Corps passed on through the gap and camped for the night.[13]

Meanwhile, on August 29, General Jackson's corps met the enemy near Groveton, Virginia. With heavy fighting, Pope attempted to cut Jackson off, thinking that the Confederates were retreating towards the mountains in the west. Longstreet's men slipped into position on the field to the right of Jackson's line. On the thirtieth of August, after Pope's forces were committed to fighting Jackson's Corps, Longstreet attacked the Union left flank. Having no coherent contingency plan for this situation, Pope finally sent forces to check Longstreet's advance. This move saved his army from a certain disaster.[14]

In spite of the defending Union forces, the surprise and strength of the Confederate forces overwhelmed them, and the entire Union army retreated toward Centreville that evening. The Fifteenth Georgia, with its brigade led now by Colonel Benning, routed the Yankees back beyond the farms on Chinn Ridge and Henry Hill as the corps pushed to the east. At the engagement below Henry Hill, with D.R. Jones assaulting in a half-mile-wide front, Fifteenth Georgia initially cracked the center of the Union line, thus

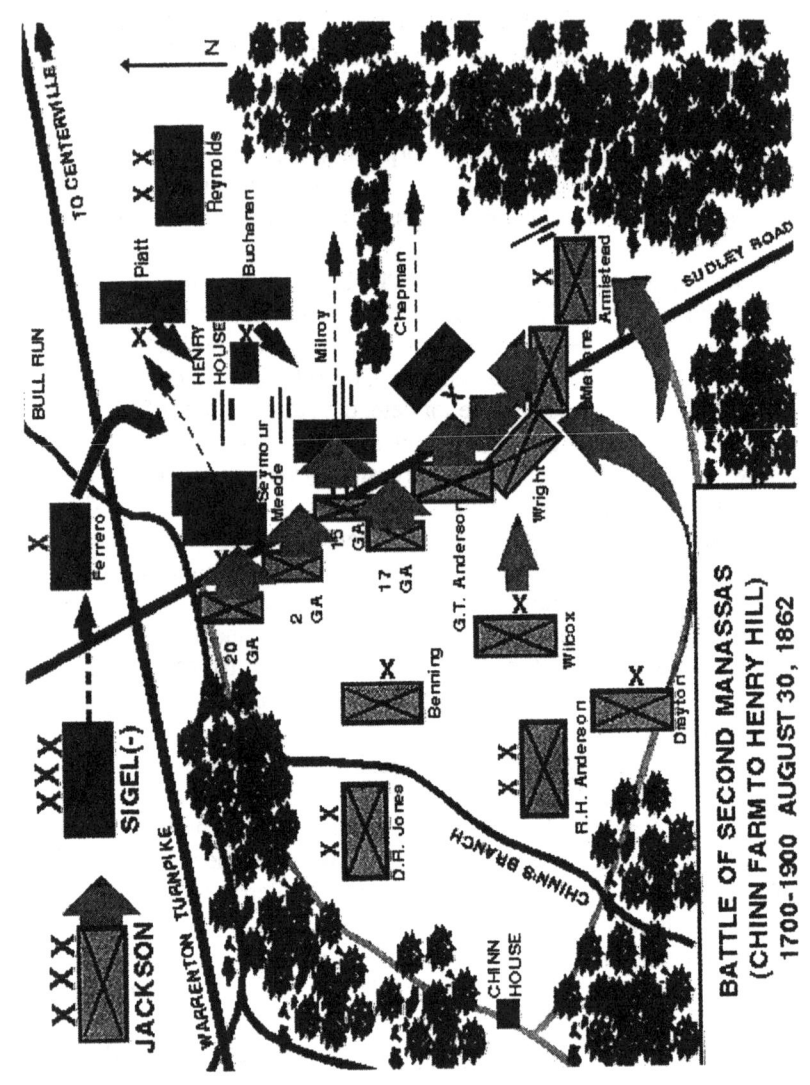

initiating the Yankees' retreat from the field and their maneuver to seek refuge at Centreville. Just as the Union line was broken, General Longstreet allowed Toombs to return to the command of his brigade. Toombs, in his finest political form, charged to the front of the advancing forces and led them with a yell up Henry Hill. This battle became known as the Second Battle of Manassas or Bull Run. It was an astounding Confederate victory, but not without great cost to the Fifteenth Georgia.[15]

Report of Major P. J. Shannon, Fifteenth Georgia Infantry, of the battle of Manassas:

I have the honor of submitting through you to Colonel Benning, commanding brigade, the following report of the portion of the engagement that my regiment was engaged in on August 30, at the battle of Manassas:

On the day previous to the engagement we were assigned the position we occupied a portion of the day of the fight. Two companies (G and K) had been detached as skirmishers on the right of our position and near the Manassas Gap Railroad the day before the fight and remained there during a portion of the 30th. A third company (B) was ordered forward as skirmishers in front of the regiment, and occupied a position near a house about 600 yards from the enemy's line. Remained in that position until 4 p.m., when the whole line was ordered to advance. The company of advance skirmishers joined the regiment when we arrived at that point. We continued the march for a distance of 1 1/4 miles across an old field, exposed to a deadly fire of grape and canister, frequently interspersed with musketry. On approaching near the enemy's line we changed direction by the right flank across a small stream into a skirt of woods. Then we moved forward by the left flank through the woods toward a road that skirted and ran parallel with the woods, in the mean time encountering a deadly fire from the enemy's battery immediately in front of our position and heavy musketry. We marched on, however, until we gained the road, with our right resting near the summit of a hill or elevation. We received orders to lie down and fire. On discovering that the enemy were about to turn our right we were ordered to fire by the right oblique, which we did with great havoc to the enemy. The troops on our right being forced to fall back about 150 or 200 yards and then change direction by the left flank; recrossed the branch, and ascended the hill across the old field immediately on the left of our position in the wood, all of which was done in good order, not withstanding the continuous fire

CHAPTER
3

FIGHTING THE ENEMY AT BURNSIDE'S BRIDGE

Once again, the South had tasted victory in northern Virginia. General Lee decided to capitalize upon their success. He immediately dispatched Jackson with his forces to take the Union garrison at Harpers Ferry, while he boldly led the remainder of his Army of Northern Virginia across the state line into Maryland. The South was on a roll, gaining recognition, respect, and badly needed resupply. Food was plentiful in the region, and the men of the Fifteenth Georgia now marched on, with heads held high and bellies full of sweet Yankee cherries.

Lincoln once again put McClellan in charge of a quickly reorganized Army of the Potomac. Immediately, he put his troops on the march in hot pursuit of Lee. Lee had expected Maryland to welcome the southern army, but she did not. The Fifteenth Georgia, in line of march with the Army of Northern Virginia, had crossed the Potomac near Leesburg, Virginia, on September 3, marched through Frederick, Maryland, and arrived in Hagerstown on the eleventh, seriously displaying a threat to Pennsylvania.[1]

Meanwhile, Lee had split his army as McClellan's forces gave chase on a broad front, following behind Longstreet's forces through Maryland. Lee ordered Longstreet to block the Union movement at South Mountain, so as to gain time in retrieving Jackson's forces.

Longstreet succeeded in delaying the Union forces, but he had to retreat from the field under the cover of darkness because of opposition consisting of three corps. Lee then ordered all of his forces to converge, on September 17, upon the heights west of Antietam Creek at Sharpsburg, Maryland. This is where Lee chose to fight. On the morning of September 17, Longstreet's Corps only had three divisions to defend the sector of the battlefield assigned to him, which protected the Confederate right wing. Two divisions had not yet rejoined the Corps; however, the terrain was advantageous to the Confederates. Gen. D. R. Jones wisely deployed Toombs's Georgia Brigade in an overwatch position, just above the lower bridge on Antietam Creek.

The Battle of Sharpsburg began at 5:30 A.M., September 17, 1862. It commenced on the Confederate left, with a bloody assault from the Union I Corps. This action ended in a stalemate several hours later with little tactical consequence, except for the incredible loss of life. Around 07:30 A.M., the Union XII Corps attacked the Confederate left, and the Union II Corps commenced their attack about 09:15 A.M., attacking the center and pushing the Confederate lines back to the vicinity of the Hagerstown Turnpike. Again, the fighting ebbed after several hours of human carnage, but on a scale that had not yet been witnessed in this war.[2]

Meanwhile, on the Confederate right, the Georgians repeatedly repulsed Gen. Ambrose Burnside's IX Corps (13,819 men). His attempts to cross Antietam Creek on the lower bridge were successfully delayed for about three hours by less than a brigade (four hundred men, a ratio of thirty-four to one). From that day forward the lower bridge across Antietam Creek has been known as Burnside's Bridge. The following report summarizes their actions:[3]

> Report of Col. Henry L. Benning, Seventeenth Georgia Infantry, commanding Toomb's brigade, of operations September 15-17.
>
> Headquarters Toomb's Brigade
>
> Captain: I have the honor to submit to you the following report of the part taken in the battle of Sharpsburg on the 17th ultimo by Toombs' brigade, the command of which devolved on me by his being in command of the division:
>
> On the morning of the 15th I was ordered by General Toombs to place the brigade across the road leading from Sharpsburg to Rohrersville at the Stone Bridge over Antietam Creek and to defend the bridge. Hardly had I received this order and commenced to execute it when I received another order from him to detach two regiments of the brigade and send them toward Williamsport in pursuit of the enemy's calvary, which the night before had escaped from Harper's Ferry and gone toward Williamsport to the peril of our wagon train, proceeding to that place from Hagerstown. Accordingly, I detached the Fifteenth and Seventeenth Georgia and sent them off under Colonel Millican on this duty. This left me for the defense of the bridge only two small regiments, the Second Georgia, under Lieutenant-Colonel Holmes, and the Twentieth Georgia, under Col. John B. Cumming. With these two regiments I proceeded to the bridge and there put them in position as ordered. For a long distance below the bridge, and for some distance above it, the ground rose very steeply

Fighting the Enemy at Burnside's Bridge

from the creek for fifty or sixty yards. The face of this slope was clothed with rather thinly scattered trees, and in one place on the left it had a sort of pit large enough to hold twenty or thirty men. Behind the trees at the top of the steep slope ran a rail fence. Along the face of this slope among the trees, in a rather irregular line, to suit the ground, I placed the two regiments, the Second on the right and the Twentieth on the left, with the line of the Twentieth extending forty or fifty yards above the bridge. Thus the greater part of the general line was placed below the bridge. This disposition was adopted because the road to the bridge on the other side of the creek ran from below up the bank of the creek near the water for 100 or 200 yards. The rails were taken from the fence and built up against such trees as were in suitable situations, and where there were no such trees the rails were laid in simple piles. These rude barricades, few and far between, afforded to men lying down behind them tolerable shelter against small arms. Such was the protection on which the regiments had to rely. The creek was fordable everywhere above and below the bridge; in most places was not more than knee deep. The hill-side occupied by the regiments was on its left commanded by a sharp ridge about 200 yards beyond the creek, and throughout by good positions for cannon at the distance of from 500 to 600 yards beyond the creek. Pickets and skirmishers were soon thrown across the creek several hundred yards to the front. The day passed off with perhaps an occasional shot from these; and so passed the next day, except that the skirmishing was heavier and that a number of well directed shells were thrown across the creek from Captain Eubank's battery at small parties of the enemy as they showed themselves and at spots in which it was supposed the enemy lay concealed.

The next morning early (that of the 17th) the skirmishing was renewed. It continued growing heavier on the part of the enemy, till about 9 o'clock, when our skirmishers were driven in. At about 8 o'clock Captain Eubank discovered a large body of the enemy opposite to him in a wood within range of his guns. He opened fire on them and drove them in confusion from the wood, and with loss, to judge from the movement of their ambulances. Not long after his battery had finished this work it was ordered away. Thus the two regiments were left at the bridge without any artillery supports whatever. The general line of battle of our army was nearly, if not quite, three-quarters of a mile in their rear, and not a soldier was between them and that line. The intervening ground for a great part of the way was a long slope facing the enemy's batteries, and thus commanded by those batteries, so that re-enforcements, if they had been sent, would have been cut up by shells before they could have reached their destination. A regiment had been posted on the right farther down the creek, but this soon after the battle commenced abandoned it's post and went to the rear. Thus the two regiments were without infantry supports, and without the expectation of receiving any re-enforcements. The two together numbered not more than 350 men and officers, the Second having only 97, and the Twentieth not more than 250. In their front was Burnside's whole Corps of not fewer than 12,000 or 15,000 of the enemy's best men, with a numerous artillery. In this forlorn condition were the two regiments at about 9 o'clock, when the fight opened in earnest. At this time the enemy's infantry, aided by the fire of many pieces of artillery, advanced in heavy force to the attack; and soon the attack opened on our whole line as far as the bridge. It was bold and persevering. The enemy came to the creek. The fire not only from their infantry, but from the artillery, was incessant, the artillery being so placed that it would fire over the heads of the infantry. It was met by a rapid, well directed, and unflinching fire from our men, under which the enemy, after a vain struggle, broke and fell back. This attack was succeeded by two similar ones from apparently two bodies of troops, and with likely results, the last of the two extending above the bridge to the upper part of our line. At length, toward 12 o'clock, the enemy made preparations for a still more formidable attack. A battery was placed in position from which it could command at almost an enfilade the whole face of the hill occupied by our troops. Soon it opened fire, and the infantry, in much heavier force than any time before, extending far above as well as below the bridge, again advanced to the attack. The combined fire of infantry and artillery was terrific. It was, however, withstood by our men until their ammunition was quite exhausted, and until the enemy had got upon the bridge and were above and below it fording the creek. I then gave the order to fall back. Colonel Cumming, with two companies which had a few rounds of ammunition left, remained near the bridge as a little rear guard, and was, with these, the last to clear the ground. When he left it the enemy had crossed above and below him, and were coming up on both his flanks. They indeed cut off a few of his men by getting to his rear. The men of both regiments, though retreating different ways, were exposed for a long distance to the shells of the enemy. Under an order received from General Toombs they retired to a position near the right of the general line of battle. Thus at near 1 o'clock we were driven from the bridge, but we had held it long enough to enable the advance troops of General A. P. Hill to reach their position in the line of battle; and this, I suppose, was obtaining the great object of defending a place so far in front of the line—a place so untenable as the bridge.

The Second Regiment lost in killed and wounded forty-two, nearly half of it's number. Among it's killed was Lieutenant Colonel Holmes, a good officer, and as gallant a man, I think, as my eyes ever beheld. The loss of the Twentieth in killed, wounded, and missing was sixty-eight, more than a forth of it's number. No words of mine in praise of officers and men are needed. The simple story is eulogy enough. I must, however, bear witness to one fact: During that long and terrible fire, not a man, except a wounded one, fell out and went to the rear— not a man. The loss of the enemy was heavy. Near the bridge they lay in heaps. Their own estimate, as a paroled sergeant of ours taken at the bridge told me, was at from 500 to 1,000 men killed. He also told me that they informed him that at about 12 o'clock an order came from General McClellan to take the bridge, cost what it might, and that when the whole corps advanced to the attack, and Colonel Cumming counted seven flags near the bridge. Shortly before the fight at the bridge terminated the Fifteenth and Seventeenth by forced marches had returned from Williamsport by way of Sheperdstown, and when that fight terminated they were in line of battle on the right and 400 or 500 yards in advance of general line of battle, which was along the summit of the ascent from Antietam Creek. This position they, together with the Eleventh Georgia, under Major Little, had been placed in by General Toombs, who ordered me, when I returned from the bridge, to take command of the whole. I did so. All remained in this position until, I think, near 4 o'clock. The enemy, except a few skirmishers, were too far off to be fired upon. These skirmishers were driven back by ours, and themselves got out of range. Shortly after I was put in command by General Toombs, he informed me that we would be relieved by General Gregg's brigade, and that then I must carry the men, much exhausted by their late long and rapid march to the right of the general line for rest. At about 4 o'clock General Gregg brought his brigade down and took our place, and we commenced marching to the position assigned us. Before, however, we got half way there, an order was sent to me to hasten the march and carry the command some distance to the left of that position along the road running into Sharpsburg until we came opposite to the enemy advancing from the bridge. This point was distant, I suppose, half a mile.

Again and again was this order repeated, the last time with the starting addition that the enemy had broken our line and were nearly up to the road with not a soldier of ours in their front. The pace was accelerated to a double-quick, which in a short time carried the head of the line beyond the corn field and in sight of the enemy. A brigade of them was standing composedly in line of battle not 200 yards from the road, apparently waiting for the nearer approach of our supports, and neither in their front nor far to their right (our left) was a man of ours to be seen, but three abandoned pieces of ours were conspicuous objects about midway between the road and the enemy's line. Major Little, with his battalion was in advance. The Seventeenth, under Captain McGregor, was next, the Fifteenth, under Colonel Millican, was next, and a large part of the Twentieth, under Colonel Cumming, again ready for action, notwithstanding the severe work of the morning, brought up the rear. All, however, made but a short line. I carried the head of the line opposite to the right of the enemy, and ordered it to commence firing on the enemy without waiting for the rest of the line to come up. It did so with promptness and spirit. The rest of the line as it came up joined in the fire. The fire soon became general. It was hot and rapid. The enemy returned it with vigor, and showed a determination to hold their position stubbornly. In about ten or fifteen minutes a cannon or two opened on them, and their line, which had already showed signs of wavering, broke, and fled down the hill and was soon out of sight, concealed by the crest of the hill. General Toombs ordered pursuit, and our whole line rapidly advanced after them. We could not see what was below the crest of the hill, but I knew a very large force of the enemy must be somewhere below it, for I had from our late position seen three or four long lines of them march out from the bridge. I therefore suggested to General Toombs the propriety of halting the line, as its numbers were so small and it had no supports behind it, just before it reached the crest of the hill, and sending to that crest only the men armed with long range guns. This suggestion he adopted, and the men armed with those guns quickly advanced to the crest and opened on the retreating enemy. Their other forces under the hill soon commenced falling back also. After getting near the creek, however, a large portion of them halted and formed behind a fence. On discovering this General Toombs ordered down the greater part of the command to dislodge them, soon following himself. After a very hot fight, in which Colonel Millican fell mortally wounded, he succeeded in his object. But it is for him to relate what took place there, as I remained behind with the small reserve. Our loss in this part of the battle was in numbers light, considering the large force of the enemy and the short distance of the fire. Their loss was very heavy. The conduct of both officers and men was, as far as I could observe it, as good as it could be. To mention some names without mentioning all would therefore be unjust. The service they rendered, to say nothing of the saving of the three abandoned guns, was, I think, hardly to be overestimated. If General Burnside's corps had once got through the long gap in our line it would soon have been in the rear of our whole army, and that anybody can see would have been disastrous.

> I am, captain, your obedient servant,
> Henry L. Benning
> Colonel, Commanding Toomb's Brigade[4]

The Fifteenth Georgia began this battle with 112 men and 13 officers. The total casualties of the regiment were:

Killed	Wounded	Captured
10	17	1

After the death of Colonel Millican, General Toombs assigned Capt. T. H. Jackson as commander of the Fifteenth Georgia. At nightfall on the seventeenth, having suffered 160 casualties during the battle, the forces of General Toombs reoccupied the same positions they had held on the previous day. General Ambrose Burnside's IX Corps was back on the eastern side of Antietam Creek and had suffered in excess of 2,300 casualties. The Battle of Antietam had ended in a bloody stalemate. Once again, the Union forces had gone into battle with superior strength, but armed with fortitude and dogged determination the Confederate troops proved to be worthy of the Yankees' respect.[5]

Throughout the evening, the Fifteenth Georgia and its sister regiments scoured the field of the day's battle, collecting weapons and prisoners. The night was warm and pleasant. Finally, with their duties for the day accomplished, they stretched out their weary bodies upon the blood-soaked field and slept.[6]

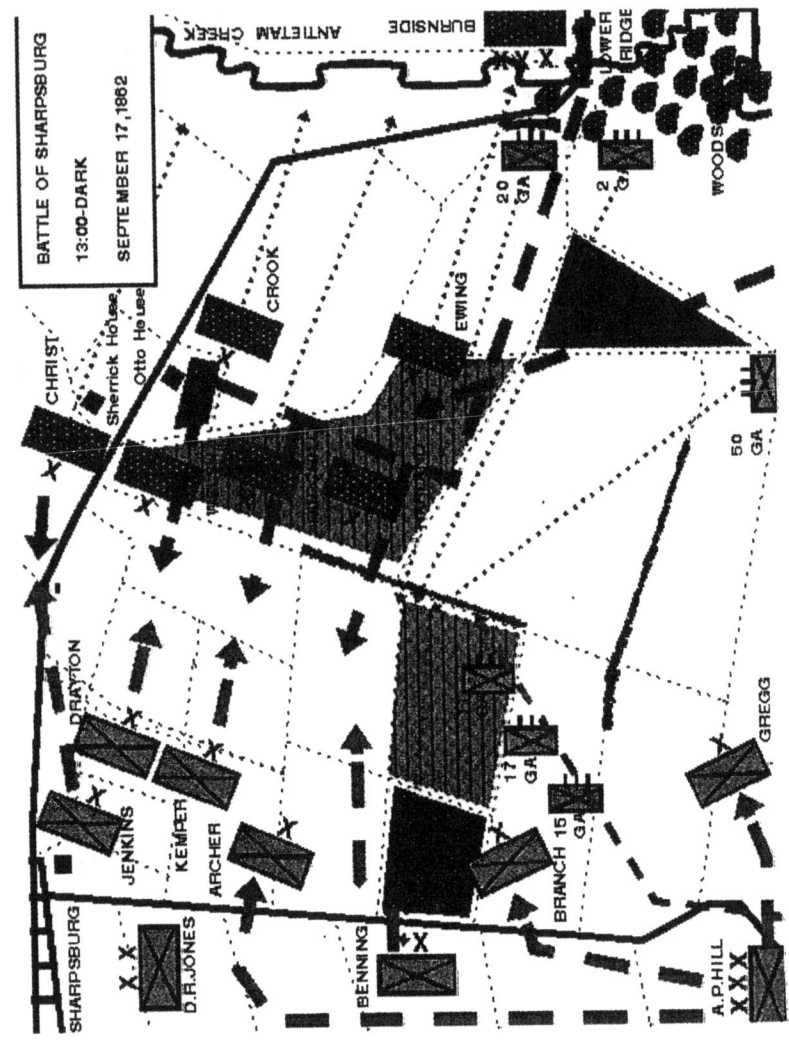

Unit Arms Report Toombs Brigade (E.P. Alexander File, UNC Collection)

CHAPTER

4

"THE HEROES ARE WELCOMED, WITH FAIR LADIES WAVING HANDKERCHIEFS."

On September 18, 1862, Lee's forces retreated from Sharpsburg, Maryland. Although not defeated, the southern army had been significantly reduced in number, while the Union troops had been re-enforced. Luckily for the South, General McClellan overestimated his opponent's size and failed to strike again at the weakened Army of Northern Virginia. Lee recrossed the Potomac and sought refuge within his home state of Virginia. The Army of Northern Virginia moved to Winchester on the twenty-fifth and concentrated their efforts on reorganization.

On September 30 General Toombs and his son-in-law, Capt, Dudley M. Dubose, departed for Washington, Georgia on a leave of absence. Captain DuBose was also General Toombs's adjutant. Both of them had received accolades for their brilliant display of leadership at Sharpsburg; however, General Toombs had been wounded. Physically, he had been shot in the hand, but his most painful injury had been one of emotion. Prior to the war Robert Toombs had served his home state of Georgia with great distinction. Previously he had represented Georgia from 1845 to 1853 in the House of Representatives and in the Senate from 1853 until 1861. He then served the Confederate States of America as its secretary of state until he joined the army and was commissioned as a brigadier-general and brigade commander.

As a general, Robert Toombs was deeply admired by his men, but he frequently infuriated his peers. His temper flared on several occasions; one incident resulted in a near duel and another in his being arrested and confined by General Longstreet. In 1862 General Toombs was a fifty-two-year-old man who was accustomed to being in charge, but in the company of younger West Point men with military backgrounds, he frequently found himself having to respect their orders. Additionally, General Toombs openly disagreed with the political and tactical strategy of President Davis. General Toombs and Captain DuBose extended their leave of absence for a total of seventy days while the general pondered his future in the Army of Northern Virginia.[1]

Meanwhile, President Lincoln was infuriated with General McClellan, who had consistently failed to exploit his advantage over Lee's smaller forces. McClellan was replaced with General Burnside. The Union forces restructured their Army of the Potomac into three "Grand Divisions," which consisted of well over a hundred thousand men. Slowly, the Union moved its tremendous military machine south once more, towards the heart of the southern cause, Richmond.[2]

On the home front in Georgia, not only had many families lost their husbands, fathers, and sons, but Lincoln had further insulted them with rumors of emancipation for the negroes. Recruitment of new troops swelled and they were rapidly dispatched to the field.[3]

In November 1862 Burnside and his "Grand Divisions" of the Army of the Potomac departed Warrenton, Virginia, en route towards the Rappahannock River at Fredericksburg. He planned to cross the river at this location and continue on to Richmond. Fortunately for the Confederacy, heavy rain had swollen the river, thus creating a natural obstacle for the Union army. This movement caught Lee off guard, but he swiftly put his army into motion, moved parallel to Burnside, and then fishhooked in front of his adversary on the opposite side of the river. The Fifteenth and her fellow Georgians arrived in Fredericksburg on November 22. Jackson's forces swung east and also were emplaced at Fredericksburg. Lee had his army place lines of defensive trenches along the high ground overlooking the town. They had soon established an extremely formidable barrier to Burnside and his grand plan. Meanwhile, the Union forces waited for the arrival of their pontoon bridges, which were urgently required to cross the river.

The Army of Northern Virginia had been restructured since the Battle of Sharpsburg, and now the Fifteenth, Second, Twentieth, and Seventeenth regiments comprised Benning's Georgia Brigade, of General Hood's Division, Longstreet's Corps. Maj. P.J. Shannon was now the Fifteenth's commander, since the death of Colonel Millican at the Battle of Sharpsburg. The Army of Northern Virginia was now at a strength in excess of seventy-two thousand men.[4]

Finally, on December 11, 1862, Burnside began his attempt to emplace bridging equipment across the river, thus initiating hostilities. The actions of the Fifteenth Georgia in this battle were minimal and reported as follows:[5]

Report of Colonel Henry L. Benning, Seventeenth Georgia Infantry, commanding Toomb's Brigade.

Major I have the honor to report to you that the part taken in the action of the 13th instant by Toomb's Brigade was slight. The brigade occupied a position near the center of the second general line of battle. The enemy never approached near enough to that line to draw its fire. Still, the brigade was near enough to his batteries to suffer some casualties from the artillery fire directed at our batteries or other troops in its front and on its flanks. A list of these casualties I send you. The brigade showed the most commendable activity and energy in strengthening its position to resist attack. In a single night, with eight spades, six or eight picks, and a very few axes, it rendered its position impregnable to small arms, and to every kind of attack, except one by artillery, conducted on the principles of a regular siege. On the day of the battle it was without any of these artificial defenses, hence the casualties it sustained. Shells were bursting on its line, especially that part of the line occupied by the Fifteenth and Twentieth Georgia, every few minutes during the whole battle; and it is cause for thankfulness that the casualties were so few. The men were quiet and firm under this long ordeal. Only one other thing deserves mention: From the time the signal guns were fired on the night of the 11th to the time when the enemy retreated across the river in the night of the 16th, the number of men for duty remained about the same, rather increasing toward the last. The desire to meet the enemy was universal.

I am, major, very respectfully, your obedient servant,
Henry L. Benning,
Colonel, Commanding Brigade.[6]

The casualties of the Fifteenth Georgia during this battle were:

Killed	Wounded	Captured
1	5	0

Although fate had been kind to Benning's Brigade, the Battle of Fredericksburg was the final tragic episode in the series of human slaughter during 1862. General Cobb and his legion of Georgians bore the brunt of battle for the South, behind a stone wall on Mayre's Heights. Sadly, General Cobb was mortally wounded. Although he was wounded in the calf, an artery was severed and he bled to death. He was one of approximately seventeen thousand men that fell upon the cold ground in

Fredericksburg, just ten days before Christmas. With the gray wintry skies overhead, both sides collected and buried their dead. After lying overnight in freezing temperatures, the stiff and distorted bodies had to be pried from their fixated positions and covered with clods of frozen dirt. Some were stacked in buildings and not buried until spring. Both Armies then moved a safe distance apart and began preparing their winter quarters for another season in the field.[7]

On December 28, 1862, the Fifteenth Georgia settled into winter quarters near Guinea Station, Virginia. Although the Union forces were still located just on the other side of the Rappahannock River, the weather made another assault impractical. Once again the southern army concentrated on enduring the cold. Now, with winter well entrenched, the year 1863 made its silent debut.[8]

Private Thomas L. Ware and his regimental brothers in arms were now beginning their second holiday season, far from home, in the Army of Northern Virginia. Thomas recorded his feelings and the activities of the first few days of that year in his small diary:

> **January the 1st. 1863. "Thursday."**
> Very cold morning, clear & all in fine health.
>
> The old year with its sorrows has passed and numbered with things of eternity. Its shadows are stamped upon the heart of the nation. Its sorrows and sad bereavements are felt around every hearthstone. Many who greeted the last new year morn with bright hopes, and beaming prospects, now lie cold and still upon the battlefields, where midnight winds sing a requiem o'er their graves, "Peace to their Ashes." The new year is upon us. May its sorrows be few; and ere its declining sun shall set, may the halcyon days again open and may we all meet around our firesides once more with our friends. So mote it be.
>
> Election came off today for Col. (which was glad news to us all as we had been anxious for it to come off for some time) DuBose of Gen'l Toombs staff & Capt Edwards of Co. F Candidates, the former elected by a large majority. (DuBose 310 votes & Edwards 102. Scattering a few) the election caused great joy over most the Reg'mt as we were anxious for his election.
>
> Most the Co. doing nothing. Several Apples & Cakes in Reg'mt for sale. But few sick. A.H. Hardy arrived in camps.
>
> Clear & pleasant Eve, nothing new. The band are playing some very good pieces, are playing at a late hour.
>
> I am up reading at 10 p.m. the moon shines beautiful. Cold night.

January the 2nd. "Friday." 1863
Very cold & frosty morning. Quite a lively & Jolly set in the "Co" as they seem to be taking their Christmas. Some are quite "funny." "Co" "B" having furnished enough to nearly treat the "Co." "Brigade" inspection of guns, ammunition by Lieut. "Perry" of the 2nd Geo Vol.

The Reg'mt marched over to Gen'l "Toombs" quarters where they called upon him for a speech, which was short, thanking them for the election of his SON for their Col. This speech was short as he spoke of the gallant Fifteenth at the battle of Sharpsburg. He then closed by saying "Lets take a drink boys, I have not made a speech in 5 yrs." He then took a toast "for the gallant "Edwards"(the Col's competitor) & said "Pitch in boys there is enough for us all" The Reg'mt then pressed up to his tent so close but few could get a toast, the Keg was taken from his tent by Boy Bob. & such a crowd running over & most of it was poured out & few tasted any. The affair wound up with quite a mob affair, when it was stopped by some officers & all returned to their quarters. So the treat did but few any good.

The night was quite a cold one, the moon shone pleasant. I was up quite late reading, sitting by a hot fire while the boys slept.[9]

During this time several of the men were allowed to take a thirty-day furlough. Each regiment was limited in the number of leaves allowable. Most everyone wanted to go home, but the commanders had to determine who were the most deserving. The determining factors were marital status, behavior, and service of no less than eighteen months with the regiment. Only the fortunate ones received the ultimate blessing of a trip home. For most of them, life went on in camp. A few men got sick and died, while some returned from the hospitals in Richmond, having recovered sufficiently from their wounds or illnesses.

Upon the field, the weather grew increasingly brutal. With the enemy just across the river, the posting of pickets in the open field was an unpleasant necessity. Soldiers of both armies dreaded this task with equal passion. The cold rains soaked their woolen blankets, and the wind chilled them to the bone.

On January 21 the pickets of the Fifteenth Georgia, received a surprise from across the river. With a stern wind behind it, a piece of plank with a sail on it arrived at their post. This vessel carried with it a cargo of coffee and some papers. The senders on the opposite bank indicated that they were members of the Thirteenth New Jersey Regiment, and below them was the Second Wisconsin. The boys of the Fifteenth, attempted to return the favor but the wind was unfavorable.[10]

On January 26 elections were held in the regiment for major. Major Shannon had been promoted to lieutenant colonel under DuBose. Captains Hearnsberger and Jackson of Company H vied for the vacancy caused by Shannon's promotion. Hearnsberger won, receiving the majority of the popular vote. Private Thomas Ware was voted into the position of orderly sergeant (1st SGT). The troops enjoyed their elections and they all had a "rich time."

Time passed slowly but peacefully and the Fifteenth Georgia wrote letters home, practiced their manual of arms (weather permitting), and waited with great anticipation for news and parcels from home. In the latter days of January, Sergeant Ware, the newly elected orderly sergeant, received some good fortune. He had the distinct pleasure of accompanying the newly elected Major Hearnsberger to Richmond on official business.

The travelers started out very early in the morning, trudged their way down the muddy road to the train station, and spent the remainder of the day enjoying their casual ride to the capital. They arrived in town at sunset, checked into a boarding house, ate a hearty meal, visited some sick members of their unit, and then slept in a bed for the first time in over a year.

The next day they had their heads shampooed, ate heartily, visited their sick friends, shopped, and went to the "Varieties" until very late in the evening. On Sunday they slept late, ate heartily, and spent the evening with Miss Anna and Alice Willis, "two nice young ladies." The next day was pleasant and warm, so the pair went downtown. Private Ware "stopped at Doctor Blankman's (Dentist), who I got to plug 6 teeth and extract 3 at a cost of $40.00, which was very painful and suffered considerable for a while. I was unwell at night suffering from my teeth."

The next several days were spent taking care of regimental affairs, which included picking up parcels from home. Sergeant Ware received a package from his "Ma" which included "sausages, tomatoes, sugar, lard, cakes, preserves, butter and pinders. Of course we lived very well for a time." The next day, Sergeant Ware and the major reluctantly returned to camp.[11]

On February 16 the regiment received orders to prepare to march at sunrise. Sergeant Ware received a letter from home stating that his youngest brother was dead. Early the next day, the regiment formed on the telegraph road, in line of march, heading south. There was rumor that Longstreet's Corps was marching to Suffolk, Virginia, and then on to North Carolina. As they marched, it began to snow. The snow quickly piled up to a depth of eight to ten inches. When they halted that afternoon, they had only marched eight miles. The next several days of marching were almost equally depressing, as the snow had turned to rain and the road was a slippery mess. The corps trudged on, arriving at Richmond on February 21. They proudly marched down Main Street. The entire town welcomed the heroes warmly with the "fair ladies waving their handkerchiefs." That evening the corps camped on the outskirts of town near Manchester, but close enough for the young at heart to trudge back for an evening on the town. The corps remained encamped just outside Richmond for the next five weeks. While there the units were replenished and the men enjoyed some well deserved rest and relaxation. When Colonel DuBose returned from his furlough, the regiment returned to drilling and preparing for the next campaign.[12] General Toombs decided to resign his commission and in an eloquent letter dated March 5, 1863, he expressed his farewell address to his soldiers as follows:

> Soldiers, today I cease to command you. I have resigned my commission as brigadier general in the Provisional Army of the Confederate States. The separation from you is deeply painful to me. It is only necessary now for me to say that, under existing circumstances, in my judgement, I could no longer hold my commission under President Davis with advantage to my country or to you, or with honor to myself. I cannot separate from you without the expression of my warmest attachment to you and admiration of your noble and heroic conduct from the beginning of this great struggle to the present time. You left your wives and children, kindred, friends, home, property, and pursuits at the very first call of your country, and entered her military service as soon as she was ready to accept you. From that day to this you have stood, with but few brief intervals, in sight of the public enemy or within hearing distance of his guns.
>
> Upon your arrival in Virginia, in the summer of 1861, you were incorporated into the Army of the Potomac. You have shared with that army all its toils, its sufferings, its hardships and perils, and contributed at least your share to its glorious career. You have been in the front, the post of danger and of honor, on all the great battlefields of Northern Virginia and Maryland, from Yorktown to Sharpsburg. Neither disheartened by the death of comrades or friends, nor by disease or toil, or privations or sufferings or neglect, nor intimidated by the greatly superior numbers of the enemy, whom you have been called upon to meet and vanquish, you have upon all occasions displayed

that heroic courage which has shed undying luster upon yourselves, your State, your country, and her just and holy cause. Nearly one-thousand of the brave men who originally composed your four regiments have fallen, killed or wounded in battle. Your dead have been buried on the battlefield, shed a manly tear over them, left "glory to keep eternal watch" over their graves, and pressed on to new fields of duty and danger.

Though it may seem to be the language of extravagant eulogy, it is the truth, and fit, on this occasion, to be spoken. You have fairly won the right to inscribe on your battered war flags the proud boast of Napoleon's Old Guard: " This brigade knows how to die, but not to yield to the foe."

Courage on the field is not your only claim to proud distinction. Since I took command over you I have not preferred a single charge against or arraigned one of you before a court conduct never demanded such a duty. You can well appreciate the feelings with which I part from such a command.

Nothing less potent than the requirements of a soldier's honor could, with my consent, wrench us asunder while a single banner of the enemy floated over one foot of our country. Soldiers, comrades, friends, farewell!

R. Toombs[13]

After the resignation of General Toombs, Col. Henry Lewis Benning, who had recently been promoted to the rank of brigadier general, was now officially assigned to command the brigade. On the second day of the coming month, April, Henry Benning would be forty-nine years old. Prior to the war, Benning had been well educated and graduated with honors from the University of Georgia in Athens. He then studied law and was admitted to the bar in 1835. He had earned great respect as a prominent Georgia lawyer until 1853, when, at the age of thirty-nine, he was elected to the Supreme Court of Georgia, where he served a complete six-year term. In 1860 and early in 1861, he served as a Georgia delegate and was very instrumental in the adoption of the Ordinance of Secession. In August 1861 he entered the Confederate service as a colonel and the commander of the Seventeenth Regiment Georgia Infantry. He had well proven his abilities of command during the previous campaigns and had earned the admiration of his superiors, peers, and subordinates. He was described as being a very physical man, nearly six feet tall and of noble presence and bearing. His attributes of courage, candor, and high ethical values had been displayed throughout his life. General Benning was referred to affectionately as "Old Rock" by the men of his command for his steadfastness and courage. Although the Confederate army lacked material wealth, it was well blessed with good leadership.[14] Ware wrote in his diary, March 12, 1863, "Drill at 10 A.M., 1 mile from camp, good drill ground. It was Col. DuBose first time & he did very well (all well pleased with him). He is a brave & kind man & will do all for his men. If any are punished they will deserve it by him." All too soon, with spring on the horizon, Longstreet's Corps assumed their line of march. They departed on the twenty-ninth, en route for Suffolk, Virginia, arriving there on April 16, 1863.[15]

Their mission was two-fold. By sending Longstreet to the vicinity of Suffolk, the Army of Northern Virginia was now defending Richmond from all possible threats. As a secondary mission, he was to obtain badly needed forage for the army from the local farmers in North Carolina. The Fifteenth and the rest of Benning's Brigade were sent forth to accomplish this task.

The brigade spent the next several weeks traveling throughout Chowan and Gates counties obtaining food stuffs, loading them on the wagons, and generally building rapport. It was reported that many people in this region were disloyal to the southern cause. The soldiers could hear heavy cannon fire in the distance around Suffolk. On May 3 the brigade rejoined the corps, on line before the enemy at Suffolk, with enemy shells bursting in the camps. The brigade was issued ammunition and moved toward the front of the action. Suddenly, they were halted and ordered to return to their original positions. The regimental commanders were all summoned to General Hood's headquarters. When they returned, they relayed the plan to their men.[16]

Unbeknown to the regiments, while they were away on foraging detail, General Hooker had taken control of the Union forces north of the Rappahannock River. Hooker was a much more aggressive commander than Burnside. With one corps of the Army of Northern Virginia away, Hooker was presently attempting to outflank and attack Lee. Longstreet's Corps had been called upon to march immediately and rejoin the Army of Northern Virginia. Hooker's Army of the Potomac now had over 135,000 men. Within their own ranks were only 60,000. Immediately, all units were to retreat from the field as quietly as possible. The men marched rapidly throughout the night, stopping in Franklin at eight o'clock the next morning. They had marched a distance of forty miles in twenty-four hours.[17]

The corps ultimately arrived in Richmond on May 10. Meanwhile, without Longstreet's Corps, Lee defeated Hooker in a brilliant victory at the

Battle of Chancellorsville. He forced the Union forces to retreat back to the north side of the Rappahannock River. Longstreet's Corps continued their march, arriving at Racoon Ford on the Rapidan River on the seventeenth of May.[18]

On May 27, having recuperated from their grueling forced march, the men of Hood's Division celebrated with a division review. Sergeant Ware wrote:

> At 10 a.m., all four brigades formed a line across a great field. "Texas" Brigade on the right, "Laws" (Ala. Brig.) next "Bennings" and then "Andersons" on the left, the position was hilly. 4 Batteries of 24 pieces on the extreme right; line being formed. Officers to the front, General Hood and Staff rode up the lines and all the bands played, drums beat and flags dipped. Many local citizens from the country & Orange Court House came out to observe and cheer for the boys in gray."
>
> "So it was a gala day with Hoods Division. Everything passed off finely. Gen'l Hood was well pleased, the Div. numbering on review near 8,000; all was well pleased with the different maneuvers, and formed a greater liking to their brave chivalric leader; News encouraging from Vicksburg that we repulsed them 6 different times with small losses, their loss heavy."[19]

On June 6, 1863, the Army of Northern Virginia was whole once more. Lee had his entire forces located around Culpeper Court House, in the heart of Virginia. Refit and emerging from an astounding victory, they were well prepared for a new campaign. In the Fifteenth Georgia, although their ranks had dwindled, their spirits soared. The men rested their weary feet and awaited the inevitable command of forward march.[20]

CHAPTER
5
WITH BENNING'S BRIGADE IN THE "DEVIL'S DEN"

On June 15, 1863, the Fifteenth Georgia was back in motion, this time, heading northwest with the entire Army of Northern Virginia on yet another campaign into enemy territory. On June 16 the regiment marched seventeen miles to Marcum Station on the Manassas Railroad. Because of the heat, several men died of sunstroke. Lee marched them hard, but it was for a good reason. Once his troops reached the fertile Shenandoah Valley, they could march north, flanked on either side by high mountains. These ridges were protected by his cavalry and flanking forces. But first they had to beat the Yankees to the mountain passes. This resulted in a difficult forced march during the hot swelter of the summer sun. On June 17 Sergeant Ware recorded in his diary that, as a result of the excessive heat and hard marching, over a hundred men of the Fifteenth Georgia fell out. Everyone agreed that it was by far their most difficult march of the war. Lee's army succeeded in its quest. Longstreet's Corps entered the lush valley through Ashby's Gap on the eighteenth of June. Sergeant Ware recorded the day's events as follows:

> June 18th. "Thursday." 1863.
> Very dusty day. Received orders to leave by sun rise which we did; about faced & marched back through the village on the Winchester pike (at Upperville the "Piedmont" pike joins the "Winchester" & Alexandria pike)
> Our aim in coming such a crooked route was to get possession of "Ashby's" Gap by coming in at "Upperville" & thus in the rear.
> We marched up the pike & soon came to "Paris" a small village in the mountains, the village is very old. Here we rested 2 hours, mountains all around & a gradual ascent from the village to the top of the mountain. Excellent water all around, few people living along the road.
> We soon passed through the Gap & the scenery was grand, mountains & plains could be seen as far as the eye would permit & now a

descent down to the noted "Shenandoah" which is only 2 miles at the foot of the mountain. Where runs the river is a beautiful country, fine farms & dwellings, & one the beawtifulest country to live in I ever saw. Here we crossed the Shenandoah which we waded, it was waist deep & 200 yards wide. Beyond the river & near it is a limestone spring so bold the current a few feet below would turn a mill. Here the cooking detail of the Division were preparing rations & all the sick & those unable to march yesterday were at this noted spring. Water very cool, fine farms & houses around.

We marched 1 mile beyond the river & took up Camp. "Laws" & "Andersons" Brig were sent down the river to Snicker's ford as guard. We stopped at 3 P.M. & drew Beef & bread (flour) & no Salt. Marched only 8 miles today.

Heavy rain with thunder & lightning fell this eve & continued slowly most the night. Several quite sick in the Co. Wrote a letter home.

As they passed through the valley, the men crossed the Shenandoah River several times. On June 20 the Fifteenth Georgia crossed the Shenandoah for the third time and in spite of orders from the high command, according to Sergeant Ware, they crossed half-naked. No doubt the river crossings were a splendid reprieve from the dusty trails. On the twenty-fourth, the Fifteenth Georgia passed by the village of Middleway, where Sergeant Ware wrote, " a large crowd of girls came out to see us & waved their handkerchiefs, we passed them with music."

The corps continued northward and crossed the Potomac River at Williamsport on the twenty-sixth. Once more the Georgia infantry marched through Maryland with heads held high, as they once again enjoyed those sweet Yankee cherries. Although the regiment marched sixteen miles that day, several men in the regiment celebrated with a dram of liquor during a rest halt. Ware wrote, " We got a great many cherries & living finely."

On the twenty-seventh, the regiment marched through the town of Greencastle, Pennsylvania. The Georgians were not at all welcome there. Ware reflected the tone in his diary, "People strong Unionist & looked mad & sullen at our appearance a great many closed doors; stores all closed the Streets & Hotels crowded with young men just out of service. Some nice looking girls dressed very fine as every thing is cheap. Several Federal Flags were seen the girls had them on their bonnets. We marched through quick time with music."

The regiment continued marching northward and along the route the Southerners began collecting honey, poultry, horses, and cattle from the local civilians. Twelve miles north of Greencastle the Georgians passed through the large town of Chambersburg, Pennsylvania. Thus far, this was the furthest north the Southerners had been during the war. The people of Pennsylvania were very loyal and fervent members of the Union. Many of their men had been killed or permanently maimed by the Army of Northern Virginia and being invaded did not make them happy. The southerners were used to marching through towns and receiving cheerful admiration from the ever-present ladies waving their handkerchiefs, but not here. Again, Ware recorded in his diary, " Stores all closed & a great many people out to see us & looked frightened & mad." In spite of their cold reception, Ware, with his eagle eye for beauty noted, "I saw more girls than I have seen at any one time before, some very good looking ones."

On Sunday, June 28, 1863, the Fifteenth Georgia finally received a day of rest. Sergeant Ware recorded, "We will remain in Camps today, passes granted & a great manv the boys out foraging, the soldiers are taking every thing. Camps full of chickens, butter & milk. Our mess had a chicken stew, cherries in great abundance."[1]

Meanwhile, Hooker maintained his army on a northerly course, parallel to Lee's, but east of the Blue Ridge Mountains. The cavalry units of both armies maintained flank security for their respective forces, frequently skirmishing throughout the campaign trail. General Lee's ultimate goal was to exploit the rich farmlands of Pennsylvania and gain international support from Europe, all the while achieving tactical victories against the consistently larger Union forces. Unfortunately for the South, this strategy was soon curtailed by two separate events.

Most importantly, General Hooker was relieved of his command and replaced by General Meade. Meade proved to be a worthy opponent, a man of action, and an excellent tactician; however, the most ominous event occurred just as Lee's forward elements arrived within several miles of Harrisburg, the capital of Pennsylvania and an excellent target. Two divisions of Gen. A. P. Hill's corps ventured into the little town of Gettysburg, Pennsylvania, in search of shoes for themselves. Unfortunately, a Union cavalry division was already there, as well as two corps of Union infantry. A heated battle ensued, and the Yankees were beating them very badly until help arrived that afternoon and drove the Union forces back towards the east of Gettysburg. This latter event occurred on July 1, thus beginning the Battle of Gettysburg, the three bloodiest days of warfare in the history of the United States.[2]

The battlefield at Gettysburg was quickly established. The two opposing armies faced one another and prepared for hostilities. The Union forces were established in a defensive front four and one-half miles long, on the high ground extending from the east at Culps Hill and hooking around Cemetery Ridge and then south to two hills known as Big and Little Round Top. Meade strengthened the areas in the north facing the town of Gettysburg and to his western front, the regions where Lee concentrated his forces. Meade certainly had the advantage, with a larger army and the occupation of the most prominent terrain features in a defensive posture. Lee, on the other hand, would meet his adversary with the disadvantage of a smaller army attacking a larger one in fortified positions, across open fields with sparse opportunity for cover and concealment.

Lee established his forces in attack formations, north, in and around Gettysburg, and in a line extending southwest, facing the enemy from the west and parallel to the Emmitsburg Road. General Lee felt confidence in his men's ability to win the impending conflict; however, General Longstreet voiced disagreement. Longstreet's Corps would initiate the battle by charging his forces into the Union forces located on and in front of the Round Tops. This action would then be followed by the other corps attacking to their respective fronts. Lee respected Longstreet's opinion but declined to alter his plan.[3]

For the next two days, the second and third of July, casualties mounted as the Confederate corps repeatedly charged the Union left and right flanks. On several occasions it appeared that Southern forces would capture key terrain, but the Union forces maintained their positions. Finally, on the afternoon of July 3, Lee sent fresh forces charging into the weakened Union center. The charge, led by George Pickett, was gallant and determined, but ultimately a staggering defeat for the Confederacy. Throughout the battle, the Fifteenth Georgia, as an element of Benning's Brigade, Hood's Division, Longstreet's Corps, fought on the Union left. For two full days, the Fifteenth waged war at the very epicenter of the fight to destroy the Union left flank. This struggle could have changed the tide of battle and redirected the resulting course of events, but it was not to be. General Hood, in the early moments of his assault, relayed to Longstreet that by going around the high ground, he could trap the enemy in their exposed rear area. Unfortunately, this suggestion was not taken.[4]

Just prior to the opening moments of the battle of Gettysburg, Private Ware, Fifteenth Georgia, wrote: " Drizzly, wet evening, have a splendid place to sleep, some dry straw. Had a splendid nights rest."[5]

For the next several days, the men of both sides struggled to survive the raging tide of war. The ensuing conflict, as experienced by the Fifteenth Georgia, was recorded by the commander, Col. Dudley M. DuBose:

> Report of Col. D. M. DuBose, Fifteenth Georgia Infantry
>
> Sir: In obedience to orders No. ____, received today, I herewith submit to Brigadier General H. L. Benning a report of the part taken by my regiment (the Fifteenth Georgia) in the battle of Gettysburg on the 2d and 3d of July, 1863. My regiment occupied that portion of the ground on the extreme left of the brigade. On the 2d of July, after moving for a considerable distance across an open field under a heavy shelling from the enemy's batteries, I reached my position from which I was to move in line of battle to assist in supporting Brigadier General Law's brigade, which I learned had moved forward to attack the enemy. After marching forward four or five hundred yards, I, with the rest of the brigade, was halted and rested until an order came to me from General Benning to move forward at once, in good order, under fire of the enemy's artillery. After getting within a hundred and fifty yards of the advanced troops, I was again halted by General Benning for a few moments, my regiment having gotten a short distance ahead of another portion of the brigade lines, owing, I suppose, to the difference in the nature of the ground, over which we had to march. General Benning then left the position where he was, then near my right, and went towards the right of the brigade. I rested a few minutes in this position, until I saw the balance of the brigade had moved up even with my position and were still advancing. I immediately ordered a forward movement, and soon gained the point where our advance troops were fighting behind a stone fence, a little above the foot of a high, wooded, rocky hill. At this point my regiment commenced the engagement with the enemy who occupied the hill. At this point the nature of the ground was such that I could not see the other portion of our brigade. After fighting the enemy in this position for a short time, I saw from the heavy fire of musketry on my right that the other portion of the brigade were hotly engaged in trying to carry the hill in their front, which was destitute of trees. I immediately ordered my egiment to jump the stone fence and charge that portion of the hill in my front; which order they obeyed willingly and promptly, driving the enemy from my part of the hill, turning that portion of their right flank which occupied the barren hill in front of the troops of our own brigade, on my right, and thereby assisting them in gaining the hill in their front. In this charge a portion of one

of the Texas regiments joined me (the First Texas) and behaved well. After gaining the hill I continued to move forward, driving the enemy before me at a rapid rate, capturing between one hundred and forty and two hundred prisoners, including officers as well as men. I had gone on rapidly from the top of the hill between a quarter and a half mile ahead of the other portion of our brigade, which I found had halted at the top of that portion of the hill in their front, when I discovered a large body of the enemy moving so as to put themselves between me and the troops on my left and in my rear, and thereby cut me off entirely from support. As soon as I saw the danger to which I was exposed I ordered a halt, and also ordered my regiment to fall back.

I fell back to the stone fence before referred to, and there very soon arranged my line and fought the enemy in this position until I saw the troops on my left getting ready for another charge. I at once ordered my regiment to charge, which they did well, driving the enemy from their position. The troops on my left then fell back to their original position and the enemy commenced advancing upon my left. I took a small party of men, threw them out as skirmishers on the left and drove back the enemy's advance, but very soon a heavy column of the enemy came upon my left flank, drove in the skirmishers, and not being supported on the left in that position, I fell back to my original position, and continued the fight at this point until I received a message from the commander of the troops on my left, stating that he was going to charge the enemy again, and desired me to do the same on my part of the line, which proposition I agreed to at once, and immediately ordered my regiment forward, and again did they obey my order with alacrity and courage, driving the enemy in the open field at the foot of the mountain on my right. In this position my line was almost at a right angle with the line of the brigade. I placed them in a position so as to assist the troops on the left, who had followed the retreating column of enemy, and were then attempting to charge a portion of the mountain height. I ordered my men to pour in a heavy fire upon the enemy as soon as the troops on the left commenced falling back, as I thought they would have to do, and thereby protect their retreat as much as possible. This they did very effectually. I remained in this position a considerable length of time, and until late in the evening, when it became so dark that objects in the woods could not be so easily discerned. I then learned that the enemy were again moving round upon my left in heavy force. Upon learning this, I changed my line back about two hundred yards and fronted differently. I had not gotten through this movement before I discovered that the enemy were moving forward rapidly and were within two hundred yards of the left of my line. I halted, faced about and commenced fighting them, and after a few well directed volleys, succeeded in checking their advance. They then fell back, and I moved my regiment back to the stone fence in my rear, formed them in a few moments and rested in this position until General Benning ordered me to rest for the night upon the hill in my front. It was now after dark; I moved up and occupied the position he had directed me to, and also collected together all the fragments of regiments and companies from other commands, and formed them upon the same line with my own regiment, and stationed pickets in front. In this position I remained until just before daylight on the morning of the 3d of July, when I was ordered by General Benning to move my regiment back to the stone wall, from which he had ordered me the night before. I remained in position behind this wall until late in the evening of the third of July, keeping a body of skirmishers in my front. In the latter part of the evening the enemy pressed so heavily upon my skirmishers that I was compelled to reinforce them with two additional companies, and very soon thereafter a heavy skirmish commenced.

The enemy had commenced moving around upon my left in heavy force. The troops upon my left having been withdrawn, I notified General Benning of the movement being made by the enemy. He immediately came down to my position and there received orders through a courier to move the left of his brigade so as to unite with the right of General McLaw's division. Brigadier General Benning ordered me to move to the position pointed out by the courier, which order I obeyed at once, calling in my skirmishers. The new position to which I had been ordered and occupied left a space of fully a quarter of a mile between my right and the then left of General Benning's brigade. This space was entirely unoccupied except by a few skirmishers from my regiment. I had not gained my new position but a short time before a brisk skirmish commenced between the enemy and my left wing. At this time I received an order from General Benning by one of his couriers to hold the hill I was on and that General McLaws would support me on the left. By the courier who brought me this order I notified General Benning that I could see nothing of General McLaws, but instead of finding his troops upon my left, that the enemy were moving around upon my left in heavy force. After this time I received no further orders or notice of the movement of our troops from any one. The enemy came on rapidly in heavy force, turning my left entirely, and also advancing in front, and moving upon my right, in the space between my right and the left of the position where I had left the balance of the brigade.

After fighting in this position until I saw the enemy had greatly the advantage of me by his flank movement, I drew my line of battle back about seventy or eighty yards, changing at the same time my front.

At this position I secured my men as best I could behind rocks and trees, seeing that I was compelled to fight greatly superior numbers. In this position I had a desperate fight, the enemy moving up on my right and left flanks and front. I fought them until they had gotten within twenty to forty yards of my men. Seeing no reinforcements coming to my relief, and finding that in a few moments more my whole regiment would be either killed or captured, I ordered a retreat through the only space open to me by the enemy. After falling back three or four hundred yards, I rallied my regiment behind a stone fence, and there checked the advance of the enemy; but after fighting in this position for a time, the enemy made the same movement upon this position that he had done upon the one I had last left, by throwing a force around my left flank, and moving up on my right flank, by this means hoping to surround me, and entirely cut off all means of retreat. As soon as I saw that the position of the enemy rendered my position untenable, I again ordered my men to retire. After retreating some four hundred yards further back I again rallied the remnant of my regiment, and fought them until driven from my position by one of the enemy's batteries, which completely enfilade my position, throwing shells among my men who were lying behind the stone fence. I again ordered a retreat and fell back to where the balance of the brigade had been ordered after I left it.

During each of the four separate fights I made that evening I looked for and expected support either upon my right or left, which did not come, nor did I retire from either position until I had ascertained that there was no support to be had. My men and officers fought bravely, but my loss was immense. How any of us escaped, I do not see. In the battle of the 2d July I went in with 330 or 335 muskets, and lost seventy men killed, wounded and missing. In the battle of the third I lost one hundred and one, making a total loss of one hundred and seventy one men in the two days' fighting.

During the battle of the 2nd July I was greatly assisted by Lieutenant Colonel Hearnsberger and my Adjutant Lieutenant, L. Pierce, both of whom behaved with coolness and courage. I am also indebted to all of my officers who were present, for the assistance rendered by them. My men behaved well and worthy of their former reputation. All of which is respectfully submitted. I am, sir, very respectfully, your obedient servant,

D. M. DuBose, Colonel Fifteenth Georgia Volunteers[6]

Near the end of the battle, as the Fifteenth Georgia was being overwhelmed as a result of confusion among the commanders, Sgt. James B. Thompson, Company G, First Pennsylvania Rifles, managed to capture the Fifteenth's regimental colors; however, before the day was through, Sergeant Thompson was carried from the field, a prisoner of the Confederacy.[7]

Total casualties of the Fifteenth Georgia as a result of this battle:

Killed	Wounded	Captured
18	39	119

In two days of battle, the regiment was reduced in size by one-half of its strength. The Army of Northern Virginia lost twenty-eight thousand men of its seventy-five-thousand-man army. The Union Army of the Potomac suffered approximately twenty-three thousand casualties. But the cold, hard statistics fail to reflect the pain and anguish of personal tragedy.[8]

The following entry in the diary of Pvt. Thomas L. Ware was not recorded in his handwriting:

July 2nd. "Thursday." 1863.

We received orders to be ready to march at 7 O'clock. Soon we were in marching order and left for the Scene of action. Passing through Cashtown and marching one hour we came in sight of Gettysburg. Here we rested in an old field until 2 o'clock, at which time we left to attack the enemy. After passing through a very heavy shelling for 20 minutes we rested and then formed a line of battle. We charged the enemy, driving them from their position. Here at the foot of the mountain the engagement became general and fierce and lasted until 8

O'clock at night. And in the third and last charge the fatal blow was struck.

My Brother: You have offered your life as a sacrifice upon your country's altar.

Today concludes the terms of life of my Brother. He now sleeps upon the battle field of Gettysburg with

> *There Brothers, Fathers, small & great,*
> *Partake the same repose*
> *There in peace the ashes mix*
> *Of those who once were foes.*

Many of our brother soldiers whose life was made a sacrifice upon our country's altar. There the weeping willow gently waves over his grave. And there we prayed that God would guard that little mound."[9]

Tragically, the life of Thomas L. Ware was violently ended. He had made the ultimate sacrifice. Somewhere, strewn amidst the multitude of shattered, malodorous corpses were the repulsive remains of a once proud and determined young man. Perhaps his brother had found time to bury Thomas in a shallow grave below a weeping willow, as he wrote in his diary. In reality, however, it is not very likely. Chaos reigned and his brother Robert was captured the day after Thomas was killed. The terrain that the Fifteenth Georgia and Benning's Brigade struggled so hard to conquer and hold was the "Devil's Den" and the once peaceful "Plum Run Valley" below Little Round Top. Since those days of violence, it has been referred to as the "Valley of Death."

The Army of Northern Virginia began a long and agonizing retreat on July 4, 1863. As a violent summer storm swept over the field, the army staggered back to Virginia. The Union pursuit was mercifully slow and what remained of Lee's crippled army survived to fight another day. Meanwhile, upon the fields of Gettysburg, it would take weeks to clean up the carnage that remained. Masses of noxious, distorted human remains and horse flesh were in dire need of disposal. They lay where they had been violently tossed, in rotting heaps, and fully exposed to the sweltering summer sun. Most of them were eventually dumped into massive trenches. Many could not be identified and are known but to God.[10]

Many important commanders and officers were wounded or killed at Gettysburg. The Fifteenth Georgia's division commander, General Hood, suffered the loss an arm.[11] Despite the pathetic slaughter at Gettysburg, the Fifteenth trudged south, crossed the Rapidan River, and encamped in the vicinity of Chancellorsville, Virginia, on the first of August. There, as always, the Fifteenth Georgia silently awaited the inevitable order to march and fight. All too soon, the shadow of the specter of death would be cast upon them once more. The Battle of Gettysburg proved to be the "high tide" of the Confederacy. For the remainder of the war, the Fifteenth Georgia Infantry would staunchly continue the fight; however, the constant surge of Union forces would remain ever present and unrelenting in the zealous pursuit of their foe.[12]

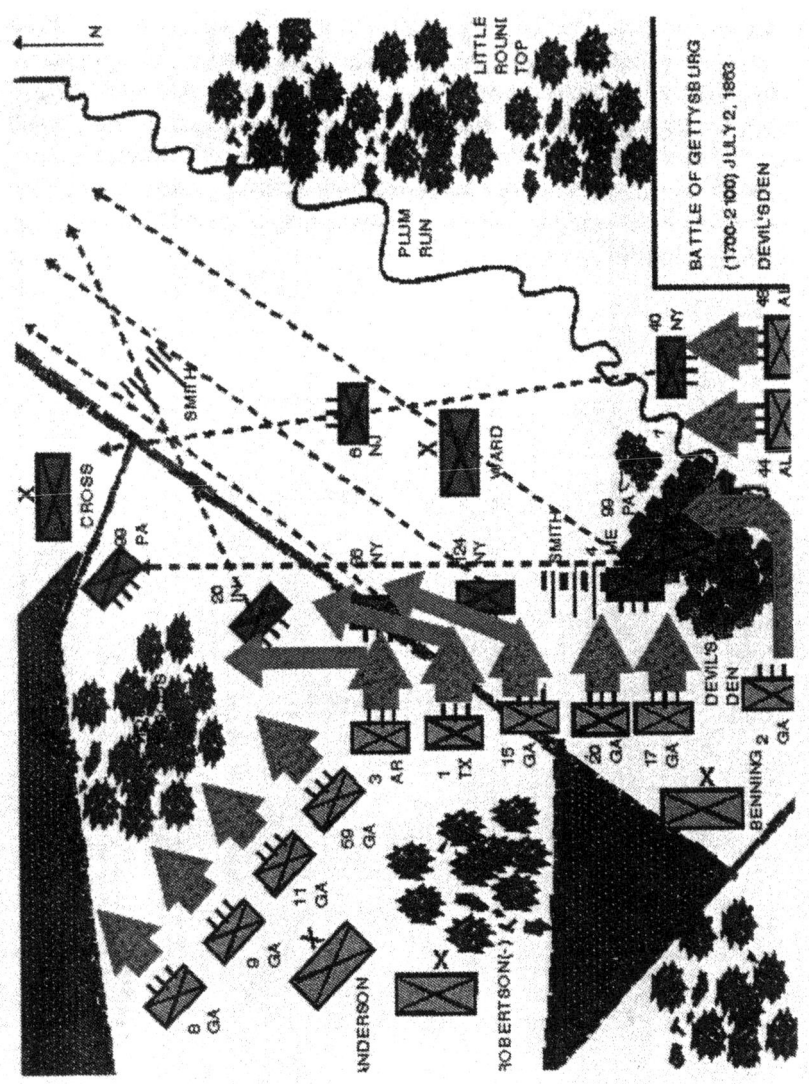

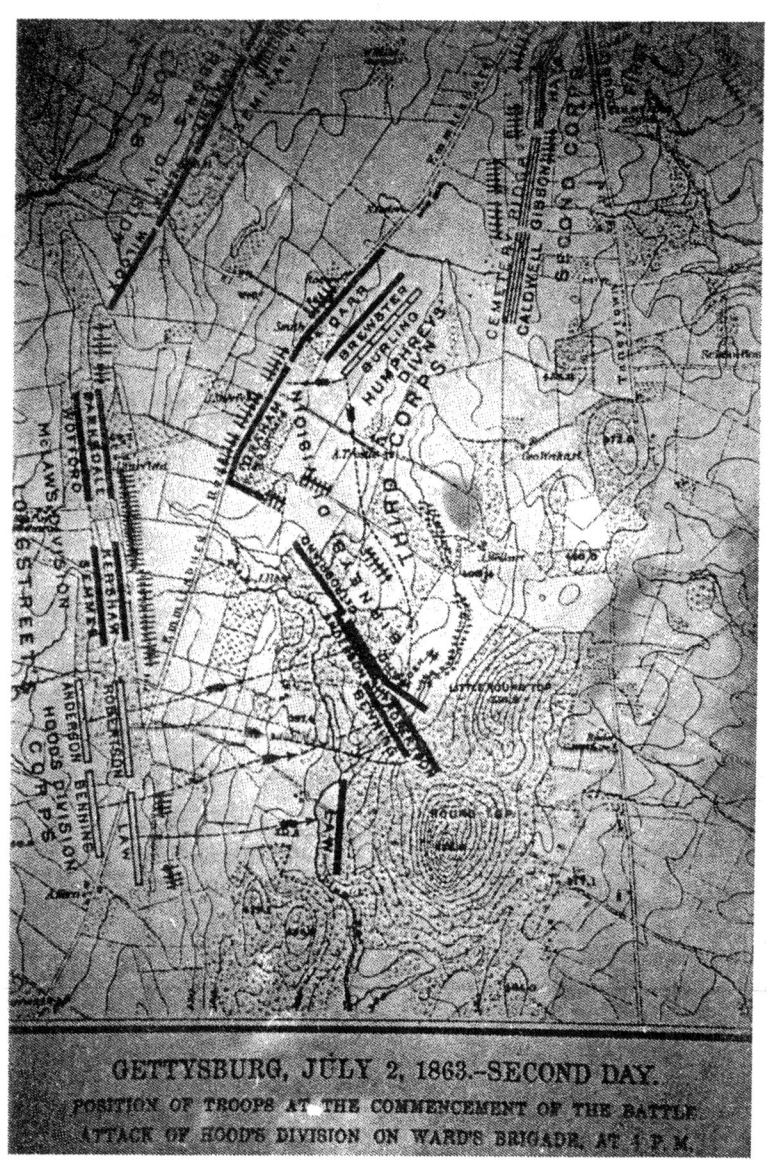

Map of Gettysburg, July 2, 1863
(from E.P. Alexander File, Wilson Library, UNC Collection)

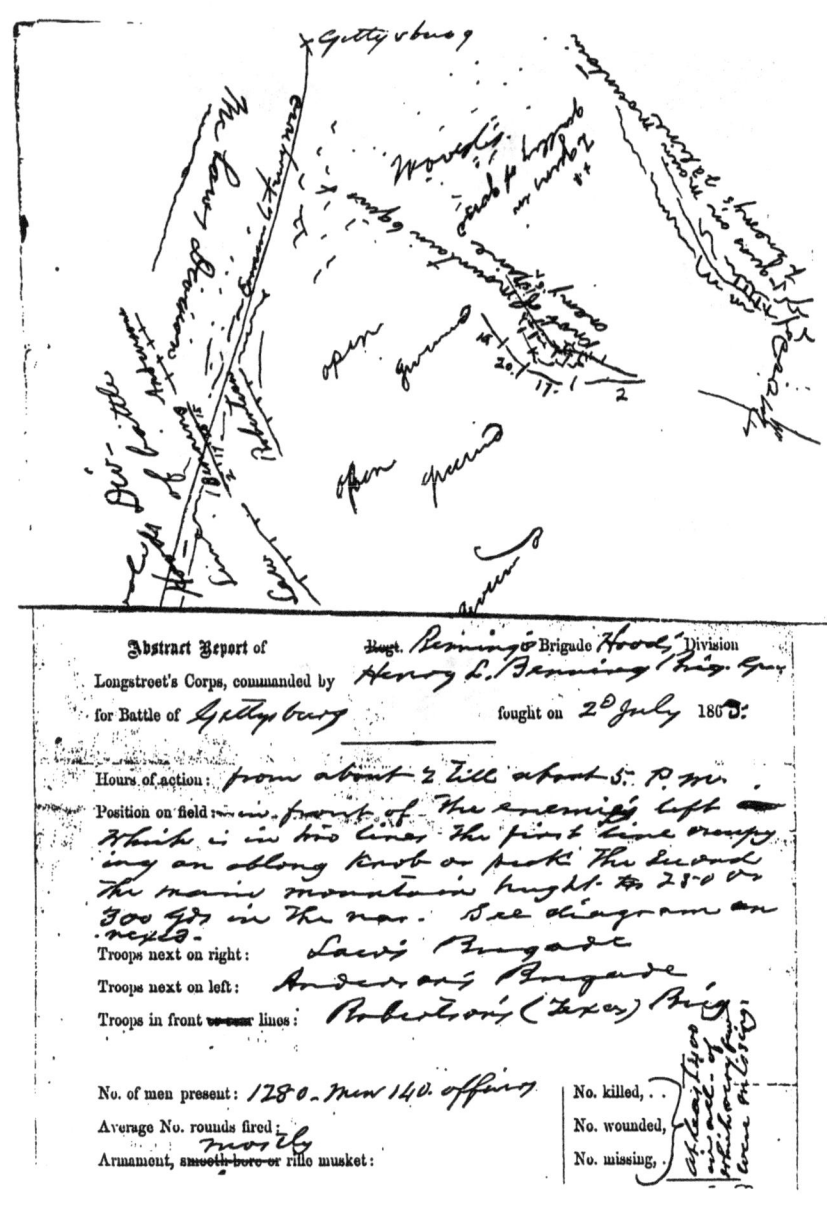

Hand-drawn battle map and report by General Benning, submitted to Edward Porter Alexander. (From the E.P.A. file, UNC Chapel Hill.)

CHAPTER
6
"I Then Marched upon Them and Attacked Them!"

Once again Lee was busy attempting to reorganize his forces. The Battle of Gettysburg had proven to be a very costly endeavor. He was slowly losing his most trusted and competent subordinate commanders. Replacements for the foot soldiers lost in battle were difficult to find. Desertions became more frequent. Many men had suffered the trials of battle for two years, and most of them had never received a furlough. Army life was difficult at best, and the pain of separation from loved ones, for some men, became too intense. President Davis had to declare an amnesty before many would return to their units.

Meanwhile, the Union army was drafting men into compulsive military service. Their industrial might continued to fuel the northern military machine at a fervent pace. Additionally, the North continued choking the South with its maritime blockade.

In spite of its gloomy predicament, the resilient Army of Northern Virginia was far from defeat. The Fifteenth Georgia, although maimed and reduced in size, was now hungry for retaliation. Their veteran chain of command would soon be intact once again and ready to meet the foe. The men would proudly follow Colonel DuBose, and sooner than expected, they did.

On September 7, 1863, Longstreet was deployed with Hood's and McLaw's divisions to the western theater to reinforce the Army of Tennessee. Most of these men were Georgians and their own state was now in peril. The Army of the Cumberland, led by General Rosecrans, had pressured General Bragg's forces to retreat below Chattanooga, Tennessee, and into the state of Georgia.[1]

With a renewed fighting spirit, the Georgians packed up their gear and marched towards Petersburg, Virginia. Here they boarded the trains en route to Georgia. As they passed through Richmond, General Hood rejoined his division. Still suffering from his wound received at Gettysburg, he resumed his post.[2]

Although riding was much preferred over marching, the men suffered through the next several days crammed into box cars. Along the seemingly endless ride, the Georgians had plenty of time to contemplate the seriousness of future events. The 850-mile route entered their beloved state at Augusta, passed through Atlanta, and terminated at Catoosa Station, four miles from Ringgold, Georgia. Thus ended the longest and most famous Confederate troop deployment via rail during the war. The anxious reinforcements of Longstreet's Corps arrived on September 16, disembarked from the trains, immediately rushed to their positions, and were emplaced as the battle began on the nineteenth.

General Longstreet assumed command of the entire left wing of the Army of Tennessee, which consisted of General Buckner's corps and General Hood's corps, the latter being comprised of the divisions of Generals Johnson, Law, and Kershaw.

Benning's "Rock" Brigade remained in its original form, consisting of the Second, Fifteenth, Seventeenth, and Twentieth Regiments.

Although the battle began on September 19, the twentieth marked the "high tide" for General Rosecrans and his army. General Longstreet took immediate advantage of a tactical error committed by the Union forces. He seized the initiative and drove his forces deep into the Union right wing. This tactically brilliant maneuver caused the Union right wing to turn and flee from the field. The ecstatic Georgians screaming their "rebel yell" pursued the Yankees mercilessly. General Rosecrans himself fled to the rear.[3]

Unfortunately, General Bragg failed to complement the situation with additional support. Longstreet's forces had effectively driven a giant southern wedge deep into the Army of the Cumberland and severed its ability to fight. Throughout the evening the Union forces hastily retreated to Chattanooga, Tennessee. Bragg's army, now exhausted, pursued too slowly to destroy them. The following report describes the specific events experienced in Benning's Brigade at the Battle of Chickamauga:

> Report of Brig. Gen. Henry L. Benning, C.S. Army:
> Headquarters Benning's Brigade
> Captain: I have the honor to submit to you the following report of the part taken by this brigade in the battles of the 19th and 20th ultimo on the Chickamauga:
> At about 3 p.m. of the 19th, I was ordered to advance and support Brigadier-General Robertson, who was a little to my left. On advancing, I found him with his brigade hotly engaged with a superior force of the enemy's infantry aided by a battery. The place was on the Chat-

tanooga road near a small house, and a smaller out-house with open ground for 150 or 200 yards in front, and stretching to the right and left, through which ran the road from front to rear. Beyond the open ground all was forest, in which, on the right of the road, was the enemy's battery. Thus the missiles from this battery not only swept over nearly all of the open ground, but passed on with effect far into the level wood in the rear.

When we first encountered the enemy they were at the two houses and on the near side of the open ground. After an obstinate contest they were driven from this position and across the open ground into the woods beyond. We then occupied the ground about the houses. My numbers were too few to venture with them alone to follow the enemy into the woods and into the battery. The place we held was much exposed to the enemy's fire, but with the little cover furnished by the houses, some stumps, and a few scattered trees, I thought I could hold it till the re-enforcements (every minute expected) should arrive, when a general advance might be made and the enemy swept from the opposite wood. We did hold it for a long time, driving back several charges of the enemy to retake it. No re-enforcements came. Finally toward sunset the enemy's fire from his battery and from his infantry, protected by the wood, became so heavy, and so many of our officers and men had fallen, that we had ourselves to retire a short distance. We accordingly took up a new position 100 or 200 yards in the rear of the houses, where we remained till the close of the fight.

We felt much in this engagement the want of artillery to oppose not only to the enemy's artillery but to his infantry; but none came to our aid. None had been attached either to my brigade or to Brigadier-General Robertson's.

My loss was very heavy to my numbers. In the Twentieth Regiment 17 officers out of 23 were killed or wounded. In the other regiments the proportion though not so great was very great. The proportionate loss among the men was but little less. The command fought with a dogged resolution.

On the next day, the brigade was in line a little to the right of the place where it had fought the day before, and a short distance in the rear of Law's brigade. At about 12 m. I was ordered to follow and support that brigade at the distance of from 300 to 400 yards. After advancing, in obedience to this order, 400 or 500 yards, and after having passed the Chattanooga road, Law's brigade, which had moved a little faster than mine, became lost to view in the thick woods. At the same time I saw the enemy in considerable force on his right apparently preparing to attack his flank and rear. I immediately changed the direction of march by bearing to the right and advancing my left, so as to face this enemy. I then marched upon them and attacked them. After a sharp contest they gave way and we pursued them. They made a stand at some artillery in the wood, but were driven again from this position and pursued several hundred yards beyond the guns, when they disappeared in the wood.

In a short time they returned in heavy force and made a desperate effort to recover their ground. Here their was a very obstinate fight. At length I saw them turning my right to get into my rear. We then fell back behind the cannon, facing so as to meet this new demonstration. The enemy followed a short distance, but not far enough to retake the artillery, and for some time kept up with us at long range a desultory fire. Finally they disappeared.

The artillery taken consisted of seven or eight pieces. According to my count there were eight—four brass and four iron pieces. Some of the officers thought that the iron pieces were only three. A flag was taken with the guns.

The brigade, reduced as it was to a handful by the fight of the day before, again suffered heavily. Lieutenant-Colonel Matthews, commanding Seventeenth Georgia, fell mortally wounded while acting in a most heroic manner.

On the previous day 4 field officers had been wounded, 1 I fear mortally—Lieutenant-Colonel Seago, Twentieth Georgia. The other 3 were Colonel DuBose, of the Fifteenth Georgia; Lieutenant-Colonel Sheperd, commanding Second Georgia, and Capt. McLewis, acting major of Second Georgia. Many other officers of the line fell killed or wounded in fight or the other.

Lieut. Herman H. Perry, brigade inspector and acting Adjutant, had his horse shot under him. Owen T____, one of my couriers, had two horses shot under him. Joseph D. Bethune, another, had his horse shot under him and was at the same time himself wounded. The remaining courier (S. Sligh) was knocked from his horse by a piece of shell, which, however, only bruised him. Hardly a man or officer escaped without a touch of his person or clothes.

Colonel Waddell, of the Twentieth; Major Shannon, of the Fifteenth, and Major Charlton, of the Second Georgia, the only field officers left, set a shining example to their men, as did those that were wounded.

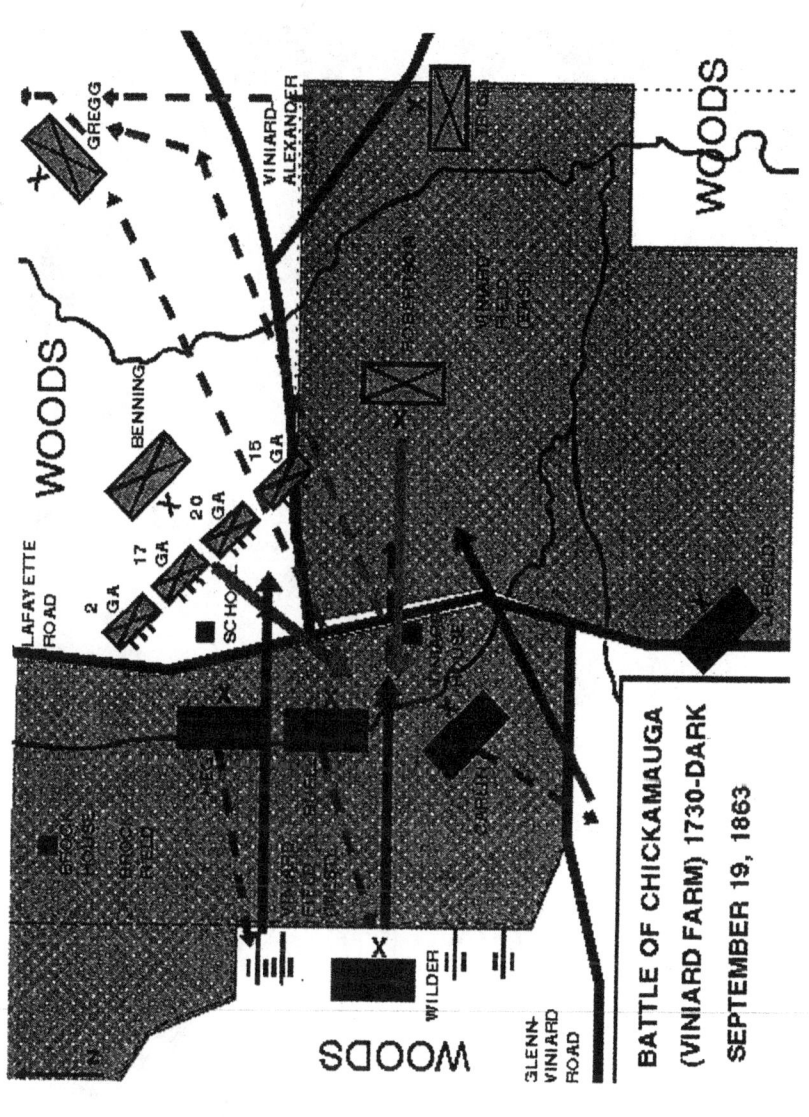

Map of Chickamauga
(Official Record Atlas, Library of Congress)

A list of the casualties has already been forwarded; also a tabular statement of the strength of the brigade on each day. I am, captain, very respectfully, your obedient servant,

Henry L. Benning,
[Brigadier-General, Commanding Brigade][4]

Casualties of the Fifteenth Georgia, as a result of the battle:

Killed	Wounded
12	19

Additionally, General Hood was wounded again. This time his wound resulted in the amputation of a leg. The poor man had now lost the use of an arm and a leg, but he continued to serve the Confederacy. General Benning humbly failed to mention in his report how the conflict affected himself. Several accounts of this battle state that Benning had three horses shot out from under him. Additionally, his clothing was pierced by small arms fire. Near the end of the battle, he mounted an artillery horse and rode it bareback. Upon the suggestion that he throw a saddle on the horse, Benning reportedly stated: "There is no time to saddle horses, we have them going and must keep after them!"[5] The fighting at Chickamauga was conducted at close range and with a murderous tempo that rivaled the action at Gettysburg. Benning again led the brigade by example, and he had certainly earned the respect and admiration of his men.

General Bragg slowly moved his Army of Tennessee into defensive positions overlooking Chattanooga. His army stretched from the heights of Lookout Mountain east across the Chattanooga Valley, and then it hooked north along the heights of Missionary Ridge. In this position Bragg was content to lay siege upon the Union forces of Rosecrans, now encamped in and around Chattanooga. Bragg shelled him daily from the heights.

General Longstreet, in concert with most of the army's high command, was appalled and verbally protested General Bragg's tactics. Longstreet pleaded with President Davis to send General Lee. President Davis and General Lee declined this suggestion. Soon thereafter, President Davis visited the Army of Tennessee and discussed strategy with his field commanders.

As a result of the conference, Bragg continued to lay siege upon the Union forces of Rosecrans, and Longstreet's Corps was detached from General Bragg and sent on a mission to repulse General Burnside's forces. Burnside's Corps had been recently dispatched from Virginia to reinforce

Rosecrans. Unbeknown to the Army of Tennessee, Generals Hooker, Grant, and Sherman were on the march to aid their comrade as well.

Shortly after General Hood was wounded at Chickamauga, Gen. Micah Jenkins was appointed as his replacement. General Jenkins had amassed a fine reputation and his abilities would soon be tested. Upon the arrival of Generals Hooker and Grant, they immediately set forth on a plan to break through the siege by stealthily flanking the Confederate left, under cover of darkness, and gain control of Lookout Valley. This task was soon accomplished, and on October 28, 1863, Hooker marched his men into Lookout Valley and encamped five thousand men. At Wauhatchie, about three miles upriver near the rail depot, he stationed about fifteen hundred men.[6]

This area was the responsibility of General Longstreet, who immediately formulated a plan to attack the smaller force at Wauhatchie. Longstreet decided to dispatch the divisions of Jenkins and McLaws on the mission. Jenkins dispatched Law's Brigade, to keep the larger force from rescuing the smaller one, while Jenkins attacked it. Longstreet intended the division of McLaws to assist Law's brigade, but General Bragg never relayed the order to General McLaws. Meanwhile, Jenkins commenced his mission and attacked with a force of inadequate strength.

The following report was submitted by General Benning concerning the engagement at Wauhatchie, Tennessee, on October 28-29, 1863:

> Report of Brig. Gen. Henry L. Benning, C.S. Army, commanding brigade.
>
> Headquarters Benning's Brigade
>
> Captain: I have the honor to submit to you the following report of the participation of this brigade in the action of the 28th beyond Lookout Creek:
>
> It was, I think, about 8:30 or 9 p.m., when the brigade reached the railroad, having crossed the mountain since dark. There it was halted, and I was informed by the Brigadier-General commanding the division that Law's brigade had already crossed the creek at the lower bridge; that Robertson's was then crossing there; that these two brigades would be on the right of the line of battle, occupying ridges so as to command the road on the other side of the ridges and prevent the force of the enemy encamped on the right from moving up that road to the assistance of the force encamped on the left when that should be attacked; that it would be attacked by Colonel Bratton with Jenkins' brigade; that Jenkins' brigade was already across the creek, having

crossed it at the upper bridge, and was advancing toward the enemy's force encamped on the left; that my brigade must follow Colonel Bratton and occupy the crest of the hill in front of the bridge as soon as Colonel Bratton had passed the hill in marching forward, and that, connecting on the right with the two brigades on the right, I should co-operate with them in preventing the enemy's force on the right from moving up the road to that on the left. In an hour or two, I was ordered to advance.

I crossed the creek, and had to halt again for some time till the troops in my front could get out of my way. At length my brigade ascended the ridge indicated and formed in line of battle on it. I discovered almost immediately that the road was too far off to be commanded from that line. The distance could not have been less than 300 yards, and the intervening ground was a thickly wooded mountain side, in some places very steep, the wood entirely excluding a view of the road. I thought the spirit rather than the letter of my instructions was to be obeyed, and therefore I advanced the brigade until it came within thirty yards of the road. There I halted again in line of battle. Shortly after assuming this position I received an order to march to the left to the railroad. I did so by the flank, thus leaving a wide gap between my brigade and the two on the right.

On arriving at the railroad the brigadier-general commanding informed me that he wished me to select the best position there for covering Colonel Bratton on his return from the attack on the left, whom he had ordered back, or was about to order back. I then placed my line in the road which passes to the right out of the road from the bridge and makes a short cut-off into the valley road from which I had come. Thus my line faced sufficiently toward the left to oppose any force moving from that direction, and yet on the right commanded a part of the valley road, by which it could intercept an attack from that side. Here I ordered a breast-work of rails to be erected as quickly as possible. A pretty good one was put up in a short time. When this was about completed the pickets reported to me that the enemy were near on the right. I then turned the breastwork at right angles, and ran it thirty or forty yards into the woods. The men formed behind this rectangular work. Soon afterward Colonel Logan with the pickets of the division, who having after night-fall been relieved on the other side of the mountain had lately come up and been placed under my command, was ordered by me from his position on my left to a position on my right in continuation of the line across the road into the woods. This order he executed promptly. These dispositions made, we awaited the approach of the enemy. Little firing had taken place. Our pickets had shot down several cavalrymen attempting to dash up the road from the right to the left where the fight was going on, and had taken a few prisoners. The enemy, however, were still near at hand, and a part of them had got into the wood and on the ridge which I by the original order was to occupy. I heard them talking myself, and their line was visible to the pickets. Thus they were threatening to cut us off from the bridge. About the time Colonel Logan had established himself in his new position on my right in the woods, I saw the first of Colonel Bratton's troops returning down the road. They proved to be two regiments, the foremost commanded by Major _____. They were moving in perfect order, and without any sign of hurry or excitement. Knowing that the enemy were in the wood toward the bridge, I requested the major to form his regiment in front of the bridge and face the hill instead of crossing over. He did so. I afterward found him in line there. The rest of Colonel Bratton's command passed down to the bridge by another way nearer the creek, which was out of my sight. When the whole command had crossed the bridge, except that part of it lately formed in line in front of the bridge, I moved my brigade back to the bridge, leaving in the breast-works a strong line of skirmishers. Colonel Logan pursued a similar course with his command. Arriving near the bridge, I deployed the Fifteenth Regiment Georgia Volunteers as skirmishers in front of the bridge and of the line referred to. This line then crossed the bridge and I followed it with the three other regiments of my brigade. My skirmishers were sent for when I commenced moving to the bridge with the three brigades. They all came in safely, having repulsed two attacks of the enemy, one a dash of a small cavalry party on the breast-work across the road, the other an attack of infantry skirmishers on the angle of the work. Thus, captain, I have given you an account of the part this brigade had in the night affair of the 28th, and I regret much having to use so many words for so little matter. We had two or three wounded, not dangerously, and two are missing, no doubt taken prisoners, as they went toward the part of the wood occupied, as we afterward found out, by the enemy. It was important to know where General Robertson's left was. These two young men volunteered to go and ascertain. They were gallant fellows. Their names are John J. Boswell,

Company C, Seventeenth Georgia, and David Zachary, Company H, Seventeenth Georgia.

I am, captain, very respectfully, your obedient servant,
Henry L. Benning, Brigadier-General.[7]

The engagement at Wauhatchie was tactically unimportant; however, it was in actuality the first hostile action to occur in the battles of Chattanooga. It is also important to note that General Jenkins had accomplished a well executed night raid against a superior force. His men had engaged a far superior force than planned (twelve thousand enemy). Additionally, they successfully returned to friendly lines, suffering approximately the same number of casualties that they had inflicted upon the enemy. A large raiding force operating in darkness is very difficult to coordinate on the modern battlefield. The report of General Benning reflects the tactics his forces employed in providing the security and support elements of a daring mission.

General Longstreet undoubtedly had firm confidence in the abilities of the commanders and the men of Benning's Brigade. Their ranks over the past several years of battle had diminished tremendously. In October of 1863, the Fifteenth Georgia consisted of approximately two hundred soldiers. Many of them were still suffering from wounds received during the Battle of Chickamauga. Despite their pain and suffering, the men of the Fifteenth Georgia still maintained a stern devotion to duty.[8]

From "Mountain Campaigns in Georgia" by Joseph Brown. Drawn by Alfred R. Waud.

"Confederate line of battle in the Chickamauga woods" (Battles and Leaders of the Civil War).

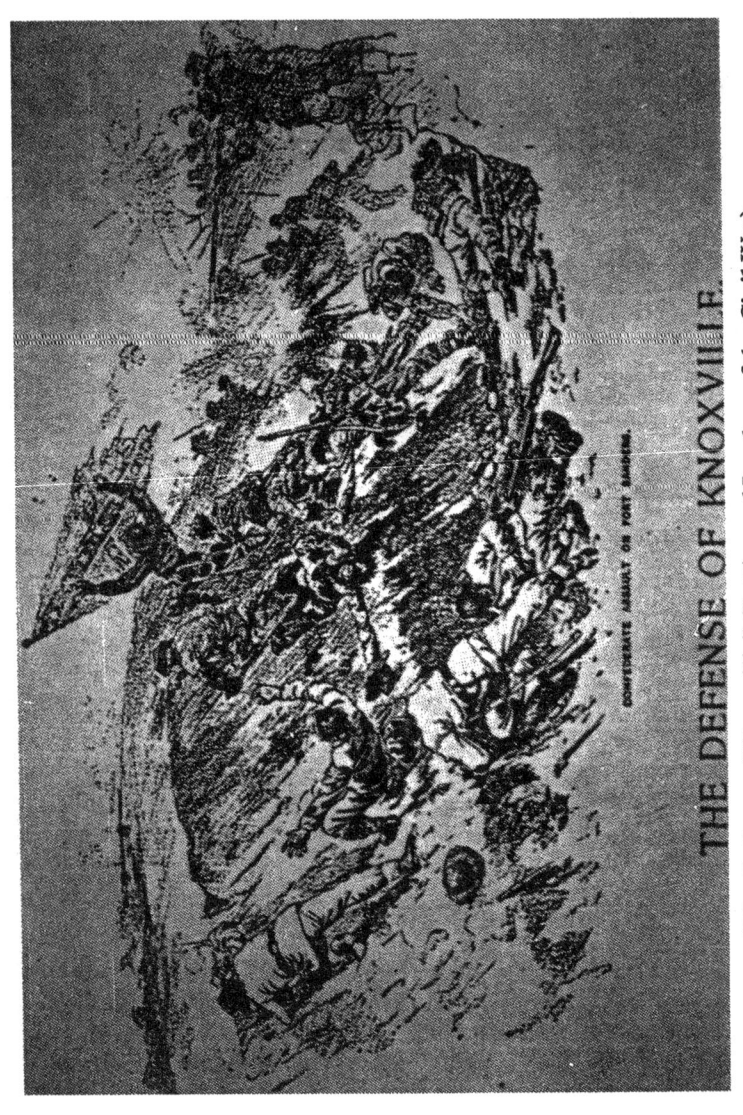

"The Defense of Knoxville" (Battles and Leaders of the Civil War)

CHAPTER

7

THE UNION LINES WERE "ROLLED UP LIKE A WET BLANKET"

On November 3, 1863, General Bragg ordered General Longstreet to move his two divisions and attack General Burnside's Union forces, located in the vicinity of Knoxville, Tennessee. Longstreet had been in favor of this move in the past, but now General Grant had replaced General Rosecrans as commander of the Union army in the western theater. The Union army was also increasing in size and posed a serious threat to Bragg's forces. Grant had already taken control of Lookout Valley. Longstreet was reinforced with four brigades of cavalry and dispatched on his mission.[1]

General Longstreet and his men were certainly happy to be relieved of General Bragg's defensive positions, but winter's cold fury was rapidly approaching. Additionally, the departure of Longstreet's forces weakened Bragg's defense; however, the general had confidence in his positions among the heights overlooking Chattanooga. In spite of the growing threat, Longstreet prepared his forces and set forth on a new campaign.

On the fifth of November, the Fifteenth Georgia and the rest of Longstreet's Corps began their journey. They rode the trains northeast to Sweetwater, Tennessee. Here they disembarked and began a pursuit of Burnside's forces. They slowly forced the Yanks into a defensive posture around Knoxville. A breastworks had been established on the west side of the town, and it was here that Longstreet decided to press battle. Before starting the attack, however, Longstreet waited for several brigades which were being sent up as reinforcements. Finally, just before dawn on November 29, in bitter cold weather, Longstreet assaulted Fort Sanders with the infantry. The attack was spearheaded by the Georgian troops of General McLaw. Although his men were highly capable veterans, the parapets of the fort could not be scaled. Longstreet withdrew his forces, seeing the impracticality of pressing the fight. The Fifteenth Georgia was in line of battle in front of Fort Sanders, but not committed to the fray.[2]

That afternoon a shocking telegram was delivered to General Longstreet. President Davis had sent news of Bragg's defeat at Chattanooga on November 25 and his rapid retreat towards Dalton, Georgia. Longstreet was instructed to quit the siege of Knoxville and rejoin General Bragg. Then another message arrived. This one stated that General Sherman was marching up to join forces with General Burnside.

Longstreet decided to evacuate the siege of Knoxville and move northeast towards Bristol, Tennessee, to establish winter quarters. Perhaps they could rejoin Bragg in the spring. On December 4 Longstreet stealthily withdrew from his positions at Knoxville. His corps of hardened rebel veterans was now on its own; however, it was also in a position to repulse General Grant's grand plan to dominate Tennessee.[3]

Many of the men in the Fifteenth Georgia and the rest of Longstreet's infantry were without shoes. They wrapped cloth and beef hides around their feet and continued the march. The weather was brutally cold with frequent rain and sleet. Out of necessity, they had to burn the fence rails of local citizens in order to survive the long harsh nights. Grant pressed them hard with rear cavalry skirmishes, which resulted in the capture of several beleaguered Confederates. As the barefoot men marched along the frozen mud roads, the sharp, jagged terrain cut their feet. As a result, it was easy for the Union forces to track the Confederates' blood-stained trail. On December 23 Longstreet's forces established winter quarters in various locations throughout East Tennessee. The Fifteenth Georgia settled into an area near Morristown.[4]

Several minor skirmishes and cavalry clashes kept both forces occupied during the next few months, but Longstreet's troops were fairly secure, as the winter weather made open battle impractical for both sides.

The men of Longstreet's Corps managed to survive the difficult winter in East Tennessee, all the while acting like a painful thorn in Grant's side.[5]

As a result of the operations that winter, the Fifteenth Georgia lost:

Killed	Wounded	Captured
0	0	44

The Confederate administration was deeply moved by the tenacity displayed by General Longstreet's men in the face of such difficult challenges. They were so impressed that they passed the following resolutions:

> No. 42. Joint Resolutions of Thanks to Lieutenant-General Longstreet and the officers and men of his command.
> Resolved by the Congress of the Confederate States of America, That the thanks of the Congress are due, and hereby cordially ten-

dered, to Lieutenant-General James Longstreet and the officers and men of his command, for their patriotic services and brilliant achievements in the present war, sharing as they have in the arduous fatigues and privations of many campaigns in Virginia, Maryland, Pennsylvania, Georgia, and Tennessee, and participating in nearly every great battle fought in those States, the commanding general ever displaying great ability, skill, and prudence in command, and the officers and men the most heroic bravery, fortitude, and energy, in every duty they have been called upon to perform.

Resolved, That the President be requested to transmit a copy of the foregoing resolutions to Lieutenant-General Longstreet for publication to his command.

Approved February 17, 1864.[6]

Special recognition in the Confederate States Army was seldom received, especially from the administration in Richmond. Everyone was expected to give a hundred percent at all times, and if you showed aptitude or special capabilities, perhaps you would be promoted and assigned to more difficult duties. All the Confederate forces were worthy of praise, but Longstreet's men had been tasked extensively.

Throughout February and March of 1864, the Confederate hierarchy debated strategy concerning the future deployment of Longstreet's Corps. Finally and thankfully, it was announced that Longstreet and his men would rejoin General Lee's Army of Northern Virginia. Longstreet's forces slowly made their way to Bristol, Tennessee. The troops remained in Bristol for several weeks, awaiting the trains that would carry them on the first leg of their route back to Lee. They departed in mid-April and disembarked at Charlottesville, Virginia. Ironically, they were retracing the same route of arrival as in 1861. They even encamped on the University grounds where they had seen their first victims of the war.

The corps marched from Charlottesville to the vicinity of Mechanicsville, Virginia, arriving there on April 22. The Fifteenth Georgia was once again proudly assigned to the Army of Northern Virginia. Colonel DuBose had recovered from his wounds in Georgia and was again their regimental commander. General Field had returned also and was assigned as their division commander. As always since the resignation of General Toombs, the "Old Rock," General Benning, commanded their brigade. Additionally, the regiment was reunited with several old companions who had been paroled from Union prisons, and the regiment had received 24 young recruits while in

East Tennessee. The regiment was now back up to a strength of approximately 250 officers and men.[7]

General Lee officially welcomed the return of Longstreet's forces with a "Grand Review." General Lee, mounted upon his horse, reviewed his men in an emotional ceremony. Once again, the renowned Army of Northern Virginia was ready to march and fight with a renewed spirit. Lee's army had shared incredible victories against overwhelming forces, but they had also endured the hardships of loss and death. Additionally, every man present realized that there were ominous challenges ahead. General Grant was now in charge of the entire Union Army and had come to Virginia also. He would exercise direct personal supervision over General Meade's forces and soon launch headstrong into a new campaign.

On the first day of May, 1864, the armies of Grant and Lee faced one another from opposite sides of the Rapidan River near the Orange and Alexandria railroad. The Union forces, mostly consisting of fresh troops, numbered nearly 120,000 men. Lee's Confederate troops of 60,000 men were comprised of mainly staunch veterans of previous campaigns. Grant had superior forces but the battleground was on Southern soil. Grant's strategy was to constantly wage war on Lee, press him back against Richmond, and crush him with overwhelming, unending assaults.

Grant launched his plan in the pre-dawn morning on the May 4, 1864, when four Union corps crossed the Rapidan River at Germanna Ford and Ely's Ford. His intent was to crush Lee's right wing. Lee's Second and Third Corps were immediately maneuvered into positions to offset the threat. Longstreet's First Corps, which was stationed further south, marched up the Catharpin Road to establish Lee's right wing. This area was known as the Wilderness. Fighting had occurred nearby at Chancellorsville in 1863. The Wilderness region consisted of dense forest with very thick underbrush. The wooded area where the battle occurred was bisected by two east-west roads: the Orange-Fredericksburg Turnpike was located in the northern region and the Orange Plank Road in the southern sector. The resulting Battle of the Wilderness lasted for two days. The fighting in the northern region was a stalemate throughout the battle; however, the southern sector was Grant's primary objective, as he attempted to flank Lee's right wing, with the prize of Richmond behind it.[8]

On the morning of May 6 two Union corps, in depth, led by Generals Hancock and Getty, attacked the Confederate right wing, defended by General A.P. Hill's Third Corps. The Union forces initially met with great success; however, Longstreet's First Corps came forward at three o'clock that

Battle of the Wilderness (Battles and Leaders of the Civil War)

morning to reinforce Hill's Corps. Benning's Brigade, with the Fifteenth Georgia, was last in line of march, but was ordered to swing around the left of the enemy in concert with several other brigades. This resulted in the collapse of the Union lines.[9] The effect was later described by the Union Corps commander, General Hancock, as "rolled up like a wet blanket."[10]

That afternoon, when everything was going so well for the Army of Northern Virginia, tragedy again befell the South. In the midst of the confusion within the dark forest, Confederate soldiers fired upon approaching men on horseback. General Micah Jenkins, the former Field's Division commander, fell mortally wounded. Additionally, General Longstreet was shot through his throat. His horse came to a halt; the soldiers, realizing their grave mistake, helped him off his mount and propped him against a tree. With a bloody froth emanating from his mouth, General Longstreet managed to encourage his men forward, saying, "Tell General Field to take command, and move forward with the whole force and gain the Brock road." Ironically, this event occurred within the same area in which General Stonewall Jackson had been shot by his own men in 1863.[11]

Unfortunately, General Field was unable to follow through with Longstreet's command. The assault slowed as fire erupted within the dense underbrush. General Burnside's corps reinforced the Union front just as darkness fell upon the field. Throughout the night, the wounded screamed in agony as they were helplessly consumed by the flames.

The casualties suffered by the Fifteenth Georgia during the Battle of the Wilderness:

Killed	Wounded	Captured
16	11	5[12]

On the morning of the seventh, Grant left some of his men on the front, as he slipped the majority of his forces around to the southeast towards Spotsylvania. Lee, in anticipation of Grant's plan, dispatched Gen. Richard Anderson, now commanding General Longstreet's forces, on a sixteen-hour forced march to Spotsylvania. Immediately, in order to halt the enemy's advance, the exhausted Confederates constructed breastworks and hasty defensive fighting positions.

During the engagement on May 6 General Benning was very seriously wounded in the shoulder and carried from the field. Therefore Colonel DuBose now commanded Benning's Brigade. The commander of the Fifteenth Georgia was now Maj. P.J. Shannon. DuBose was assigned the right center brigade on the front line of Field's Division, facing north, one-and-a-half miles northwest of Spotsylvania Court House. Breastworks had been established to their front, as they rested and awaited the inevitable assault from Grant's forces. The other two Confederate corps soon joined them. By May 10 Lee's forces were fully entrenched within a north-pointing-"V" defensive posture.

On the afternoon of the tenth of May, General Warren's Fifth Corps assaulted the section of the Confederate line defended by Anderson's (Longstreet's) Corps. The men of the Fifteenth Georgia, in concert with their Southern brothers, repulsed the Yankee charge. The Union casualties were nearly three thousand men. Several hours later the Union forces consolidated their efforts on the apex of the "V," referred to by the troops as the "Mule Shoe." Here the Union Army made great headway, but they were unable to maintain their advance and withdrew. On May 11 both sides reconsolidated their forces as a heavy rain soaked the field.

On May 12 at 4:30 A.M., Grant launched an assault wave of twenty thousand men into the "Mule Shoe." Lee reinforced this section of the line. The battle raged for several hours and resulted in approximately fifteen thousand casualties. After that fateful day, the "Mule Shoe" was referred to as the "Bloody Angle." Smaller attacks and skirmishes continued throughout the next week. Slowly, on May 20, Grant slid around Lee's left wing, continuing the march towards Richmond.[13] Fortunately for the men of the Fifteenth Georgia, their casualties were light. The casualties suffered by the Fifteenth Georgia at the Battle of Spotsylvania Court House:

Killed	Wounded	Captured
6	10	0[14]

Again, on May 22, Lee sent troops to intercept Grant's forces—this time at Hanover Junction on the North Anna River. Again the Fifteenth Georgia and the rest of the Army of Northern Virginia established defensive lines. They held the line until May 27, when they departed at 11 A.M. for Cold Harbor, once more anticipating Grant's move. Lee began establishing defensive lines at Cold Harbor on the thirtieth of May, as the gigantic Union machine lumbered further southward, on towards Richmond. Grant's forces were now dangerously close to their ultimate goal, the Confederate capital.

Lee bolstered his defense with additional troops from the Richmond and Petersburg perimeter lines. Grant decided to make an assault and prepared his massive army for the task. In the first three days of June 1864, Grant sent wave upon wave of Union forces to their death. During three days of battle the Union forces lost approximately twelve thousand men. In the month since Grant had begun his trek towards Richmond, his losses had reached a total of fifty thousand men.

In comparison, within the Confederate defenses, losses during the Battle of Cold Harbor did not exceed fifteen hundred men—once again, a ratio of thirty-four to one. The Fifteenth Georgia was entrenched on the Confederate left. The Union assaults focused primarily on the Confederate right; however, the unit still suffered several casualties at the Battle of Cold Harbor.

Casualties of the Fifteenth Georgia were:

Killed	Wounded	Captured
3	2	0^{15}

General Grant decided that he could not take Richmond with a frontal assault. He changed his strategy, moved further south, and concentrated his forces on Lee's vulnerable underbelly and lines of communication, located at Petersburg, Virginia. The Southern lines were being stretched exceedingly thin. Resources of nearly everything were dangerously low. Lee and his forces now braced for the realities of a siege and a war of attrition. Even General Longstreet, miraculously healing from a dangerous wound, pondered the unthinkable Southern thought: How much longer could the Confederacy continue to repel Grant's superior forces and unending aggression?[16]

In desperation, Virginia sent old men and boys into the trenches as members of the Local Defense Forces (LDF). The local citizens began to question the uncertainty of their future. General Grant, with an army of superior forces and abundant materials of war, answered their questions with a siege.

CHAPTER
8

"THE 15TH GEORGIA CAPTURED 433 PRISONERS AND BURIED 119 ENEMY, UP CLOSE TO FT. GILMER."

Within the ranks of the Fifteenth Georgia, morale had improved. Since returning to the Army of Northern Virginia, the unit had received light casualties in spite of numerous conflicts with the Yankees. Now that the army was close to Richmond, the foot soldiers enjoyed more abundant rations, which included vegetables. Although the unit had achieved repeated success against Grant's overwhelming Union forces, they could muster only several hundred men.

As always, the Fifteenth Georgia's reprieve was brief. General Grant, on June 12, 1864, stealthily maneuvered his four corps down to the James River. Here his entire army crossed the river, catching General Lee completely by surprise. Responding to Grant's move, Lee marched his army south on June 13. The Fifteenth Georgia responded to his order and marched to a new position thirteen miles south near Malvern Hill. Quietly the Confederates awaited Grant's next assault, towards Richmond. For the next three days, the Army of Northern Virginia improved their trenches and continued to wait.

Finally, early on the morning of the sixteenth, General Lee found out where Grant had gone. His entire army was making preparations to assault General Beauregard's lightly defended entrenchments east of Petersburg. Fortunately, the Union machine moved slowly. Lee's forces immediately rushed south to assist in the defense of Petersburg. The Fifteenth Georgia and the rest of Longstreet's Corps took up positions about thirteen miles north of the main defense lines in front of Petersburg, near Bermuda Hundred. On June 17, Longstreet's Corps drove back elements of General Butler's forces, gaining valuable territory.

Meanwhile, Lee's other forces arrived to reinforce Beauregard's defensive positions and successfully spoiled Grant's initiative to capture Petersburg.[1] The men of the Fifteenth Georgia arrived at their position in the Petersburg line on the eighteenth of June and immediately went to work preparing their entrenchments. Up and down the Petersburg line, all the Confederate forces worked diligently throughout the night to improve their positions. On the nineteenth and twentieth of June, weak Union assaults began to probe the line but they were all successfully repelled. In the fighting on the twentieth, the Fifteenth Georgia suffered two more men, killed in action. They were both experienced, veteran fighters—Lt. W. R. Walters and Cpl. Samuel Roe of Company H. Thus began the Siege of Petersburg. For the next several months, General Grant launched several unsuccessful assaults at various positions in and around the Richmond and Petersburg lines.²

The siege added to the soldiers' misery. Soon scurvy began to affect everyone. As a result of the dwindling supply of fresh vegetables, the men's gums became sore and bled. A serious drought affected the region, and no rain fell for forty-seven days. This began on June 3 and ended on July 19. Body lice added their very personal form of aggravation. Sanitation was primitive, and worst of all, it became a war of sudden death from the handiwork of snipers. Anyone exposing himself to the enemy lines for just a short moment was a potential victim of human target practice.³

On July 29 the Fifteenth Georgia was relieved from its position near the center of the line at Petersburg. Field's Division was reassigned to defend the area between Chaffin's Farm in the south, up to the Darbytown road in the north, along the defensive perimeter between Richmond and Petersburg.

Meanwhile, General Grant had decided to expand his lines northward towards Richmond. On August 13 Grant dispatched two corps from City Point. They traveled north up the James River and disembarked under cover of darkness at Deep Bottom. Here they formed their line of battle. At dawn, on the fourteenth, they attacked the Confederate defenses on a four-mile front. Initially, with the element of surprise and overwhelming forces, the Union met with success. They punched a hole through the earthworks of General Law's and General Anderson's brigades, but their progress was soon halted.⁴ A news reporter from the *Richmond Enquirer* witnessed the following scene:

> Pausing in a ravine long enough to reform their lines, Colonel DuBose, being the only brigade commander then on the immediate field of conflict, assumed command of several detachments from other commands, and, acting in concert with Col. Howard and the Alabama regiments on the right and Col. Little on the left, with a yell that only rebels know how to make, charged and carried the works under a

galling fire, and, Colonels DuBose and Little throwing their commands across the fortifications, swept the enemy pell mell far beyond, inflicting heavy loss.

The observant reporter added, "Colonel DuBose, who has commanded Benning's Brigade with unvarying success since the morning of the battle of the Wilderness, acted with conspicuous gallantry on this occasion, and no other officer of my acquaintance is more deserving of promotion." The fighting continued back and forth throughout the next day, with frequent skirmishing and artillery duels. Once again the Union forces penetrated the Confederate lines, at the positions of the Alabama regiments. The reporter of the *Richmond Enquirer* continues his coverage with:

But, in the nick of time, Colonel Coward, of the 5th South Carolina regiment of Bratton's brigade, and Colonel DuBose, with the 15th, 17th and 20th Georgia regiments, reached the field, and though much exhausted by a rapid march, co-operating with each other, charged the heavy advancing columns in the center, and drove them back to the breastworks our men had vacated. . . . He (enemy) left in our hands on the Darbytown Road over 200 of his dead and many wounded, besides over 400 prisoners and 2,080 stands of arms and the colors of his "gallant COLORED TROOPS. . . . And the prisoners captured on this part of the field represent 54 regiments, which give some idea of the force with which he made the attack.[5]

The fighting in the vicinity of the New Market heights ended with the Confederates maintaining their defensive lines intact; however, the Union forces would return with a vengeance.

With the battle ended, the soldiers went back to work in the trenches. The tasks of digging, strengthening, and extending their lines were never ending. The Fifteenth Georgia now assumed a semi-permanent position on the New Market line. This line was formed in the shape of a "U," with the curve facing the enemy. The curve also served as the center of the line, through which the New Market Road bisected. The New Market Road connected the New Market community with Richmond, which was ten miles to the northwest. Immediately below the New Market heights was Deep Bottom, on the James River, where the Yankees had launched their assault on August 14-16. Benning's Brigade, commanded by Colonel DuBose, and Gregg's Texas Brigade, commanded by Colonel Bass, were the only veteran forces located between Richmond and another assault; however, Lee determined that another assault at this location was not likely. He considered the most critical threat to be directly in front of Petersburg.

Strategically, in the big picture, he was correct; therefore he concentrated his forces at Petersburg and maintained the remaining brigades of General Field's Division as a mobile reinforcement unit which could be sent up from Petersburg if Grant attacked in the vicinity of New Market.[6]

In the meantime, the soldiers of the Fifteenth Georgia worked on their line, tried to stay healthy, and read the newspapers with great anxiety. A dreadfully depressing, seemingly unreal nightmare was occurring back home in Georgia. The Union forces invading their home state were laying siege to Atlanta. Their old hero, General Hood, attempted to repel General Sherman's forces, but eventually Atlanta fell, and the Yankees took the city on September 2, 1864.[7]

Throughout the month of September, Union troops continued to lay siege to Petersburg. Suddenly, in a surprising assault early before dawn on September 29, Grant renewed the offensive. He sent General Birney's X Corps, marching all night, and attempted to take the Confederate line at the New Market heights. Almost simultaneously, he sent General Ord's XVIII Corps across the James River at Aiken's Landing. Ord's forces concentrated their immediate efforts to the northwest, up the Varina Road towards Fort Harrison. The Confederate forces standing between Richmond and the twenty-four thousand men sent to threaten the capital city numbered approximately six thousand.[8]

General Gregg, in command of the Confederate forces headquartered at Chaffin's farm, sent warning of a massive attack to General Lee. Field's mobile reserve unit, in Petersburg, was ordered to Gregg's aid, but they did not arrive until too late that evening. Meanwhile, General Lee himself moved up towards Chaffin's farm to witness the battle.[9]

On the battlefield, at the New Market line, the men of the Texas Brigade, commanded by Colonel Bass, Benning's Brigade, still under the command of Colonel DuBose, and a mixed unit of dismounted Virginia cavalry, commanded by Colonel Gary, opened fire on General Birney's "Colored Troops" advancing in mass. The Union forces bravely charged the New Market heights but they became entangled within the abatis. Unable to penetrate the obstacles strategically emplaced on the sloping terrain, Birney's troops were literally cut to pieces. A few brave men managed to reach the Confederate positions, only to be captured or, because of the hatred of negro soldiers, simply murdered. The survivors staggered or crawled to the rear, in retreat. The lead brigade of the Union corps had been virtually eliminated.

At Fort Harrison the defenders went into action against General Ord's rapidly advancing corps. Unfortunately, only four of the nine cannons within the fort were operational. Lieutenant Guerrant's "Goochland Artillery," consisting of thirty-five men, made good use of the few operational cannons, unleashing their large-caliber fury directly through the human waves rushing before them. There was a small detachment of militiamen stationed at the fort (LDF), but they were armed with old smooth-bore muskets and only had ten rounds each.

Luckily, seven companies of the Seventeenth Georgia had just arrived with a detail of convicts and negroes who were going to work on the entrenchments. Suddenly the war had reappeared. They dispatched their detail to the rear and joined the fray.[10]

Capt. Judge Martin, Company G, Seventeenth Georgia, described the chaotic pace of events as follows:

> A courier dashed up and said that the enemy were attacking the Texas Brigade, and I was ordered to go back and assist them. We returned as rapidly as possible; and when we got opposite the Phillips House, just in front of our breastworks, we saw that the Texans had killed "niggers" galore, and the fight at that point was over. Just as this attack had been repulsed a courier came down and ordered us to reinforce Battery Harrison. We then hurried as rapidly as possible along the line of breastworks; and when we came in sight of Fort Harrison, it seemed that the whole world in front was full of bluecoats. When we reached the point in our line of breastworks where they turned into a right angle to Fort Harrison, four Federal flags had gone up on the fort and on the breastworks surrounding it.[11]

With the enemy now in command of Fort Harrison and that portion of the exterior line, the Fifteenth Georgia and the rest of the forces in the vicinity of the New Market heights, fell back to the exterior line of defenses, two miles behind the New Market line. The exterior line was a long trench five miles in front of Richmond. The line was reinforced with fortifications at various locations of tactical importance. Fort Harrison was the largest and most heavily fortified. They all had been constructed with large ditches in front which served as obstacles to an attacking force; however, General Ord's Union forces now occupied the premier property on the line.

Back on the New Market line, the Union colored troops continued to press their assault as the Confederates retreated to their exterior line. Birney's Corps had finally succeeded in taking the heights but at an extremely high price. Upon seizing this valuable property, both Birney and Ord reorganized their respective corps, surveyed their situation, and continued their assaults on towards Richmond.

Meanwhile, General Gregg prepared his thinly stretched forces along the exterior line and awaited the Union onslaught. The Second and Twentieth Georgia regiments of Benning's Brigade made futile assaults to recapture Fort Harrison, but they were immediately repulsed. Colonel DuBose took charge of the situation along the exterior and intermediate lines.

Retreating Confederate artillery pieces were emplaced within Forts Johnson, Field, and Gregg. They were supported by the Second, Fifteenth, and Seventeenth Georgia regiments and the Local Defense Forces. DuBose had the artillery fire upon the enemy within and around Fort Harrison. At the same time the Texas Brigade and Gary's cavalry arrived on the line. At this point General Gregg assumed command of the line. Behind them, extending west and north, General Ewell, commander of the Richmond interior lines and the militiamen, maintained their preparedness as a reserve force.

Richmond was now in the most dire straits of the war. Two Union corps, were now just five miles from the Southern capital, but they had some angry Confederates between them and their prize.

Leading his men below Fort Harrison, General Ord was wounded and replaced by General Heckman. Slowly and with piecemeal, uncoordinated advances, the new Union commander pressed alternating brigades against the Confederate defensive positions. Fortunately for the Confederates, the terrain between their position at Fort Johnson and the Yankees at Fort Harrison was a flat, open field. This situation enabled the artillery and riflemen, behind protective earthworks, to fire repeatedly and safely into the rushing Union mobs. Shortly after being replenished with ammunition, DuBose was attacked by several Union brigades. He surprised them by sending the Second and Seventeenth regiments on a flanking maneuver around their left. With their shrieking "rebel yell" they tore into the unsuspecting Yanks as the artillery opened on their front, firing canister shot at close range. The Georgians captured men of the XVIII Corps, which confirmed to Lee that he needed to send reinforcements in larger quantity. Unfortunately, it would be several hours before they could reach the line. Although the Fifteenth Georgia and her sister units were at their smallest strength ever, they were being called upon to provide the largest service yet rendered.

As the Union line slowly inched northward throughout the day, Dubose stretched his thin line from Fort Johnson in the south, to Fort Gregg in the center, and Fort Gilmer in the north. Fort Gilmer was the largest, with a moat eight-by-ten-feet deep. The fort had two artillery pieces, fragments of Gary's men, and the Fifteenth Georgia Regiment, commanded by Capt. Madison Marcus.

Finally, in the afternoon, General Birney re-entered the battlefield, after securing the New Market heights, and reorganizing his exhausted corps. He decided to concentrate his forces against Fort Gilmer. Birney attacked toward the Confederates' front with piecemeal units of his New York and Pennsylvania regiments. They were easily repulsed with enfilade fire from the entire Confederate line, and they retreated with five hundred casualties. Next Birney sent in a colored brigade consisting of the Seventh, Eighth, and Ninth USCT regiments. These brave black men immediately began to experience the same deadly fire unleashed on the previous Yankee assault; however, this time the Georgians purposely allowed them to get closer, so as to send, up close, horrendous volleys of fire into the assaulting waves. Stumbling through the dense underbrush and over the bodies of their dead and wounded comrades with dogged determination, the colored troops managed to reach Fort Gilmer. They rushed directly down into the moat, where they could rest. The Georgians could not see directly over the parapet and into the ditch below.

The Union troops were unable to climb the vertical dirt walls and tried heaving themselves on top and over the wall. Three times they tried to attack by lifting up their fellow soldiers, but with each assault that attained the height, the Georgians shot them back down.[12] Colonel DuBose wrote that:

> Among the negroes killed was a certain Corporal Dick who seemed to be a prominent man among his fellow soldiers, as soon as he fell, some of the buck negroes cried out, " Dare now, white folks done killed Corporal Dick, de best man in de regiment."[13]

The news quickly ran along the line that negro troops were stuck in the moat. Many of the Georgians and Texans moved from their place in the line over to Fort Gilmer, looking for "a chance to shoot a nigger."[14] Shortly thereafter, the artillerymen lit fuses on several cannon shells and dropped them into the ditch. After the horrible carnage this caused, the colored troops surrendered. Some colored troops reached Fort Gregg and even managed to steal the colors of the Twentieth Georgia.

As evening fell and reinforcements arrived on the line in great number, the colored brigade retreated back to their lines. General Gregg later reported to General Lee that at the attack of Fort Gilmer, on September 29, 1864, "the 15th Georgia captured 433 prisoners, and buried 119 enemy, up close to Fort Gilmer."[15]

The Georgians of Benning's Brigade welcomed thankfully the arrival of the remainder of Field's Division, four brigades of Hoke's Division, and General Lee himself. The Fifteenth Georgia, along with the remainder of Benning's Brigade, the Texas Brigade, and Gary's forces, were relieved of their positions on the line. They fell back behind the line, where they received some badly needed rest. Heroically, they had repulsed wave after wave of Union assaults throughout the entire day without rest.

Although the Union forces, could see their objective in the distance, the tiny band of Southern veterans denied the Yankees their prize.[16]

General Grant, although robbed of what could have been a glorious victory and the capture of Richmond, had still gained a tactical achievement with the capture of Fort Harrison. This situation caused General Lee grave concern. He wanted Fort Harrison back!

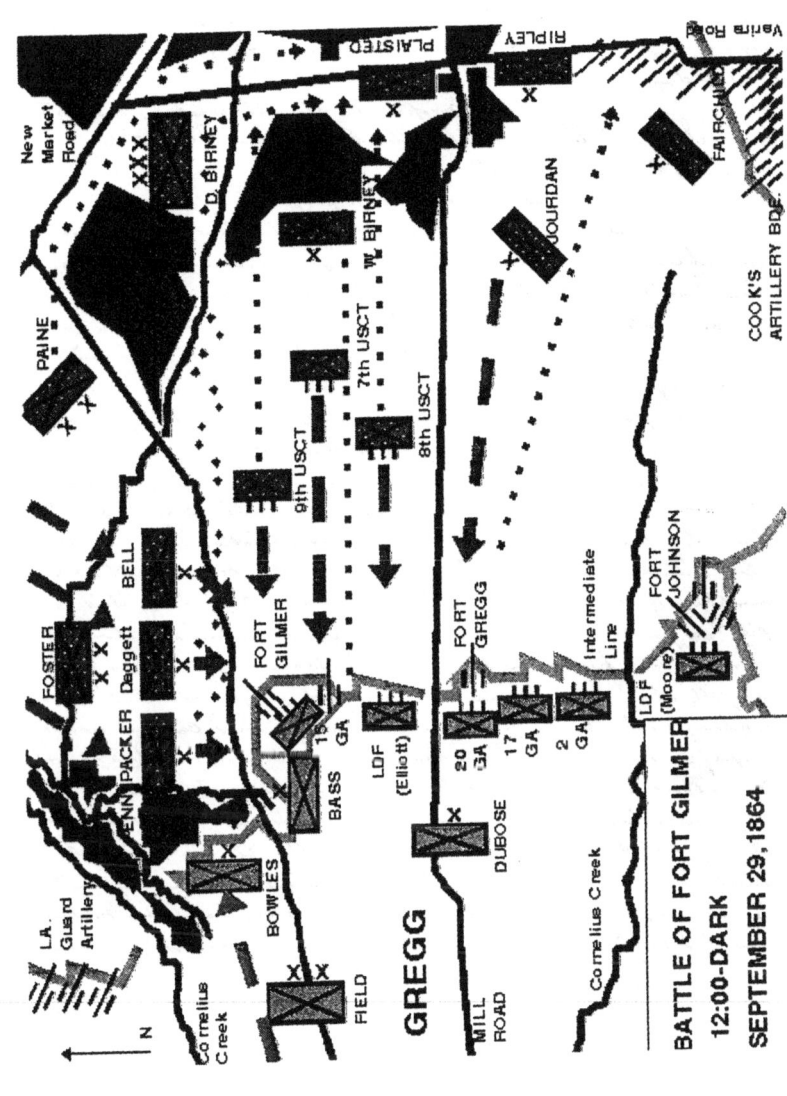

Near Richmond Va. Nov. 26th 1864.

My dear dear Mother,

    I propose to close the week by writing to you. It is Saturday night after Supper, and I am sitting at my desk & have a candle. So I thought as I may be employed tomorrow I will at least begin a letter to you tonight.

Since I last wrote home, which was to Sallie last Sunday, we have changed our Camp. We moved last Wednesday to this Camp where I suppose we will remain for the winter. We consider that we have gone into Winter quarters. We are I suppose about same distance from Richmond as our last camp, about 5 miles, and on the Darby-Town road; — about three quarters of a mile in rear of the line of works occupied by our Brigade. It is a low flat and wet spot in winter, but the best to be found, & by the pray we can make it a passable camp. Water is scarce, though it will soon be abundant. Wood is the principal object, and with Economy from the start there will be enough to keep us comfortable. Every tent, bunk, & hut will soon have a chimney, which will economise the consumption of wood, and you have no idea how comfortable it is to sit by a fire place. There are several already in pleasant operation. I would have been sitting by my own fire place too by this time, but I am all alone now. German is out with the wagons all the time, and Whitney went up the Country last Tuesday. So I can not do it by myself. This I could have done much towards it, but there are only 3 or 4 axes in our Camp & they have been in constant use.

Ben Culver has been sleeping with me for some time. Tonight I went to the hay-stack & brought in a turn to put our blankets on. So I think I will rest better to-night. Last Tuesday night it cleared off and turned very cold & has continued so ever since though it is moderating now & I think will rain Tomorrow, as it is now cloudy all over.

Wiley Letter, November 1864

CHAPTER
9
"O . . . How Long Must It Continue!"

On the morning of September 30, 1864, with the Yankees threatening Richmond at such a close distance, the citizens panicked. The local militia and reserve forces were called to duty. Businesses closed and people packed and left town. The railroad from Petersburg to the Richmond defense lines became congested with reinforcements. In the midst of confusion and chaos, General Grant threatened the Petersburg line in the south. This prompted Lee to return some of his forces to their original positions. Fortunately, the two Union corps to his front were exhausted from their actions on the previous day and had suffered nearly three thousand casualties.

Lee decided to assault Fort Harrison with his First Corps, which was still led by General Anderson. The division of General Field, minus Benning's Brigade, the Texas Brigade, and Gary's forces, would lead the attack. Around noon the Confederate artillery began its preparatory barrages on Fort Harrison.

Field's Infantry Division crept forward and at 1:45 began its assault on Fort Harrison. These highly capable veterans tried their best with several assaults, but never got close to the fort. To assault the fort, they were required to cross the same open field between Fort Johnson and Fort Harrison where the Union troops were trapped on the previous day. The entire affair was a disaster. The Union forces cut the troops in the open to pieces. That afternoon Field's Division staggered back to Fort Johnson in defeat as a heavy downpour of rain began cleansing the field. The field in front of the forts of the intermediate line was littered with mangled corpses.

Meanwhile, Union cavalry forces extended their lines due north across the Darbytown Road, moving closer and closer towards Richmond. On October 7, 1864, Generals Field and Hoke moved north to repel the advancing Union cavalry units along the Darbytown Road. The Confederates were unable to push the Union forces back; however, they did achieve the establishment of a north-to-south defense line with breastworks across the

Darbytown Road and behind Cornelius Creek. It was a costly effort, and it resulted in the death of General Gregg.[1]

On October 13 the Union cavalry attacked the new Confederate defense line on the left (north) of the Darbytown Road. This position was defended by the Fifteenth Georgia and its fellow regiments of Benning's Brigade. The Georgians successfully repelled the enemy, but Captain Madison Marcus of the Fifteenth, rallying his men along the line, was killed. Minor skirmishes continued along the line until the end of October.[2]

On October 19 General Longstreet returned to duty, having recovered from the throat wound received during the Battle of the Wilderness. General Benning also resumed command of the "Rock" brigade upon recovering from his wound received at the same battle. During the fall of 1864 the Fifteenth Georgia suffered:

Killed	**Wounded**	**Captured**
18	30	13[3]

In November the Fifteenth Georgia began construction of their winter quarters behind the lines of the Darbytown road. Heavy skirmishing continued around the south of Petersburg, but the lines in front of the Georgia troops remained quiet. As the Georgians prepared for the arrival of the wintry winds, a very ruthless storm commenced back home. General Sherman and his marauding Union forces departed Atlanta and began their horrible "march to the sea."[4]

Several members of the Fifteenth Georgia had been promoted and assigned to duties on General Benning's staff. Maj. Edgeworth Bird had been serving as the brigade quartermaster, and his clerk was his cousin, Sgt. Samuel H. Wiley. Bird had been severely wounded at the Battle of Second Manassas, and Wiley had a surgeon's certificate that kept him from the front lines. The one thing that all Georgia soldiers had in common with one another, from general to private, was the fear and hatred of Sherman. His occupation of their home state was the topic of discussion and the foremost preoccupation of the entire brigade.[5]

The misery of siege life, boredom, and constant concern for their homes dampened the spirits of the Georgia veterans. They had been fighting gallantly for so long, but there was nothing they could do about Sherman. For the common fighting man this frustration was excruciatingly painful. For Samuel Wiley, life in the army had become quite depressing. Major Bird and several of his life-long friends were transferred. He seldom saw his old friends, and he did not enjoy his work in the Quartermaster Department.

The lives of Wiley's regimental comrades were very similar during this latter phase of the war. Their sentiments were reflected in a letter from Sam Wiley to his parents:

Near Richmond Va. Nov. 26th, 1864.

My dear Pa & Ma,

How I wish I could step in to your room this morning, *if you yet have a room—if you yet have a home.* It did not rain much last night & is quiet pleasant this morning, tho it is cloudy. I have just finished my breakfast & will resume this before I am put to work. I slept unusually well and am in good health. I am restrained from enjoying my good condition and the comforts I have from the constant reflections that *you mav be stripped of every- thing*—negroes stolen away—stock & provisions all taken—all your clothing destroyed—your house burned and you all *perhaps* turned out without anvthing and even without a place to put your heads! All these reflections are caused by the knowledge that Sherman's army is abroad in Middle Georgia, and I am obliged to conclude from his having been near Macon, next near Augusta that his route must have been through *Sparta.* There is clearly room or reason to hope that you all have escaped. It is most tantalizing—distressing—Maddening. The latest we have heard from Sparta was the 16th, Capt. Forbes recd. a letter from his wife—Nothing said about the approach of an invading army. No more allusion to it than yours contained. Every one here is painfully anxious to hear. We conclude that our homes and property are scathed and plundered, and— — well we imagine the *worst.* When I think of what *may* possibly be the situation of my dear aged & infirm parents and my dear wife & little innocent children & other near & dear relatives and friends I *chide* myself for being a *drone*; for not doing something active, actual & practical. Here I am in a safe place, *behind* an army of invincible soldiers, a great part of my time with nothing to do, comfortably clad & enough to eat & a tent to sleep in—what the Govt. does not furnish me is contributed from your strained resources. Every day with you all brings its cares and anxieties.

There is no want of industry on your part—& with rigid economy & restricted indulgence in all things for *years* back, to my knowledge, *we* have only about managed to keep together. We have not grown *rich before* the *war* began & are rapidly going down hill now. What is the cause? I will tell you what I think. It is the *presence* & expense of an idle lazy sickly deceitful discontented family of negroes.

I believe they have been as a *sponge* to soak up all the substance & increase of profit of a few who have always rendered reluctant compulsory service. With you especially there is work so far behind, so many sick, the demand of the Govt. for a tithe of what is produced when the negroes do not produce *enough* to support *themselves*, & when every article of necessity which is not produced at home commands such a fabulous price, how can I drive these thoughts away & find comfort in the future. In the midst of all this state of things comes the probability of the coming disaster: Sherman's raiders among you in your house—stealing, plundering, & destroying everything—then burning your house dear old "Rocky Hill," & my home & you all perhaps disported of everything, turned out to seek the charity of a district equally impoverished. My only hope is that Shermans peculiar situation obliged him to be very hurried in his forays & therefore we are not clean striped of everything. I say I often chide myself for occupying such a place of comparative ease & freedom from danger, and feel compelled to rush to the front, regardless of my "Surgeons Certificate" and—well, if I should, everything is quiet there, and what could I do to avenge your private wrongs & insults. O that I could resolve *myself* into a *host* & throwing myself among them utterly destroy them from the face of the earth. Indeed I would disregard my privilege of remaining in the rear, rouse and shake off my frailty, and assume the strength & will of a defender of dear & sacred rights. I am not well pleased any how as I once was. Pat is gone. Edge is gone. The Culvers are always away, Capt. Perry whom I liked very much is transferred—Capt. Forbes is trying to get an assignment somewhere. Q.M's (Quartermasters) and their *attachees* are subjects of universal disrespect. Selfishness, blasphemy, obscene conversations, gluttenous, ghastly indulgence & disreputable & sinful practices which I witness, make me shudder, & long & pray for restoration of the *pure* precincts of *our own* humble & dear circle. As in the days preceeding the *flood* God saw that the wickedness of man was great in the earth, so it seems to me it is now. O *how long* must it continue! I am so anxious to hear the *fate* of you all & our neighborhood—particulars. Well, I reckon I have written enough. Give my love to sister and brothers & to all the children."[6]

On November 16, 1864, Colonel DuBose was promoted to the rank of brigadier general. He was then placed in command of Wofford's Brigade in Kershaws Division. The men of the Fifteenth Georgia were happy for him, but with the cold of winter, the scarcity of food, and Sherman's devastation of Georgia, any cause for celebration had been effectively ruined.[7]

The months of January and February of 1865 passed slowly. Both armies remained within their positions, guarding the lines and trying to stay warm. Further south, however, General Sherman had turned his forces north and was now cutting a path through South and North Carolina towards Richmond. Throughout the dreadful winter, many Confederates deserted and returned to their homes. Sadly, many men from Georgia realized their worst fears. During their absence, Sherman and his army had struck at the very soul of the Southern cause. For many, the Georgia of their past had been vanquished forever.[8]

Just as the weather began to improve, on April 1, 1865, Grant launched his forces into the Petersburg line. Southwest of Petersburg at the Battle of Five Forks the Confederates suffered a costly defeat. This assault was immediately followed on April 2 with a massive Union assault from the east, which resulted in the collapse of the defensive lines. Lee had no choice but to retreat to the west or be annihilated. The Fifteenth Georgia and her sister regiments served as the rear guard for the Confederate army. With great honor and pride, they protected the army's retreat. To their immediate front, they anxiously observed the vast Union Army. Stealthily it began to rise and cautiously maneuver into a position to strike. Fortunately, the retreat proceeded rapidly. Benning's Brigade was able to efficiently disengage and joined the march.[9]

Lee dispatched his forces on different routes. Their initial goal was Amelia Court House, where his army was to be given rations. But the food never arrived. Lee's army was now being closely pursued by Grant's Union forces. They only slowed down as they cut through and finally achieved the prizes of Richmond and Petersburg. Lee's ultimate goal was to link up with General Johnson's western forces but this would never occur.

For the next week the Army of Northern Virginia marched incessantly westward. Lee followed a route parallel to the rail line to Farmville. Longstreet's Corps arrived at Farmville first, after fighting back pursuing Union forces at High Bridge on the Appomattox River. In Farmville his beleaguered forces linked up with the wagon trains, which were carrying their badly needed rations.

Unfortunately, much of Lee's army failed to outmaneuver their pursuers. On April 6, at Saylers Creek, Anderson's Corps fought bravely but was defeated. His men were utterly exhausted and starving. Among the captives was Gen. Dudley M. DuBose. General Lee lost one-fourth of his remaining army during this battle, about eight thousand men.

After Generals Lee and Longstreet evacuated Farmville on the seventh of April, they marched with the intention of reaching Lynchburg to the west. Unfortunately, the Union forces successfully kept them from retreating along their desired route by continuously blocking them with superior forces. Longstreet's troops established a line of battle northeast of the Cumberland Church, a short distance north of Farmville. The Fifteenth Georgia, with Benning's Brigade, was assigned to the center of the line. In a "U"-shaped formation, facing northeast, the remaining forces of Field's Division and the bulk of the Army of Northern Virginia awaited the Union's next move. That afternoon at three o'clock, General Miles assailed the Confederates with his corps of Union infantry. Several Union brigades were launched towards the Confederates that afternoon and they were all repulsed.[10]

Late in the evening, the Union corps was reinforced and Grant sent Lee a note which offered him an opportunity to surrender. Lee read the note and gave it to General Longstreet. The First Corps commander quickly passed it back to Lee, saying "Not yet."[11]

That night the Confederates slipped away from their positions and began an all-night march to the west. The Union cavalry of Sheridan and Custer rode on to Appomattox Court House, arriving on the eighth of April. This move effectively cut off Lee's continuing westward march. Meanwhile, the bulk of the Union army was right behind him. The Fifteenth Georgia, as an element of Fields Division, was emplaced south of New Hope Church along the Lynchburg Stage Road. Field's Division formed its final line of battle facing the Union's entire II and VI Corps, which had a combined effective strength of twenty-four thousand men. Field's Division had dwindled to barely four thousand veteran warriors.[12]

Since retreating from the defenses of the Richmond front, the Fifteenth Georgia had lost seventeen men captured and one killed. Fighting in the vicinity of Farmville, Virginia, on April 6, 1865, Pvt. James Fain of Company H lost his life. Fain achieved the sad distinction of being the last battlefield casualty from the Fifteenth Georgia Infantry Regiment—tragically, just three short days before the Fifteenth Georgia laid down their arms.[13]

Seeing the futility of continuing combat against incredible odds, General Lee wisely decided to discuss terms of surrender. While the soldiers waited on the line in great anticipation, Generals Grant and Lee determined fair conditions of surrender and confirmed them with their signatures. Upon Lee's return to his men, he somberly announced their fate, and simply told them : "Go to your homes and resume your occupations. Obey the laws and become as good citizens as you were soldiers."[14]

The stalwart men of the Army of Northern Virginia wept. They were officially paroled on April 9, 1865. For the survivors of the Fifteenth Georgia, the war was over. Approximately 258 officers and men from the 15th Georgia surrendered at Appomattox. They turned in their weapons, the Union forces fed them, and then they began their long journey home. Most of the Georgians had formerly been farmers. It was early spring and not too late to set out crops and rebuild their lives.[15]

One of the common soldiers that set forth to rebuild his life as a new citizen of the United States of America was Fourth Sgt. James Clayburn Brown of Company H. Prior to the war he was a typical Georgia dirt farmer and proud son of the South from Hart County. Answering the Southern call to arms, he left his new bride, Mary Matilda, and his baby girl Rebecca at home. He left for the field of battle with his two brothers, A.R. and Samuel. Within one year, Samuel's young body was consumed by disease. He was buried alongside many other young men just like him, whose final resting place became one of the many Confederate cemeteries in Richmond. A.R. was shot in the leg at Second Manassas. Consequently his leg was amputated and he spent the rest of his life as a one-legged farmer. James survived the ravages of disease, but he was captured at the Battle of Gettysburg and later exchanged. He returned to duty and continued fighting until the fateful events of April 1865. After he got home, he rebuilt his life and his farm. James and Mary made up for their separation and they were soon the proud parents of fourteen children. James lived to be a great-grand father and died at the age of eighty. He was one of the few survivors from Hart County and he is buried there.[16]

Robert Ware, the younger brother of Sergeant Thomas L. Ware, survived nineteen agonizing months of prison in the federal facility at Point Lookout, Maryland. He was paroled on February 18, 1865. He was then exchanged for a Union prisoner at City Point, Virginia. Three days later he was released. He returned to his family in Georgia, carrying with him his brother's precious reflections of the war. The five-volume diary of Thomas L. Ware has since become a wealth of information and insight into his own private life and death and that of the Confederacy.[17]

Major Edgeworth Bird and his "Cousin Sam," Samuel H. Wiley, survived the war and returned to Hancock County. Both Bird's beloved "Granite Farm" and Wiley's home had been missed by Sherman and his despised raiders. The region just a few miles from their homes, from Sparta to Gordon, Georgia, had been dubbed the "burnt country."[18]

After the defeat of the Confederacy, Robert Toombs fled the nation. Toombs, through his anti-union attitude and very visual insurrectionist behavior, had made himself one of the men who were most wanted by the federal government. After resigning from the Army of Northern Virginia, he helped defend Atlanta and Macon, Georgia, from Sherman's army while serving with the state troops in Georgia. He refused to swear an oath of allegiance to the United States of America, and for the next two years he lived in Cuba, France, and England. He returned to his beloved state of Georgia in 1867 and died there in 1885.[19]

Dudley M. DuBose, the son-in-law of Robert Toombs, after being captured at the Battle of Sayler's Creek, was taken to Fort Warren in the Boston harbor as a prisoner of war. Several months later he was finally released and returned home to Washington, Georgia. He resumed his former career as a lawyer. After several years of practicing law he was elected to serve his state in the Forty-second Congress. He died at his home on the fourth of March, 1883, at the age of forty-nine.[20]

Henry L. Benning, after being paroled at Appomattox Courthouse, Virginia, returned to Georgia and resumed his highly successful career in the practice of law. He continued to uphold his high convictions and ethics, living up to the title of "Old Rock." His wife Mary preceded him in death in 1868, and Henry Benning followed her on July 10, 1875. In honor of the great respect and admiration General Benning had earned, the United States Army named its post on the outskirts of Benning's home in Columbus, Georgia, "Fort Benning." Established in 1918, Fort Benning is the home of the U.S. Army Airborne and Ranger Schools, as well as the U.S. Army Infantry Center. Today at Fort Benning, the professional ethics and tactics of "Marching and Fighting" are taught to soldiers from around the world.[21]

On the Confederate Line of Battle "With Fate Against Them" (from the painting by Gilbert Gaul)

Gen. John Bell Hood, division commander
(Courtesy of the Museum of the Confederacy, Richmond, Va.)

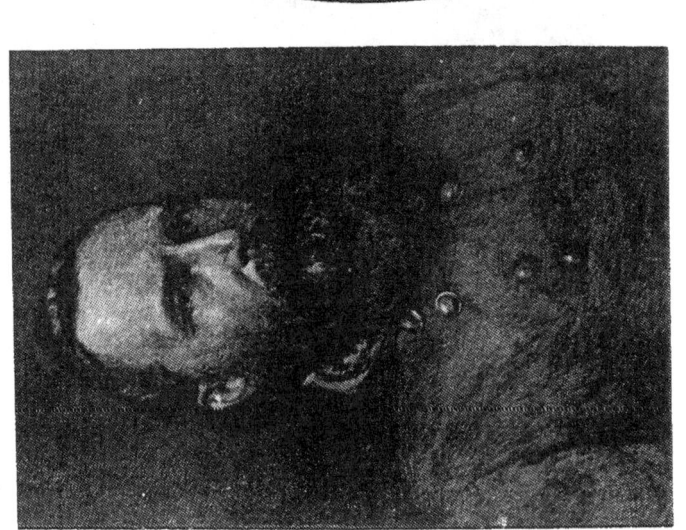

Gen. James Longstreet, First Corps commander, Army of Northern Virginia ("Battles and Leaders of the CivilWar")

Brigadier General Henry Lewis Benning, brigade commander (1862-1865), replaced Gen. Toombs (UNC Photo Collection, Wilson Library, UNC, Chapel Hill, NC)

Gen. Robert Toombs, brigade commander, 1861-1862 (Washington-Wilkes Historical Museum)

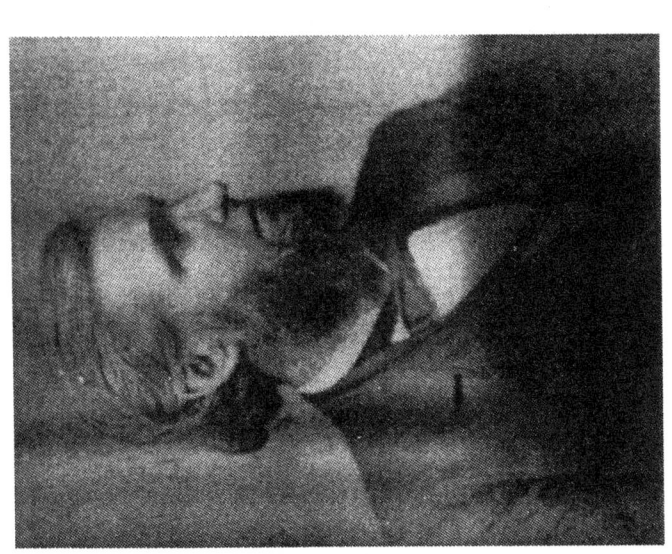

Col. Dudley M. DuBose, Fifteenth Georgia commander (1862-1865), later promoted to brigadier general near end of war (Washington-Wilkes Historical Museum)

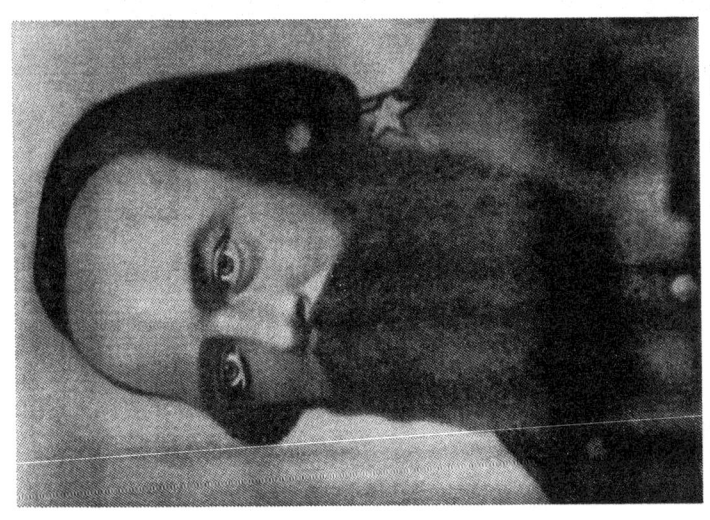

Lt. Col. William McIntosh, Fifteenth Georgia. Killed while leading the attack at Garnett's Farm, Virginia, June 27, 1862

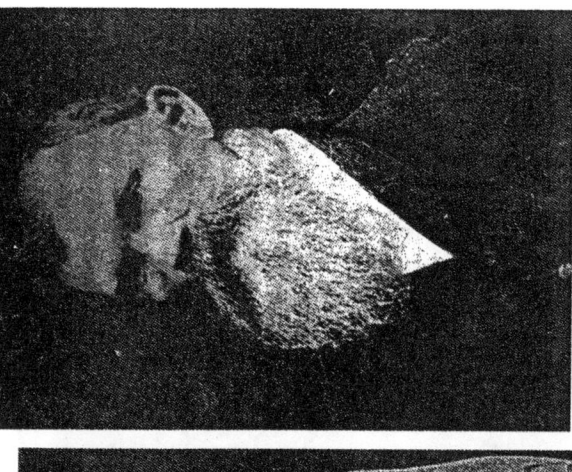

Lt. P. G. Veazey, 1862-1865, Fifteenth Georgia (*Confederate Veterans Magazine*)

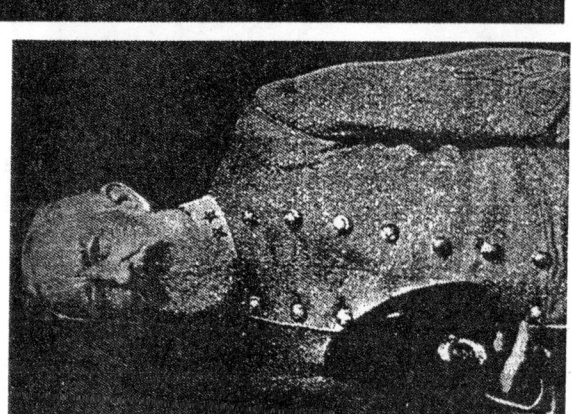

Lovick Pierce, Jr., Fifteenth Georgia, Company E Pvt, regimental adjutant 1862-1865 (*Confederate Veterans Magazine*)

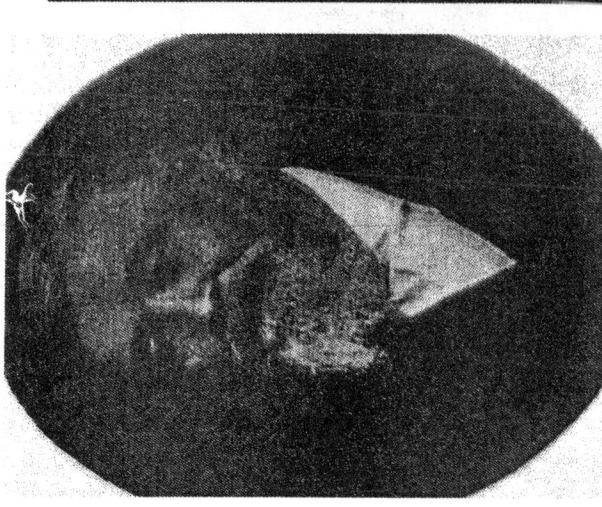

Dr. G. M. Burdett, Fifteenth Georgia, joined 1861 as 3rd cpl, Co. D, assigned 1862 as surgeon to General Lee's staff (*Confederate Veterans Magazine*)

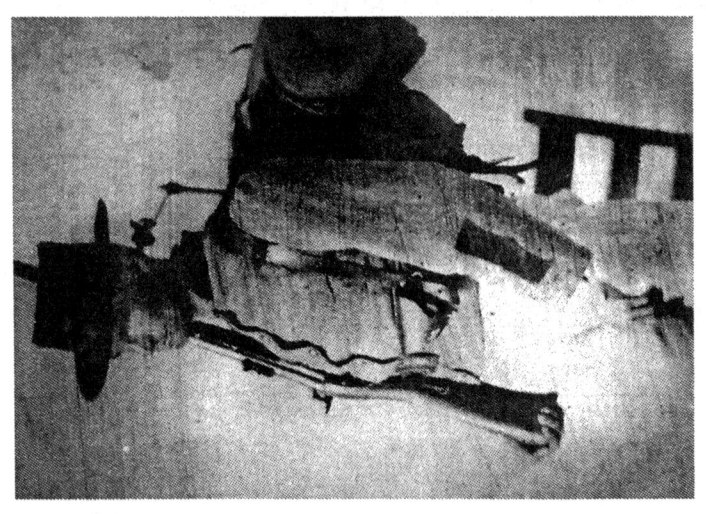

Ivy W. Duggan, private Company K, 1862 (The Museum of the Confederacy, Richmond, Virginia)

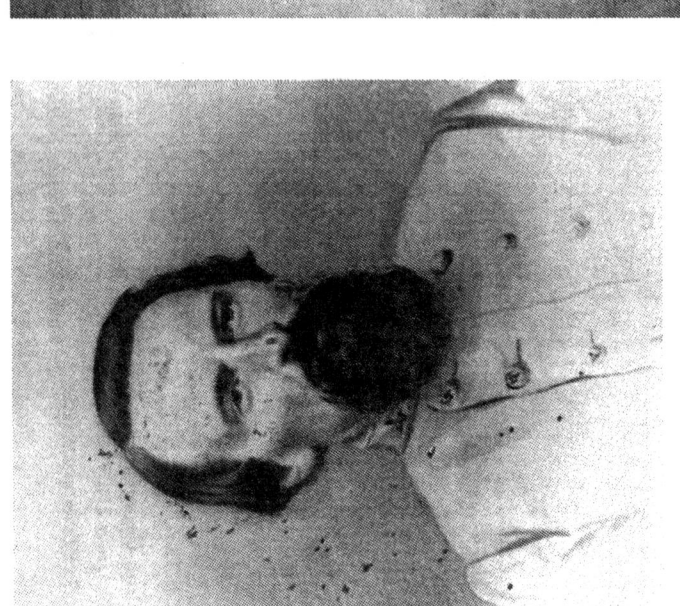

William Edgeworth Bird, first lieutenant Co. E, 1862; brigade QM 1863-1865 (University of Georgia Libraries)

Privates, Georgia Volunteeer Infantry (from the Vanishing Georgia Collection, Courtesy Georgia Department of Archives and History)

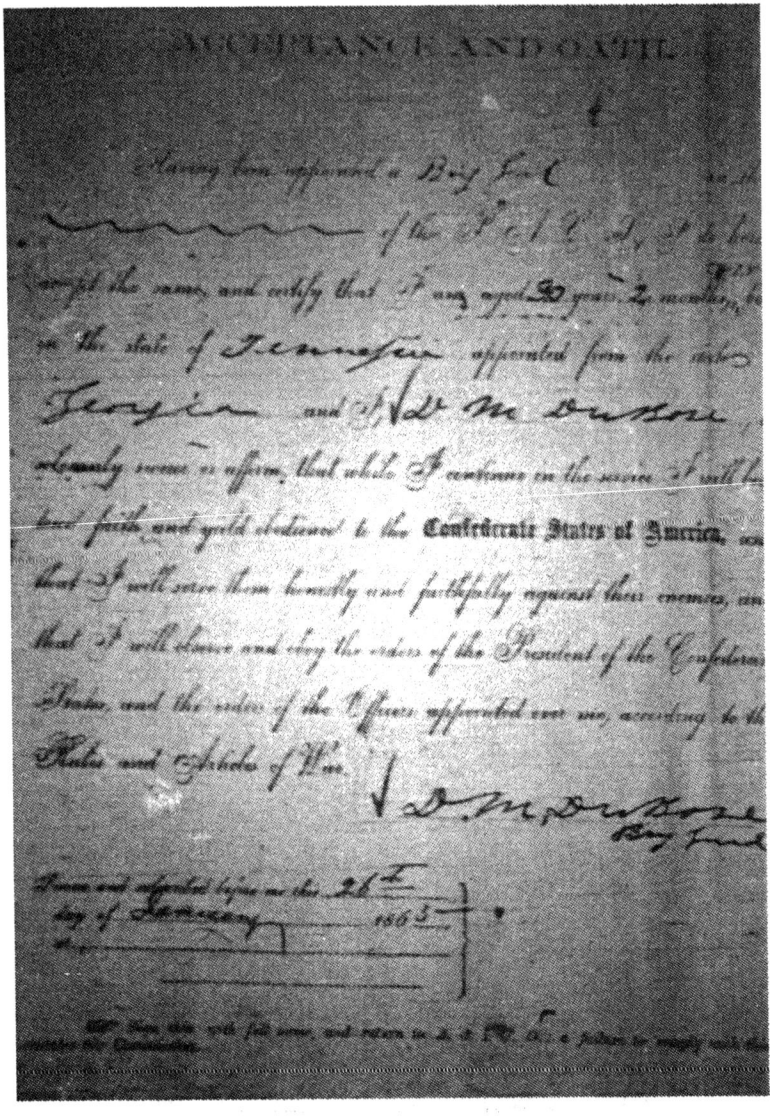

Gen. D. M. DuBose, Oath and Acceptance to the rank of brigadier general (National Archives Record Group 109)

Unit Statistics and Charts

5th GEORGIA REGIMENT
Battle Statistics- (Chart #1)

	WIA	KIA	CAP	TOTAL
Yorktown, Va.	3	1	0	4
Garnett's Farm, Va.	22	23	0	45
Malvern Hill, Va.	20	5	1	26
Thoroughfare Gap, Va.	5	1	0	6
2nd Bull Run, Va.	21	8	3	32
Antietam, Md.	17	10	1	28
Fredericksburg, Va.	5	1	0	6
Gettysburg, Pa.	39	18	119	176
Chickamauga, Ga.	19	12	0	31

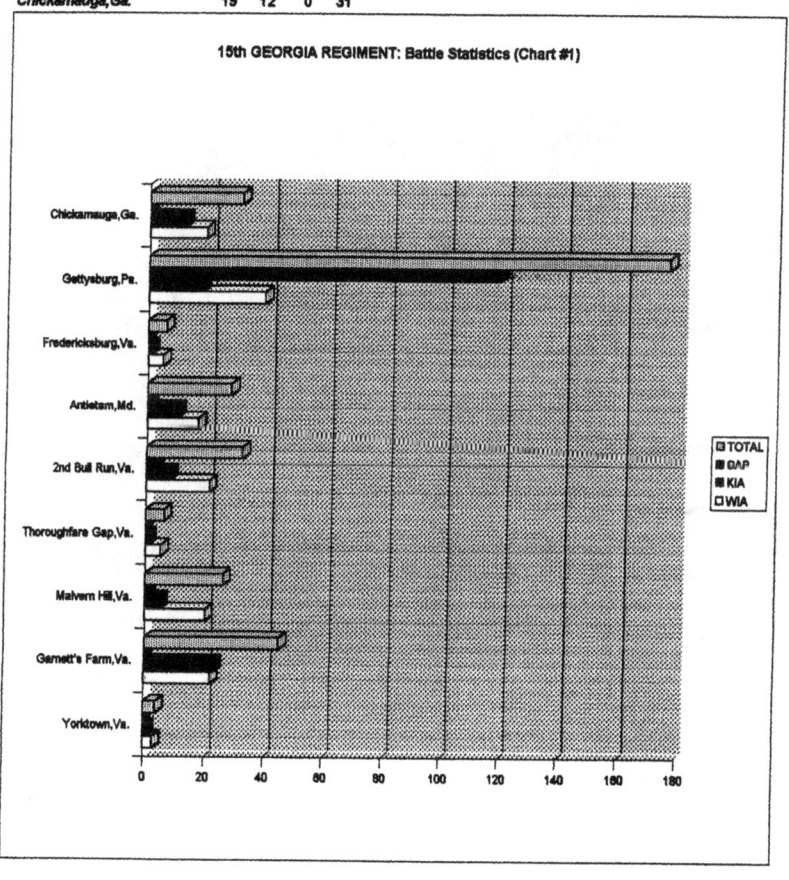

15th GEORGIA REGIMENT
Battle Statistics- (Chart #2)

	WIA	KIA	CAP	TOTAL
East Tn.Campaign	0	0	44	44
Wilderness,Va.	11	16	5	32
Spotsylvania,Va.	10	6	0	16
Cold Harbor,Va.	2	3	0	5
Petersburg,Va.	13	5	2	20
Fussell's Mill,Va.	2	2	0	4
Ft.Gilmer,Va.	9	9	11	29
Darbytown Road,Va.	6	2	0	8
Retreat to Appomattox,Va.	0	1	17	18
TOTAL	204	123	203	530

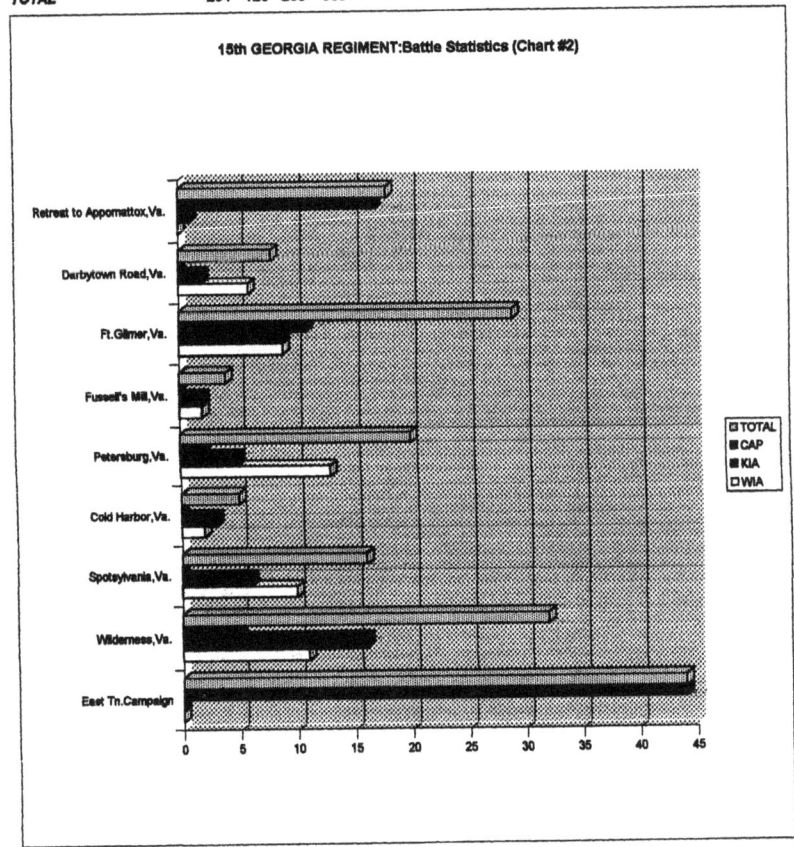

Unit Statistics and Charts

15th GEORGIA INFANTRY REGIMENT

OFFICERS & MEN ASSIGNED (7/15/1861)
OFFICERS & MEN PAROLED (4/9/1865)

	Cmd	Co.A	Co.B	Co.C	Co.D	Co.E	Co.F	Co.G	Co.H	Co.I	Co.K	UNK	TOTAL
	17	141	146	144	96	98	74	88	78	92	100	41	1074
	8	26	32	30	23	29	15	28	7	29	32	0	259

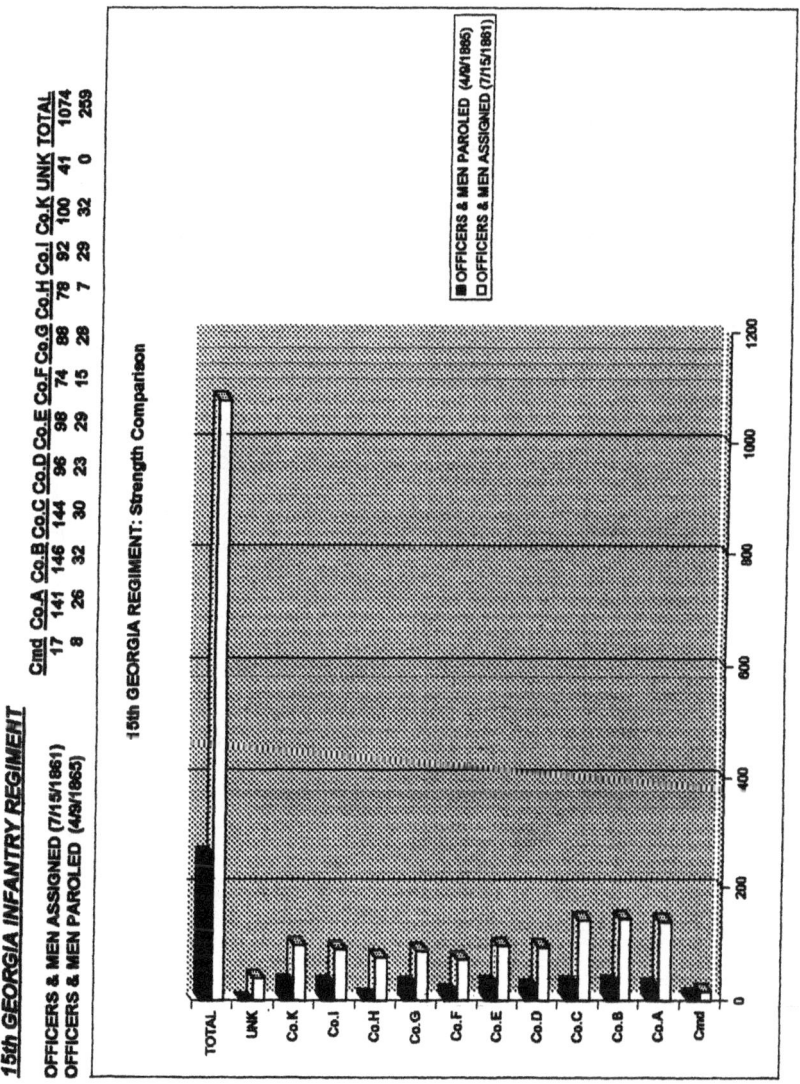

15th GEORGIA REGIMENT: Strength Comparison

■ OFFICERS & MEN PAROLED (4/9/1865)
□ OFFICERS & MEN ASSIGNED (7/15/1861)

Unit Statistics and Charts

15th GEORGIA INFANTRY REGIMENT

	Co.A	Co.B	Co.C	Co.D	Co.E	Co.F	Co.G	Co.H	Co.I	Co.K	UNK	TOTAL
Recruits received 1862-1865	9	22	24	12	17	21	25	29	29	21	0	209
Captured troops returned (Exchanged)	7	11	9	4	7	4	4	4	7	9	0	66
TOTAL: GAINS (1861-1865)	16	33	33	16	24	25	29	33	36	30	0	275

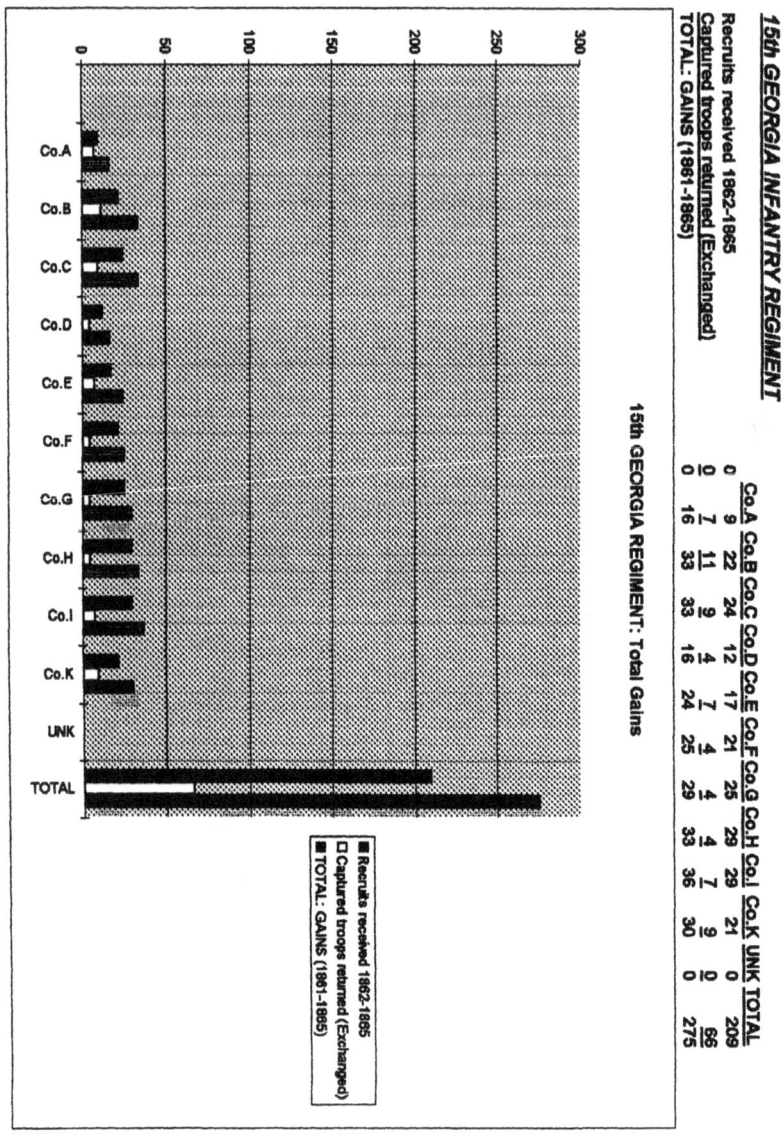

15th GEORGIA REGIMENT: Total Gains

■ Recruits received 1862-1865
□ Captured troops returned (Exchanged)
■ TOTAL: GAINS (1861-1865)

Unit Statistics and Charts 107

15th GEORGIA INFANTRY REGIMENT

	Cmd	Co.A	Co.B	Co.C	Co.D	Co.E	Co.F	Co.G	Co.H	Co.I	Co.K	UNK	TOTAL
Battle-loss Casualties (KIA & CAP)	3	46	56	30	25	22	21	33	33	27	28	2	326
Desertions & Transfers	0	13	16	6	4	7	5	2	7	9	10	0	79
Died in Union Prisons	0	4	7	3	2	4	3	4	4	3	3	0	37
Resigned/ Discharged/ Disabled	8	28	19	32	29	32	23	22	20	33	26	39	311
Deaths due to diseases	1	33	35	22	19	17	19	17	31	15	16	0	225
TOTAL LOSSES (1861-1865)	12	124	133	93	79	82	71	78	95	87	83	41	978

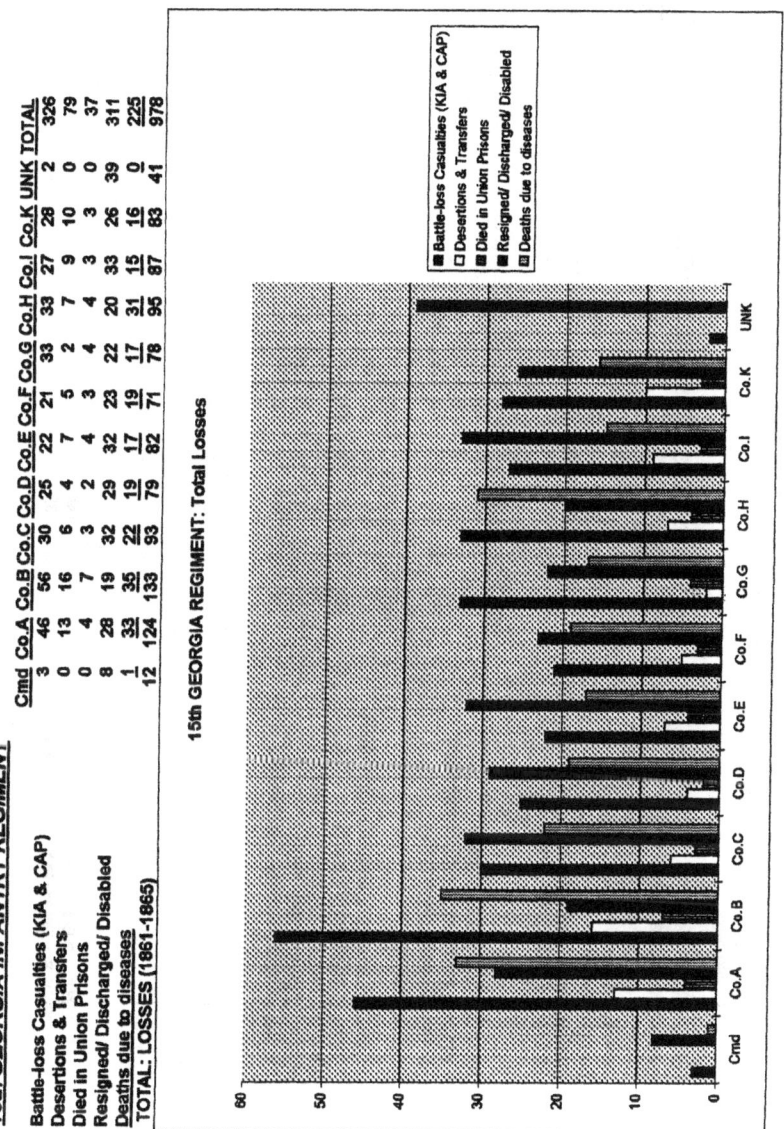

15th GEORGIA REGIMENT: Total Losses

15th GEORGIA INFANTRY REGIMENT
Statistical Data

	Cmd	Co.A	Co.B	Co.C	Co.D	Co.E	Co.F	Co.G	Co.H	Co.I	Co.K	UNK	TOTAL
Battle-loss (KIA & CAP)	3	46	56	30	25	22	21	33	33	27	28	2	326
Desertions / Transfers	0	13	16	6	4	7	5	2	7	9	10	0	79
Died in Union Prisons	0	4	7	3	2	4	3	4	4	3	3	0	37
Resign/Discharge	8	28	19	32	29	32	23	22	20	33	26	39	311
Deaths due to diseases	1	33	35	22	19	17	19	17	31	15	16	0	225
TOTAL: LOSSES(1861-1865)	12	124	133	93	79	82	71	78	95	87	83	41	978
Recruits received 1862-1865	0	9	22	24	12	17	21	25	29	29	21	0	209
Captured troops returned (Exchanged)	0	7	11	9	4	7	4	4	4	7	9	0	66
TOTAL: GAINS (1861-1865)	0	16	33	33	16	24	25	29	33	36	30	0	275
OFFICERS & MEN ASSIGNED (7/15/1861)	17	141	146	144	96	98	74	88	78	92	100	41	1074
TOTAL: LOSSES(1861-1865)	12	124	133	93	79	82	71	78	95	87	83	41	978
Officers & Men Assigned (--) losses	5	17	13	51	17	16	3	10	-17	5	17	0	154
TOTAL: GAINS (1861-1865)	0	16	33	33	16	24	25	29	33	36	30	0	275
TOTAL: ADJUSTED (Gains&Losses)	5	33	46	84	33	40	28	39	16	41	47	0	412
OFFICERS & MEN PAROLED (4/9/1865)	8	26	32	30	23	29	15	28	7	29	32	0	259
Post- Appomattox Paroles & no record	0	10	27	14	5	1	12	4	4	7	3	39	126
Released from Union Prisons-1865	0	9	2	3	1	2	1	4	1	2	2	0	27
TOTAL: OVERALL SURVIVORS	8	42	61	47	29	32	28	36	12	38	37	39	412
OFFICERS & MEN ASSIGNED (7/15/1861)	17	141	146	144	96	98	74	88	78	92	100	41	1074
OFFICERS & MEN PAROLED (4/9/1865)	8	26	32	30	23	28	17	29	7	28	31	0	259

APPENDIX A
ROSTER OF PAROLEES AT APPOMATTOX: 15TH GEORGIA

Following General Lee's surrender at Appomattox Court House, Va., on April 9, 1865, his Army was paroled and allowed to return to their homes. A total of 259 officers and men were present from the 15th Georgia Volunteer Infantry Regiment. The following roster was extracted from the Official unit records on file in the National Archives, Washington D.C.

Regimental Command and Staff

Regimental Commander: Major P.J. Shannon
Regimental Adjutant: Pierce Lovick Jr.
Regimental Sergeant's Major: Henry Middlebrooks
Regimental Surgeon: J.J. Depuy
Commissary Sergeant: W.R. Kendall
Quartermaster Sergeant: J.C. Simmons
Regimental Bandsman: George Williams
Hospital Steward: John Burroughs

Company A

Company Commander: 1st Lt. James Junkin
Company 1st Sergeant: Henry Spratling
3rd SGT: Isaac Stribling
4th SGT: Thomas Psalmonds
3rd CPL: Luke Slack

PVT's:

Mitchell Binns	David Russell	Johnathan Gill
William Partridge	George Cohron	John W. Green
Gideon Bunch	Noah Scott	Micajah Gill
Thomas Prather	Edward Freeman	Noah Hinton
William Bunch	M.L. Stribling	Thomas Lunceford
Greenbury Rhodes	Isaac Gill	Ennis Willis
Aaron Cohen	Leonard Wheatley	James W. Woodruff

Company B

Company Commander: Captain George Pace
Deputy Commander: Jr. 2nd Lt. Henry Chappelear
Company 1st Sergeant: Thomas Cawthorn
2nd SGT: Jesse Holbrook
5th SGT: Jonathan Adams
4th CPL: Alfred Carson

PVT's:

Asa Ayers	Hugh Childs	Benjamin Sammons
John James	Downs Knight	James Hembree
George T. Brown	James Davis	J.C. Stovall
Augustus Carson	Benjamin Mauldin	Kendrick Hill
Francis Carter	William Doyle	John Teague
Thomas Cary	Thomas McFarland	Nathan Holbrook
Thomas Carey	William Edwards	James Morris
John Jones	Wiley Mitchell	John Payne
	John Flangue	William Sewell

Company C

Captain: David Hudson
2nd SGT: J.M. Hudson
2nd CPL: W.T. Clark
4th CPL: Jasper Tate

PVT's:

Guilford Alexander	George Lovingood	John Cosby
John Anderson	A.V. Colwell	James Smith
P.C. Holbrook	J.W. McClanhan	Napoleon Bonaparte Cosby
Daniel Bradford	Edmond Colwell	
William Bullard	J.M. Moon	Manuel Franklin
John Hulme	Henry Colwell	Joseph Dye
Samuel Cade	J.L. Norman	W.T. Smith
Mark Heard	David Cosby	William Hubbard
J.S. Cade	Martin Ruff	Edward M. Roberts

Company D

Company Commander: Captain Samuel J. Flynt
Company 1st Sergeant: F.C. Reid
2nd SGT: J.S. Chapman
2nd CPL: G.W. Battle
3rd CPL: J.H. Lary
4th CPL: R.H. Fluker

PVT's:

Charles Brake	William Fluker	Charles Hendrick
Benjamin Jones	I. T. Smith	J.W. Woodruff
James Burnley	Thomas Ghann	C.A. Howell
W.P. Moore	Thomas Smith	John Johnson
William Clemons	Virgil Gheesling	Prior Veazey
William Pinkston	William Taylor	

Company E

Company 1st Sergeant: Joseph Herringdine
2nd SGT: Jesse Butts
3rd SGT: John Jones
4th SGT: W.H. Clark
1st CPL: Eldridge Cook
2nd CPL: Edmund Swint

PVT's:

Dudley Alfriend	Jesse Reeves	Thomas Warren
Wilber Little	Benjamin Clark	F.W.S. Johnson
James Brown	J.R. Reynolds	William Waller
James Mitchell	James Dacres Sr.	Jonathan Lary
Americus Boyer	William Simmons	Samuel Wiley
Benjamin Martin	T.W. Harris	B.L. Landers
James Coleman	George White	J.C. Rogers
	William Jackson	

Company F

Captain : James Burch
Lt : Lindsay Gaines
1st Sergeant: Ferninand Bailey
4th SGT: Theodore Rowzee
5th SGT: J.W. Jones Sr.

PVT's:

James Jones Jr.	William Craft	James Gulley
J.D. Hulme	Z.B. Taylor	Dunston Alexander
Richard Galloway	Benjamin Crawford	Vandiver Nelms
Nelson Higgonbotham	William Walseman	Andrew Webb

Company G

Company Commander: Thomas Remsen
Company 1st Sergeant: James Remsen
4th Sergeant: James Cartledge
2nd SGT: James McCord
1st CPL: Aaron Hardy
3rd CPL: Newton Stephenson

PVT's

Henry Caver	Elisha McCord	William Tatum
Peyton Florence	J.M. Crawford	Humphrey Evans
James Clary	William Murray	William S. Ware
J.H.W. Gresham	Jerry Crawford	William Flanagan
Thomas Clary	Robert Mumford	Wilkes Furgerson
Robert Harden	Leviticus Colvin	Adoniram Steed
Thomas Hawes	John Norman	Daniel Mumford
	Benjamin Elliott	Rem Remsen

Company H
Company 1st Sergeant: James Vickery

PVT's:

William Bailey	R.F. Moore
Joseph Jackson	W.M. Grubbs
G.W. Carroll	T.G. Wright

Company I
Company 1st Sergeant: Reuben Cleveland
2nd SGT: Joseph Deadwyler
3rd SGT: William Fortson
2nd CPL: J.D. Adams
3rd CPL: Livingston Gaines

PVT's:

William Anderson	Elijah Fortson	Isaac Faulkner
Francis Gaines	Alfred Mason	Tinsley White
Solomon Brown	John B. Fortson	Peter Gaines
Warren Hollingsworth	Elijah Norman	Eli Higginbotham
Martin Bond	Moses Fortson	Martin Webb
Alvin James	S.L. Pledger	Chalmers Hadden
W.H. Bond	Delancey Fortson	Alfred Teasley
Hosea Mattox	William Tenent	

Company K
Company Commander: Captain Daniel Connell
Deputy Commander: 1st Lt. Wingfield Roberson
Chaplain: William Roberson
Company 1st Sergeant: Joseph Deas
2nd SGT: Sidney Bass
5th SGT: David Warthen
1st CPL: J.J. Flury
2nd CPL: Simeon Bass
4th CPL: James Brantley

PVT's:

J.E. Medlock	J.A. Scott	John Dickson
W.R. Ray	John Wheland	William Dickson
Charles Neel	Oscar Scott	J.M. Dudley
Andrew Redfiern	Lewis Brantley	C.H. Flury
H.B. Pinkston	Robert G. Stone	William A. Flury
James Redfiern	J.J. Crawford	James F. Matthews
E.W. Redfiern	James Dickson	Joseph Wright
William Reynolds		

APPENDIX B
ROSTER OF THE 15TH GEORGIA INFANTRY REGIMENT

*The date listed after the soldier's rank indicates his service entry date. The absence of a date indicates that the soldier volunteered for service when the unit was initially formed in July, 1861.

Aaron, Melton J.–Co.B–PVT, Killed at 2d Manassas, Va., Sept. 30, 1862.

Abbie, H.–Co.A–PVT, Captured at Gettysburg, Pa. on July 5, 1863. Exchanged on Feb. 18, 1865.

Adams, Ausburn G.–Co.I–PVT, Appointed 4th CPL on Dec. 2, 1861. Died at Richmond, Va., Mar. 18, 1862.

Adams, G.–Co.I–PVT, Captured and paroled at Warrenton, Va. on Sept. 29, 1862.

Adams, James–Co.B–PVT, Captured at Gettysburg, Pa., July 3, 1863. Died in prison, Sept. 24, 1864.

Adams, James A.–Co.B–PVT, Wounded severely in the thigh at Wilderness, Va. on May 6, 1864.

Adams, James A.–Co.A–PVT, Captured at Gettysburg, Pa. on July 2, 1863. Died of Typhoid fever at Ft. Delaware, Del. on Sept. 24, 1863.

Adams, John D.–Co.I–PVT, Appointed 2nd CPL on Apr. 4, 1863. Surrendered at Appomattox, Va., Apr. 9, 1865.

Adams, Jonathan–Co.B–PVT, Appointed 5th SGT, Surrendered at Appomattox, Va. on Apr. 9, 1865.

Adams, Richard C.–Co.I–PVT–Mar. 9, 1863. Captured at Dandridge, Tn. on Jan. 22, 1864. Released at Rock Island, Ill. on June 22, 1865. Described as–Eyes–Blue/ Hair–Brown/ Height–5' 8-1/2"/ Age–42.

Adams, Rueben M.–Co.B–PVT–May 10, 1862. Captured and paroled at Hartwell, Ga. on May 17, 1865.

Adams, William C.–Co.B–PVT, Captured by the W. Va. Provost Marshalls Office on Apr. 10, 1865. Age–23/ Eyes–Blue/ Hair–Light/ Complexion–fair/ Height–5' 6"/ Occupation–Farmer.

Adams, William H.–Co.I–PVT–Feb. 8, 1864. Captured in a Richmond, Va. hospital on Apr. 3, 1865. Released at Newport News, Va. on June 16, 1865.

Adderhold, A. C.–Co.I–PVT, Discharged on Nov. 12, 1861.

Adderhold, J.H.P.–Co.B–PVT, Discharged with disability, November 12, 1861.

Adoms, J.A.–Co.C–PVT, Captured and paroled at Hartwell, Ga. on May 17, 1865.

Albea, Cyrus P.–Co.G–PVT, Discharged with disability on Dec. 16, 1861. Reenlisted Mar. 3, 1862. Present in Feb. 1865.

Albea, Thomas H.–Co.G–PVT–Feb. 24, 1862. Captured at Gettysburg, Pa. on July 3, 1863. Exchanged prisoner on Feb.21, 1865.

Albea, William H.–Co.G–PVT, Discharged with disability (Phithisis) on Sept. 18, 1863.

Alexander, Dunston B.–Co.C–1st CPL, Transferred to Co. F, May 15, 1862. Wounded (shot in the back) at Gettysburg, Pa. on July 2, 1863. Furloughed home from Chimborazo Hospital in Richmond, Va. in Sept. 1863. Surrendered at Appomattox, Va. on Apr. 9, 1865.

Alexander, Gaines T.–Co.F–PVT, Discharged with disability on May 27, 1862.

Alexander, George W.–Co.F–PVT, Appointed 2nd SGT on Apr. 21, 1863. Captured at Gettysburg, Pa. on July 3, 1863. Died at Point Lookout, Md. on Dec. 30, 1863, of Dysentery.

Alexander, Guilford L.–Co.C–PVT, Transferred to Co. I on Mar. 16, 1864. Appointed Regimental Ensign on July 26, 1864. Surrendered at Appomattox, Va. on Apr. 9, 1865.

Alexander, Henry C.–Co.C–PVT, Transferred to Co. F, May 21, 1862. Discharged with disability on July 17, 1862.

Alexander, James H.–Co.F–PVT–Jan. 7, 1864. Wounded at Cold Harbor, Va. on June 1, 1864; Petersburg, Va. on June 19, 1864. Died of wounds in a hospital on Aug. 31, 1864.

Alexander, J.H.–Co.I–PVT, Discharged with disability on Sept. 19, 1861.

Alford, James T.–Co.E–PVT, Died of disease in a Richmond, Va. hospital on July 31, 1862.

Alford, Owen–Co.K–PVT–Feb. 24, 1862. Killed at Garnett's Farm, Va. on June 27, 1862.

Alfriend, Alfred H.–Co.E–PVT–Mar. 22, 1864. Listed as AWOL in Feb. 1865.

Alfriend, Benjamin A.–Co.E–PVT–Mar. 3, 1862. Detailed with the Quartermaster in July, 1862. Listed as AWOL in Jan. 1865.

Alfriend, E. Dudley–Co.E–PVT, Wounded (severely in the thigh) at Malvern Hill, Va. on July 1, 1862. Elected 1st LT on Oct. 26, 1863. Surrendered at Appomattox, Va. on Apr. 9, 1865.

Roster of the Fifteenth Georgia Infantry Regiment 117

Alfriend, E.W.–s–Surgeon, resigned on May 11, 1862.

Alfriend, J.A.–Co.E–SGT, Discharged with disability on Nov. 26, 1861.

Algood, Elijah–Co.C–PVT, Wounded at Sharpsburg, Md. on Sept. 17, 1862. In May 1863 assigned to Division Provost Guard. Wounded at Wilderness, Va. on May 6, 1864. Died of wounds on May 16, 1864.

Allen, Elisha–Co.D–PVT, Discharged with disability on Oct. 4, 1861.

Almand, Thomas F.–Co.C–PVT–Mar. 4, 1862. Accidentally wounded resulting in amputation of arm. Discharged with disability on June 25, 1862.

Almand, William U.–Co.C–PVT, Transferred to Co. F, May 15, 1862. Wounded (shot in the hip) at Gettysburg, Pa. on July 2, 1863. Present in a Lynchburg, Va. hospital on May 2, 1864.

Almond, George M.–Co.I–PVT, Died in a Richmond, Va. hospital on Dec. 31, 1861. (Typhoid fever)

Anderson, John L.–Co.C–PVT, Surrendered at Appomattox, Va. on Apr. 9, 1865.

Anderson, William G.–Co.I–PVT, Wounded (severely in the head) at Malvern Hill, Va. on July 1, 1862. Surrendered at Appomattox, Va. on Apr. 9, 1865.

Anderson, Zacharia W.–Co.A–PVT. (No later record)

Andrews, Andrew J.–Co.A–PVT, Wounded severely in the thigh at Ft. Harrison, Va. on Sept. 29, 1864. Sent to CSA Hospital in Petersburg, Va. Transferred to Jackson Hospital in Richmond, Va. (No later record)

Andrews, Michael L.–Co.A–PVT, Appointed CPL. Captured at Gettysburg, Pa. on July 3, 1863. Released from Ft. Delaware, Del., June 16, 1865 after taking loyalty oath. Eyes–Gray/ Hair–Light/ Complexion–Light/ Ht–5'10".

Anesloy, L.O.–Co.B–PVT, Captured at Gettysburg, Pa. in July 1863. Exchanged prisoner on Sept. 30, 1864. (No later record)

Applebee, J.H.–Co.B–Captured and paroled at Athens, Ga., May 8, 1865.

Ariail, William J.–Co.B–PVT, Appointed 4th SGT. Died Oct. 9, 1861.

Armor, Claiborne R.–Co.A–PVT, Captured at Mossy Creek, Tn. on Jan. 22, 1864. Released at Rock Island, Ill. prison, June 18, 1865 after taking loyalty oath. Eyes–Gray/ Height–5'10"/ Age–26.

Armor, James N.–Co.A–PVT, Mortally wounded at Malvern Hill, Va. July 1, 1862.

Armor, Newton D.–Co.A–PVT. (No later record)

Arnold, Juluis B.D.–Co.I–PVT, Captured at Gettysburg, Pa. on July 3, 1863. Died of chronic diarrhoea at Point Lookout, Md. on May 6, 1864.

Asbell, James E.–Co.F–PVT, Wounded and captured on June 27, 1862. Paroled on Sept. 21, 1862. Absent without leave in Aug., 1863.

Asbell, William P.F.–Co.F–PVT–Mar. 4, 1862. Present in a Richmond, Va. hospital in Apr., 1862. (No later record)

Ash, John S.–Co.B–PVT, Captured at Gettysburg, Pa. July 3, 1863. Exchanged prisoner on Mar. 7, 1865.

Ashmore, Thomas L.–Co.G–PVT, Appointed 1st CPL in 1862. Wounded at Gettysburg, Pa. on July 3, 1863. Sent to General Hospital in Staunton, Va. on July 18, 1863. Transferred to a Richmond hospital in Aug. of 1863. Listed as AWOL in Feb. 1865, but noted as " serving as elected Tax Receiver of Lincoln County, Ga."

Ashworth, Robert W.–Co.F–PVT, Mar. 4, 1862. Present in a Richmond, Va. hospital in Apr., 1862. (No later record)

Askea, Martial–Co.H–PVT, Discharged with disability, July 17, 1862.

Askew, F.J.–Co.E–PVT, listed as sick in a Richmond, Va. hospital and discharged on Oct. 30, 1861. (No later record)

Aycock, Drury J.–Co.A–PVT, Captured at Gettysburg, Pa. on July 3, 1863. Exchanged at Point Lookout, Md., Feb. 18, 1865.

Ayers, Asa C.–Co.B–PVT, Surrendered at Appomattox, Va., April 9, 1865.

Ayers, John R.–Co.B–PVT, Died in Danville, Va. hospital of disease on Nov. 28, 1862.

Ayers, Obediah W.–Co.B–PVT, Charged for losing his musket, cartridge box, waist belt and shoulder belt. Transferred June 28, 1863 to Co. A, 2nd Regiment Ga. Infantry.

Ayers, Thomas J.–Co.C–PVT, Mar. 10, 1862. Died in the hospital, June, 1862.

Ayers, William R.–Co.B–SGT, Captured and paroled at Hartwell, Ga. on May 18, 1865.

Ayres, John W.–Co.H–2nd CPL, Died in a Richmond, Va. hospital on Dec. 10, 1861.

Babb, J.B.–Co.A–PVT, Sick at Jackson Hospital, Richmond, Va. with Chronic Diarrhea on Oct. 16, 1864. Captured and paroled at Athens, Ga. on May 18, 1865.

Bagwell, William A.–Co.B–PVT, Discharged with disability, Oct. 29, 1861.

Bailey, Fernando O.–Co.C–PVT, Transferred to Co.F, May 15, 1862. Promoted to 1st SGT on Apr. 21, 1863. Wounded severely (left arm) on Sept. 29, 1864. Surrendered at Appomattox, Va. on Apr. 9, 1865.

Bailey, J.A.–Co.H–PVT, Mar. 4, 1862. Appointed 1st CPL on June 20, 1864. Deserted on Feb. 26, 1865. Took a loyalty oath at Cumberland, Md. on May 18, 1865. Described as–Complexion–Dark/Hair–Dark/ Eyes–Blue/ Height–5'11"/ Age–26.

Bailey, Pascal–Co.H–PVT, Wounded and captured at Gettysburg, Pa. on July 2, 1863. Died on Dec. 2, 1864.

Bailey, Rueben, J.–Co.B–PVT, Killed in a skirmish near Gaines Cross Roads, Va. on July 24, 1863.

Bailey, Samuel–Co.B–PVT, Captured at Gettysburg, Pa. on July 2, 1863. Listed as an exchanged prisoner on Feb. 18, 1865.

Bailey, William–Co.H–PVT, Elected 3rd LT on Nov. 26, 1861; 1st LT in Jan., 1862. Severely wounded by a shell on July 1, 1862 at Malvern Hill, Va. Wounded severely again (Hemorrhage of the bowels) at Gettysburg, Pa. on July 2, 1863. Died of his wounds.

Bailey, W.J.–Co.H–PVT, Mar. 1, 1863. Surrendered at Appomattox, Va. on Apr. 9, 1865.

Balchin, Thomas–Co.F–PVT, Discharged with disability on June 26, 1862.

Barger, W.D.–Co.G–PVT, Captured and paroled at Athens, Ga. on May 8, 1865.

Barnes, James K.–Co.K–PVT, Listed as present in Feb., 1863. (No later record)

Barnes, J.J.–Co.I–PVT, Captured and paroled at Athens, Ga. on May 8, 1865.

Barnes, John T.–Co.K–PVT, Discharged in Jan., 1862.

Barnes, W.H.–Co.I–PVT, Captured and paroled at Athens, Ga. on May 8, 1865.

Barnes, W.W.–Co.I–PVT, Mortally wounded at Sharpsburg, Md. on Sept. 17, 1862. Died of wounds at Elias Groves farm.

Barr, George I.–Co.C–CPL, Discharged with disability on Dec. 16, 1861. Re-enlisted on Apr. 25, 1862 and served as Hospital Wardmaster of the 2nd Ga. Hospital in Augusta, Ga.

Bass, A. Sidney–Co.K–3rd CPL, Appointed 1st CPL in Sept., 1862; 2nd SGT on May 11, 1863. Surrendered at Appomattox, Va. on Apr. 9, 1865.

Bass, Benjamin S.–Co.E–PVT, Present in Feb. 1863. (No later record)

Bass, George E.–Co.K–PVT, Feb. 24, 1862. Captured at Gettysburg, Pa. on July 3, 1863. Died at Point Lookout, Md. on Feb. 26, 1864.

Bass, G.J.–Co.K–PVT. (No later record)

Bass, J.E.–Co.K–PVT. (No later record)

Bass, Simeon D.–Co.K–PVT, Feb. 24, 1862. Appointed 2nd CPL on Dec. 1, 1864. Surrendered at Appomattox, Va. on Apr. 9, 1865.

Bates, E.–Co.H–PVT, Captured and paroled at Andersonville, S.C. on May 22, 1865.

Battle, C. F.–Co.D–PVT, Mar. 1, 1862. (No later record)

Battle, George W.–Co.D–PVT, Appointed 2d CPL on Oct. 25, 1864. Surrendered at Appomattox, Va. on Apr. 9, 1865.

Battle, Thomas A.–Co.D–PVT, Discharged with disability on Mar. 3, 1862.

Battle, William J.–Co.D–4th SGT. Appointed 3d SGT on July 24, 1862. Wounded at Sharpsburg, Md. on Sept. 17, 1862. Assigned to Provost duty in Richmond, Va. in Feb. 1865. Captured and paroled in Augusta, Ga. on May 18, 1865.

Baxter, Richard B.–Co.E–PVT, Transferred to Co. E, 15th Georgia from Co. K, 3rd Georgia Regiment in 1862. Appointed Assistant Quartermaster. Captured at Dandridge, Tn. on Jan. 22, 1864. Released at Rock Island, Ill. on June 21, 1865.

Beall, Robert A.–Co.K–PVT, Elected Jr. 2nd LT of the 48th Georgia. Transferred there on Oct. 18, 1862.

Beard, Henry W.–Co.B–PVT, Died of Pneumonia in Camp Georgia near Manassas, Va. on Feb. 26, 1862.

Bell, George S.–Co.C–PVT, Discharged, furnished John Pickens as substitute on Nov. 3, 1862.

Bellamy, John–Co.B–PVT, Discharged Jan. 8, 1862.

Bellamy, Thomas J.–Co.B–PVT, Discharged with disability, Dec. 4, 1861.

Bellamy, William P.–Co.B–PVT, Discharged with disability, Dec. 4, 1861.

Bell, Harmon L.–Co.C–PVT, Mar. 2, 1862. Captured at Gettysburg, Pa. on July 3, 1863. Exchanged prisoner on Feb. 18, 1865.

Bell, J.B.–Co.C–PVT, Discharged with disability on Oct. 31, 1861.

Beman, Thomas S.–Co.E–PVT, Killed at 2nd Manassas, Va. on Aug. 30, 1862.

Bentley, Charles M.–Co.G–PVT, Killed at Malvern Hill, Va. on July 1, 1862.

Berry, George–Co.H–LT, Captured at Sharpsburg, Md. on Sept. 17, 1862. Paroled at Ft. McHenry, Baltimore, Md. on Dec. 14, 1862. (No later record)

Biggs, Thomas D.–Co.I–PVT, Appointed 1st CPL on May 14, 1862. Discharged, furnished Samuel J. Lumpkin as a substitute, Aug. 7, 1862.

Binns, Enoch G.–Co.A–PVT, Appointed 3d CPL in 1864. Wounded in right thigh and captured at Farmville, Va. on Apr 7, 1865.

Binns, George S.–Co.A–PVT, Appointed 4th CPL in Nov. 1861, 3rd CPL in Apr. 1862. Died of Typhoid Pneumonia in Gordonsville, Va. on Apr. 20, 1862.

Binns, Isaiah M.–Co.A–PVT, Wounded and permanently disabled in both legs at Garnett's Farm, Va. on June 27, 1862.

Binns, Joseph A.–Co.A–PVT, Died of illness at Huguenot Springs, Va. on Oct. 19, 1862.

Binns, Mitchell–Co.A–PVT, Wounded at Chickamauga, Ga. on Sept. 19, 1863. Surrendered at Appomattox, Va. on April 9, 1865.

Binns, William Lee–Co.A–PVT, Died of Typhoid Pneumonia in hospital at Orange County C.H. Hospital, Va., April 13, 1862.

Bins, J.C.–Staff–Assistant Surgeon, furloughed on Dec. 3, 1862.

Bird, William E.–Co.E–1st LT, Elected CPT on May 1, 1862. Wounded at 2nd Manassas, Va., Aug. 30, 1862. Appointed Brigade Quartermaster on Mar. 30, 1863. Paroled at Augusta, Ga. on May 20, 1865.

Black, J.M.–Co.K–PVT, Died of Typhoid fever on Sept. 25, 1861.

Black, Thomas J.–Co.C–PVT, Deserted at New Market, Va. on Feb. 23, 1864.

Blackwell, Dunston R.–Co.F–2nd SGT, Discharged. Furnished Allen Haverell as a substitute on Jan. 18, 1862.

Blackwell, L. L.–Co.C–PVT, Appointed 4th CPL in Feb., 1862.

Bledsoe, John N.–Co.D–1st SGT, Elected 1st LT on July 24, 1862. Killed at Thoroughfare Gap, Va. on Aug. 28, 1862.

Boggs, Joseph R.–Co.A–PVT, Wounded (gunshot-fingers) at Garnett's Farm, Va. on June 27, 1862. Captured at Gettysburg, Pa. on July 3, 1863. Paroled at Point Lookout, Md. on Oct. 11, 1864.

Bohler, John T.–Co.G–PVT, Wounded at Gettysburg, Pa. on July 2, 1863. Exchanged prisoner in 1864.

Bolton, Miles J.–Co.A–PVT, Killed at Chickamauga, Ga. on Sept. 19, 1863.

Bolton, William M.–Co.A–PVT, 2d CPL, Appointed 3rd SGT in Apr. 1862. Captured at Gettysburg, Pa. on July 2, 1863. Died at Ft. Delaware, Del. on Nov. 19, 1863.

Bolton, William T.–Co.A–PVT, Appointed 1st SGT; Elected 2nd LT; 1st LT; CPT Jan. 21, 1865. Paroled at Farmville, Va. on Apr. 21, 1865.

Bond, J.A.–Co.A–PVT, Died Nov. 19, 1861 in Chimborazo Hospital, Richmond, Va. of Typhoid.

Bond, Francis K.–Co.I–PVT, Discharged, furnished William R. Buffington as a substitute, Nov. 30, 1861.

Bond, John B.–Co.I–PVT, Feb. 28, 1862. Captured at Gettysburg, Pa. on July 2,

1863. Exchanged prisoner on May 8, 1864. Died at Chimborazo Hospital in Richmond, Va. on May 22, 1864.

Bond, Martin R.–Co.I–PVT, Surrendered at Appomattox, Va. on Apr. 9, 1865.

Bond, Willis H.–Co.I–PVT, Surrendered at Appomattox, Va. on Apr. 9, 1865.

Bonds, Joseph M.–Co.A–PVT, Died of illness in a Richmond, Va. hospital in Nov. 1861.

Bonds, William–Co.F–PVT, Mar. 4, 1862. Discharged due to Dropsy at camp near New Market, Va. on July 31, 1862.

Bonner, John F.–Co.A–PVT, Wounded at Sharpsburg, Md. Sept. 17, 1862. Captured at Gettysburg, Pa. on July 3, 1863. Sent to Point Lookout and Ft. Delaware Prisons and later exchanged at Aikens Landing, Va. on May 8, 1864. Furloughed on May 12, 1864.

Booth, James C.–Co.I–PVT, In Nov., 1861, he was detailed as a nurse in a farmhouse near Centerville, Va. In Jan., 1865, he is listed as serving in the Quartermaster Department in Augusta, Ga. (No later record)

Boren, Clark–Co.A–1st SGT, Elected 1st LT on Jan. 28, 1862. Died of Pneumonia at Richmond, Va. on Apr. 18, 1862.

Bourne, Powhatan B.–Co.C–2d LT, Resigned on July 19, 1862.

Bowers, Noah W.–Co.H–PVT, Died at Manassas, Va. on Mar. 4, 1862.

Bowie, J.J.–Co.K–PVT, July 15, 1863. Discharged, furnished substitute in July, 1863.

Boyer, Americus V.–Co.E–PVT, Accidentally wounded in Aug., 1861. Surrendered at Appomattox, Va. on Apr. 9, 1865.

Boyer, Jasper J.–Co.E–4th CPL, Wounded at Sharpsburg, Md. on Sept. 17, 1862. Severely wounded in the head at Gettysburg, Pa. on July 2, 1863. Captured there on 3 July, 1863. Exchanged prisoner at City Point, Va. on Mar. 20, 1864.

Bradford, Daniel W.–Co.C–PVT, Transferred to Co. F, Mar. 4, 1864. Surrendered at Appomattox, Va. on Apr. 9, 1865.

Bradford, Junius B.–Co.C–PVT, Appointed 3rd CPL in June, 1862. Transferred to Co.F on Mar. 4, 1864.

Bradford, Nathaniel M.–Co.C–PVT, Killed at Sharpsburg, Md. on Sept. 17, 1862.

Bradley, George M.–Co.A–PVT, Killed at Garnett's Farm, Va. on June 27, 1862.

Brady, James R.–Co.B–PVT, Wounded at 2d Manassas, Va. Aug. 30, 1862, Deserted near Bull's Gap, Tn. Mar. 1864. Joined Union forces.

Brake, Charles I.–Co.D–PVT, Surrendered at Appomattox, Va. on Apr. 9, 1865.

Brake, Daniel C.–Co.D–PVT, Captured in a Richmond, Va. hospital on Apr. 3, 1865.

Brake, John W.–Co.D–PVT, Mar. 1, 1862. Captured at Gettysburg, Pa. on July 3, 1863. Exchanged prisoner on Feb.21, 1865. Captured again at Salisbury, N.C. on 12, 1865. Took loyalty oath and was released from Camp Chase Prison on June 13, 1865.

Branklin, J.–Co.A–PVT, Captured on Apr. 3, 1865 and took loyalty oath. Released at Harts Island, N.Y. on June 21, 1865.

Brantley, James A.–Co.K–PVT, Appointed 4th CPL on Nov. 30, 1862. Surrendered at Appomattox, Va. on Apr. 9, 1865.

Brantley, Lewis–Co.K–PVT, Surrendered at Appomattox, Va. on Apr. 9, 1865.

Brawner, J. K.–Co.C–PVT, May 12, 1864. Captured in a Richmond, Va. hospital on Apr. 3, 1865. Paroled at Newport News, Va.

Brawner, William M.–Co.I–PVT, Detailed as a Hospital Steward. (No later record)

Brawner, William T.–Co.B–PVT, Wounded and captured at Gettysburg, Pa. on July 3, 1863. Died there on July 28, 1863.

Breedlove, Jesse M.–Co.E–PVT, Died of chronic diarrhoea at Richmond, Va. on July 17, 1864.

Brewer, John M.–Co.C–PVT, Discharged, furnished substitute on Nov. 1, 1861.

Bridges, Jeremiah–Co.E–PVT, Paroled in 1862. (No later record)

Briggs, John W.–Co.D–PVT, Captured at Salisbury, N.C. in Apr., 1865.

Brinn, Nathan–Co.C–PVT, Feb. 25, 1862. Transferred to Regimental Band on Apr. 2, 1862. **Broadwell, John M.**–Co.F–PVT, Discharged. Furnished a substitute on July 29, 1862.

Brock, Francis J.–Co.B–PVT, Appointed 3rd SGT. Wounded and captured at Gettysburg, Pa. on July 2, 1863. Paroled and sent to CSA Hospital at Petersburg, Va. Furloughed home on Aug. 28, 1863.

Brooke, C.C.–Co.A–PVT, Paroled at Farmville, Va. in Apr. 1865.

Brooke, Joseph G.–Co.D–PVT, Appointed 1st SGT on July 24, 1862. Wounded and captured at Ft. Harrison, Va. on Sept. 29, 1864.Died of wounds on Oct. 21, 1864.

Broom, Cicero–Co.K–PVT, Died of Smallpox in North Carolina, 1863.

Broom, Marion–Co.D–PVT, Captured near Knoxville, Tn. on Dec. 18, 1863. Enlisted in U.S. Army for western service on Oct. 13, 1864.

Broom, Nathaniel–Co.D–PVT, Wounded at Garnett's Farm, Va. on June 27, 1862. Listed as present in Feb. 1865.

Broom, W.C.–Co.D–PVT, Lost on retreat from Knoxville, Tn. and presumed to be captured by the enemy on Dec. 5, 1863.

Brown, Andrew F.–Co.I–PVT, Feb. 28, 1862. Wounded at Gettysburg, Pa. on July 2, 1863. Captured and paroled at Athens, Ga., May 8, 1865.

Brown, A. Ruffin–Co.H–PVT, Wounded in the right leg at Manassas, Va. on Aug. 30, 1862. Captured and paroled at Warrenton, Va. on Sept. 29, 1862. Leg amputated in 1862. (No later record)

Brown, C.–Co.A–PVT, **Captured and paroled at Athens, Ga., May 8, 1865.**

Brown, Clement C.–Co.E–PVT, Elected Jr. 2nd LT on Sept. 17, 1861; 2nd LT on May 13, 1862. Listed on Feb. 25, 1865 as AWOL.

Brown, George T.–Co.B–PVT, Surrendered at Appomattox, Va., April 9, 1865.

Brown, James C.–Co.H–PVT, Mar. 4, 1862. Appointed 4th SGT in Apr., 1862. Captured at Gettysburg, Pa. on July 2, 1863. Exchanged prisoner and rejoined his unit. Captured at Farmville, Va. on Apr. 6, 1865 and paroled.

Brown, James M.–Co.E–PVT, Surrendered at Appomattox, Va. on Apr. 9, 1865.

Brown, John M.–Co.C–1st SGT, Elected Jr. 2d LT; 1st LT on July 24, 1862. Wounded at Fussell's Mill, Va. on Aug. 16, 1864. Dropped from the rolls due to prolonged absence on Feb. 14, 1865.

Brown, L. M.–Co.C–PVT, Mar. 4, 1862. Died of Typhoid fever in a Richmond, Va. hospital on June 7, 1862.

Brown, S.C.–Co.H–PVT, Mar. 4, 1862. Died of fever at Richmond, Va. on May 7, 1862.

Brown, Samuel F.–Co.F–PVT, Wounded at Sharpsburg, Md. on Sept. 17, 1862. Died of wounds.

Brown, Solomon W.–Co.I–PVT, Assigned to the Division Rear Guard in 1863. Surrendered at Appomattox, Va. on Apr. 9, 1865.

Brown, T. J.–Co.C–PVT, Feb. 27, 1862. Discharged with disability on July 28, 1862.

Brown, Willis H.–Co.I–PVT, Wounded at Gettysburg, Pa. on July 3, 1863. Shot through the left jaw at Darbytown Road, Va. on Oct. 13, 1864. Furloughed home, unable to return.

Bruce, James A.–Co.I–PVT, Died at Richmond, Va. on Apr. 26, 1862.

Bryan, Ephraim O.–Co.B–PVT, Died of Typhoid Oct. 28, 1863.

Bryant, Joseph–Co.A–PVT, Discharged at Richmond, Va., Nov. 20, 1861.

Buffington, John H.–Co.C–PVT, Wounded May 9, 1863. Died of wounds on May 20, 1863.

Buffington, J.W.–Co.H–PVT, Appointed CPL; 2nd SGT in 1862. Deserted on Feb. 26, 1865. Took loyalty oath on May 18, 1865. Described as–Age–26/ Height–5'10"/ Complexion–Fair/ Eyes–Blue/ Hair–Fair/ Occupation–Farmer.

Buffington, Reuben T.–Co.I–PVT, Detailed as a Brigade Teamster. Listed as AWOL on Feb. 25, 1865.

Buffington, William R.–Co.I–PVT, Nov. 30, 1861. Substitute for Francis Bond. Killed at Ft. Gilmer, Va., Sept. 29, 1864.

Buffington, Willis W.–Co.H–PVT, Mar. 4, 1862. Died of fever at Richmond, Va. on May 25, 1862.

Bullard, G. F.–Co.C–PVT, Mar. 4, 1862. Died of Measles in a hospital at Richmond, Va. on May 14, 1862.

Bullard, J.B.–Co.C–SGT, Apr. 13, 1863, sick with Gonorrhoea in a Farmville, Va. hospital. Returned to duty on July 13, 1863.

Bullard, Jeptha R.–Co.I–PVT, Transferred to Company C, Apr. 4, 1862. Appointed as 1st CPL on June 28, 1862. Promoted to Orderly SGT on Jan. 1, 1863. Wounded at Chickamauga, Ga. on Sept. 19, 1863. Discharged with disability in Sept., 1864.

Bullard, William H.–Co.C–PVT, Feb. 27, 1862. Surrendered at Appomattox, Va. on Apr. 9, 1865.

Bunch, Edward A.–Co.A–PVT, Captured at Gettysburg, Pa., July 3, 1863. Released at Ft. Delaware, Del., June 16, 1865.

Bunch, Gideon B.–Co.A–PVT, Detailed as Division Commissary Guard in July of 1864. Surrendered at Appomattox, Va., April 9, 1865.

Bunch, William,A.–Co.A–PVT, Detailed as Regimental Teamster in Nov. of 1862. Surrendered at Appomattox, Va. on April 9, 1865.

Burch, John C.–Co.F–CPT, Killed at Garnett's Farm, Va. on June 27, 1862.

Burch, James J.–Co.F–1st SGT, Elected 2nd LT on Aug. 4, 1862; 1st LT on Aug. 4, 1862. Wounded at Thoroughfare Gap, Va. on Aug. 28, 1862. Elected CPT on Apr. 21, 1863. Surrendered at Appomattox, Va., on Apr. 9, 1865.

Burdett, George M.–Co.D–3d CPL, Appointed Assistant Surgeon of Georgia Hospital in Richmond, Va. on Dec. 18, 1861.Transferred on Oct. 9, 1862 to General Lee's Army.

Burnley, James T.–Co.D–PVT, Surrendered at Appomattox, Va. on Apr. 9, 1865.

Burnley, John D.–Co.D–PVT, Killed at Garnett's Farm, Va. on June 27, 1862.

Burnley, R. Henry–Co.D–PVT, Severely wounded near Petersburg, Va. on June 24, 1864. Listed as present in Feb. 1865.

Burns, E.G.–Co.A–PVT, Captured and paroled at Farmville, Va., in April, 1865.

Burroughs, John E.–Co.C–PVT, Detailed as Regimental Hospital Steward. (No later record)

Burroughs, Fred W.A.–Co.H–4th SGT, Elected Jr. 2nd LT on Nov. 1, 1861. Died on July 19, 1862 in Franklin County, Ga.

Burton, Joseph J.–Co.H–PVT, Died of Typhoid fever at Richmond, Va. on Sept. 9, 1861.

Bush, W.G.–Co.B–PVT, Captured and paroled at Hartwell, Ga., May 18, 1865.

Bush, William F.–Co.B–PVT, Captured at Gettysburg, Pa. on July 3, 1863. Sent to Ft. Delaware, Del. Exchanged prisoner on Sept. 18, 1864. Captured again at Hartwell, Ga. and paroled on May 18, 1865.

Butler, E. A.–Co.C–PVT, Mar. 4, 1862. Died of disease (Phithisis) in a hospital at Richmond, Va. on July 13, 1862.

Butler, Martin T.–Co.F–PVT, Present for duty in Apr., 1863. (No later record)

Butler, Robert–Co.F–PVT, Mar. 4, 1862. Wounded at Garnett's Farm, Va. on June 27, 1862. Died of wounds.

Butler, William P.–Co.F–PVT, died on Apr. 5, 1862.

Butler, William S.–Co.I–PVT, Discharged from a Richmond, Va. hospital, Jan. 3, 1862.

Butts, Jesse G.–Co.E–PVT, Appointed 4th CPL in 1862, then 2nd SGT. Surrendered at Appomattox, Va. on Apr. 9, 1865.

Butts, Winfield S.–Co.E–2nd CPL, Wounded at Rapidan Station, Va. on Apr. 26, 1862. Died of wounds in a Richmond, Va. hospital in May, 1862.

Byce, William A.–Co.B–PVT, Transferred in Jan, 1863.

Byrom, Samuel D.–Co.H–PVT, Sent from Knoxville, Tn., sick, and captured in winter of 1863. Died in a Bristol, Tn. hospital on Apr. 20, 1864.

Cade, Drury B.–Co.A–CPT, Resigned on Feb. 11, 1861.

Cade, J.S.–Co.C–PVT, Mar. 4, 1862. Surrendered at Appomattox, Va. on Apr. 9, 1865.

Cade, Robert B.–Co.A–CPL, Discharged with disability on Oct. 3, 1861.

Cade, Samuel R.–Co.C–PVT, Surrendered at Appomattox, Va. on Apr. 9, 1865.

Cade, William B.–Co.A–1st LT, Resigned on Sept. 1, 1861.

Callaway, John B.–Co.G–PVT, Wounded at Malvern Hill, Va. on July 1, 1862. Died of wounds in a hospital on July 13, 1862.

Callaway, John S.1–Co.A–PVT, Elected 2d LT; Later–1st LT; CPT, Aug.1, 1863. Wounded at Chickamauga, Ga. on Sept. 19, 1863. Retired from service on Jan. 21, 1865.

Callaway, Joseph–Co.A–PVT, Captured and paroled at Athens, Ga. on May 8, 1865.

Camp, Sims S.–Co.B–PVT, Died of chronic diarrhoea at Lynchburg, Va. on June 30, 1862.

Campbell, James C.–Co.F–PVT, Transferred to the 38th Georgia.

Cane, Levi–Co.K–PVT. (No later record)

Carey, Thomas–Co.B–PVT, Surrendered at Appomattox, Va., April 9, 1865.

Carpenter, Thomas J.–Co.C–PVT, Transferred to Co. H on Aug. 22, 1862. (No later record)

Carroll, A.J.–Co.H–PVT, Died of Pneumonia in U.S.A. General Hospital No. 20, in Maryland on May 13, 1863.

Carroll, Clement–Co.H–PVT, Discharged on Aug. 10, 1864.

Carroll, G.W.–Co.H–PVT, Surrendered at Appomattox, Va. on Apr. 9, 1865.

Carroll, Larkin–Co.H–PVT, Captured at Middletown, Va. on July 7, 1863. Enlisted in the U.S. Army on Sept. 18, 1863.

Carroll, Nelson–Co.H–PVT, Captured and paroled at Hartwell, Ga. on May 19, 1865.

Carroll, Thomas–Co.H–PVT, July 23, 1861. Died with fever at Richmond, Va. on May 18, 1862.

Carson, Alfred P.–Co.B–PVT, Wounded at Spotsylvania, Va. on May 10, 1864. Appointed 4th CPL, Surrendered at Appomattox, Va. on Apr. 9, 1865.

Carson, Augustus L.–Co.B–PVT, Assigned to Wagon Guard Staff. Surrendered at Appomattox, Va., April 9, 1865.

Carson, Robert H.–Co.B–PVT, Discharged with disability at Lynchburg, Va. on Aug. 13, 1863.

Carson, James M.–Co.B–Jr. 2d LT, Killed at 2d Manassas, Va. on Aug. 30, 1862.

Carter, Charles T.–Co.D–PVT, Captured at Gettysburg, Pa. on July 3, 1863. Exchanged prisoner in 1864. Died in Dec., 1864.

Carter, Francis M.–Co.B–PVT, Sept. 22, 1862. Received severe leg wound June 21, 1864. Surrendered at Appomattox, Va. Apr. 9, 1865.

Carter, James M.–Co.B–PVT, Deserted near Bull's Gap, Tn., March 28, 1864.

Cartledge, James J.–Co.G–4th SGT, Surrendered at Appomattox, Va. on Apr. 9, 1865.

Cartledge, Walton–Co.G–PVT. Listed as sick in an Augusta, Ga. hospital as late as Feb., 1865. (Sick and in hospital throughout the entire war)

Cartledge, William H.–Co.G–PVT, Detailed as a teamster in 1862. Discharged in Oct., 1864.

Cary, Thomas–Co.B–PVT, Wounded in the wrist at Wilderness, Va. on May 6, 1864. Surrendered at Appomattox, Va., April 9, 1865.

Cato, James J.–Co.E–PVT, Listed as sick in the hospital throughout 1861 and 1862. (No later record)

Cauley, Clem–Co.G–PVT, Killed at Spotsylvania, Va. on May 10, 1864.

Cauley, Henry–Co.G–PVT, Killed at Spotsylvania, Va. on May 10, 1864.

Cauley, Luke–Co.G–PVT, Sept. 3, 1862. Captured at Gettysburg, Pa. on July 2, 1863. Died at Point Lookout, Md. prison hospital on Jan. 12, 1864.

Cauthern, John G.–Co.C–PVT, Wounded at Chickamauga, Ga. on Sept. 19, 1863. Present in hospital in Aug., 1864. Died on Nov. 1, 1864.

Caver, Henry A.–Co.G–PVT, Oct. 23, 1862. Wounded at Gettysburg, Pa. on July 2, 1863. Surrendered at Appomattox, Va. on Apr. 9, 1865.

Caver, James H.–Co.G–PVT, Aug. 15, 1863. Wounded at Spotsylvania, Va. on May 10, 1864. Died of wounds at Lynchburg, Va. on June 2, 1864.

Cawthorn, Thomas J.–Co.B–PVT, Appointed 1st SGT in May, 1862. Surrendered at Appomattox, Va. on Apr. 9, 1865.

Chafin, Thomas P.–Co.A–PVT, Wounded at Chickamauga, Ga. on Sept. 19, 1863. Returned to duty on Sept. 30, 1864. (No later record)

Chandler, Howard M.–Co.C–PVT, Appointed 4th SGT on June 23, 1862. Wounded at Garnett's Farm, Va. on June 27, 1862. Died of wounds on July 2, 1862.

Chapman, James S.–Co.D–1st CPL, Appointed 2d SGT. Wounded at Chickamauga, Ga. on Sept. 20, 1863. Surrendered at Appomattox, Va. on Apr. 9, 1865.

Chappelear, Henry S.–Co.B–1st CPL, Appointed 4th SGT on Nov. 25, 1861. Elected Jr. 2d LT in Oct. 1862. Wounded in the left hip at Gettysburg, Pa., July 2, 1863. Surrendered at Appomattox, Va., April 9, 1865.

Roster of the Fifteenth Georgia Infantry Regiment

Cheek, James M.–Co.K–PVT, Wounded in the left eye on Sept. 30, 1864 and furloughed for 60 days. (No later record)

Cheek, John–Co.K–PVT, Deserted near Beans Station, Tn. in Dec., 1863. Took loyalty oath to the U.S. in 1863, at Knoxville, Tn.

Cheek, John–Co.B–PVT, Aug. 30, 1862, Deserted near Petersburg, Va. on July 28, 1864.

Cheek, Patterson F.–Co.K–PVT, Wounded at Wilderness, Va. on May 6, 1864. Died of his wounds on June 24, 1864.

Cheek, Welborn D.–Co.B–PVT, Deserted near Bull's Gap, Tn., March 28, 1864.

Childs, Hugh M.–Co.B–PVT, Mar. 4, 1862. Surrendered at Appomattox, Va. on Apr. 9, 1865.

Clark, Benjamin J.–Co.E–PVT, Surrendered at Appomattox, Va. on Apr. 9, 1865.

Clark, George W.–Co.C–PVT, Feb. 27, 1862. Died of fever in a Richmond, Va. hospital on May 23, 1862.

Clark, J. R.–Co.C–PVT, Died on May 15, 1862.

Clark, Larkin L.–Co.F–1st LT, Resigned with disability on Aug. 1, 1862.

Clark, Warren H.–Co.E–PVT, Wounded at Gettysburg, Pa. on July 2, 1863. Appointed 4th SGT on Dec. 30, 1864. Surrendered at Appomattox, Va. on Apr. 9, 1865.

Clark, W.J.–Co.I–2nd LT, Resigned on Sept. 1, 1861.

Clark, Urbin W.–Co.B PVT, Appointed 3rd CPL in May, 1862. Deserted near Bull's Gap, Tn. on Mar. 28, 1864.

Clark, William B.–Co.C–PVT, Mar. 1, 1862. Appointed 3rd SGT on July 24, 1862. Died at Winchester, Va. on Nov. 5, 1862.

Clark, William T.–Co.I–PVT, Discharged at a Richmond, Va. hospital, in 1861.

Clark, William T.–Co.C–PVT, Feb. 27, 1862. Appointed 2d CPL. Surrendered at Appomattox, Va. on Apr. 9, 1865.

Clary, James M.–Co.G–PVT, Mar. 4, 1862. Severely wounded at Garnett's Farm, Va. on June 27, 1862. Surrendered at Appomattox, Va. on Apr. 9, 1865.

Clary, Sebron Jonah–Co.G–PVT, Wounded in the left leg at Chickamauga, Ga. on Sept. 19, 1863. Furloughed due to disability.

Clary, Thomas L.–Co.G–PVT, Discharged with disability at Richmond, Va. on Dec. 18, 1861. Reenlisted on Mar. 1, 1862. Detailed as an ambulance driver in Nov., 1864. Surrendered at Appomattox, Va. on Apr. 9, 1865.

Clemons, William G.–Co.D–PVT, Surrendered at Appomattox, Va. on Apr. 9, 1865.

Cleveland, Daniel E.–Co.I–PVT, Appointed 4th CPL on Mar. 18, 1862. Captured at Dandridge, Tn. on Jan. 22, 1864. Enlisted in the U.S. Army on Oct. 13, 1864.

Cleveland, Reuben–Co.I–3rd CPL, Appointed 4th SGT on May 28, 1862. Wounded at Sharpsburg, Md. on Sept. 17, 1862. Appointed 3rd SGT on Apr. 4, 1863. Wounded at Gettysburg, Pa. on July 2, 1863; Wilderness, Va., May 6, 1864. Appointed 1st SGT on May 6, 1864. Surrendered at Appomattox, Va. on April 9, 1865.

Cleveland, William L.–Co.I–PVT, Feb. 28, 1862. Died near Strasburg, Va. on Oct. 22, 1862.

Coffee, C.–Co.A–PVT, Captured and paroled in Athens, Ga. on May 8, 1865.

Cohen, Aaron–Co.A–PVT, Surrendered at Appomattox, Va., April 9, 1865.

Cohron, George W.–Co.A–PVT, Surrendered at Appomattox, Va. on April 9, 1865.

Coker, Burgess P.–Co.I–PVT, Discharged with disability at Camp Steiner near Centerville, Va. on Nov. 19, 1861.

Coleman, James M.–Co.E–PVT, Surrendered at Appomattox, Va. on Apr. 9, 1865.

Collins, John–Co.C–PVT, Captured at Strasburg, Va. on Oct. 19, 1864. Exchanged prisoner from Pt. Lookout, Md. on Jan. 17, 1865.

Collins, Richard–Co.F–PVT, Discharged with disability on May 27, 1862.

Colson, S. D.–Co.C–PVT, Discharged with disability, Sept. 8, 1861.

Colvin, Leviticus L.–Co.G–PVT, Received a severe leg wound in May of 1864. Surrendered at Appomattox, Va. on Apr. 9, 1865.

Colvin, Preston L.–Co.G–PVT, Appointed as 1st SGT on Oct. 11, 1862. Wounded during the Peninsula campaign in Apr. of 1862. Elected 1st LT on Mar. 4, 1863. Captured near Suffolk, Va. on May 4, 1863. Exchanged prisoner on May 23, 1863. Rejoined his unit. Wounded again at Ft. Harrison, Va. on Sept. 29, 1864. Died of his wounds on Oct. 12, 1864.

Colwell, A.V.–Co.C–PVT, Wounded at Chickamauga, Ga. on Sept. 19, 1863. Surrendered at Appomattox, Va. on Apr. 9, 1865.

Colwell, Edmond–Co.C–PVT, Surrendered at Appomattox, Va. on Apr. 9, 1865.

Colwell, Henry–Co.C–PVT, Surrendered at Appomattox, Va. on Apr. 9, 1865.

Cone, Jonathan B.–Co.E–PVT, Wounded at Rapidan Station, Va. on May 1, 1862. Died of wounds in a Richmond, Va. hospital on May 10, 1862.

Connel, E.B.–Co.K–PVT, Wounded in the left ankle at Farmville, Va. on Apr. 8, 1865. (No later record)

Connell, Daniel–Co.K–Jr. 2nd LT, Elected 2nd LT on July 20, 1862; 1st LT on May 11, 1863; CPT on Nov. 17, 1864. Surrendered at Appomattox, Va. on Apr. 9, 1865.

Conwir, J.–Co.C–PVT, Captured and paroled at Athens, Ga. on May 8, 1865.

Cook, Eldridge W.–Co.E–PVT, Wounded at 2nd Manassas, Va. on Aug. 30, 1862. Appointed 1st CPL on Mar. 24, 1864. Surrendered at Appomattox, Va. on Apr. 9, 1865.

Cook, G.–Co.A–PVT, Captured and paroled at Athens, Ga. on May 8, 1865.

Cooper, Joseph P.–Co.D–PVT, Died of Pneumonia at Chimborazo Hospital in Richmond, Va. on Apr. 24, 1862.

Cosby, David C.–Co.C–PVT, Surrendered at Appomattox, Va. on Apr. 9, 1865.

Cosby, John H.–Co.C–PVT, Wounded at Sharpsburg, Md. on Sept. 17, 1862. Surrendered at Appomattox, Va. on Apr. 9, 1865.

Cosby, Napoleon Bonaparte–Co.C–PVT, Mar. 4, 1862. Surrendered at Appomattox, Va. on Apr. 9, 1865.

Craft, David L.–Co.F–PVT, Died of Pneumonia in camp near Orange Court House, Va. on Mar. 28, 1862.

Craft, E.L.–Co.F–PVT, Sick at Chimborazo Hospital, Richmond, Va., in Oct., 1861. Returned to duty on Nov. 26, 1861. (No later record)

Craft, Jasper E.–Co.F–PVT, Mar. 4, 1862. Discharged with disability on July 10, 1862. Died in a Richmond, Va. hospital in July, 1862.

Craft, John F.–Co.F–2nd LT, Appointed CPT and Assistant Regimental Quartermaster on June 16, 1863. Transferred to position of Post Quartermaster at Americus, Ga., June 30, 1864.

Craft, William A.–Co.F–PVT, Mar. 4, 1862. Surrendered at Appomattox, Va. on Apr. 9, 1865.

Craft, William M.–Co.A–PVT, Transferred to Co. F on 22 Aug. 1862.

Crawford, Benjamin S.–Co.F–PVT, May 1862. Appointed as the Brigade Blacksmith. Surrendered at Appomattox, Va. on Apr. 9, 1865.

Crawford, George H.–Co.B–PVT, Killed at Malvern Hill, Va. on July 1, 1862.

Crawford, Jabez M.–Co.G–PVT, Surrendered at Appomattox, Va. on Apr. 9, 1865.

Crawford, James C.–Co.F–PVT, Mar. 4, 1862. Died in a Richmond, Va. hospital on May 10, 1862.

Crawford, James J.–Co.E–PVT, Discharged with disability from a Richmond, Va. hospital on Aug. 1, 1862.

Crawford, Jerry–Co.G–PVT, Surrendered at Appomattox, Va. on Apr. 9, 1865.

Crawford, J.J.–Co.K–PVT, Mar. 18, 1863. Surrendered at Appomattox, Va. on Apr. 9, 1865.

Crawford, John–Co.G–PVT, Died of Typhoid fever in General Hospital #2 at Richmond, Va. on Apr. 15, 1862.

Crawford, Thomas W.–Co.G–PVT, Wounded at Malvern Hill, Va. on July 1, 1862. Sent home on wounded furlough. (No later record)

Cromer, Thomas N.–Co.B–PVT, July 3, 1862. Captured at Gettysburg, Pa. on July, 3, 1863. Died in a Union prison on Dec. 15, 1863.

Crow, James A.–Co.B–1st CPL. Sent home on Recruiting duty and died at home on Nov. 17, 1862.

Crow, P.M.–Co.F–PVT, Present in Sept., 1861. (No later record)

Crowley, John–Co.K–PVT, Mar. 3, 1863. Deserted in Oct., 1863.

Crymes, Thomas–Co.B–PVT, Captured at Gettysburg, Pa. on July 3, 1863. Exchanged prisoner on Feb. 21, 1865. Captured again and paroled at Salisbury, N.C., April 12, 1865.

Cullars, James M.–Co.G–PVT, Discharged with disability on Oct. 17, 1861.

Cullars, Robert T.–Co.G–3rd CPL, Appointed 2nd CPL on Apr. 7, 1862; Later he attained the rank of Sergeant. Captured at Ft. Harrison, Va. on Sept. 30, 1864. Released at Point Lookout, Md. on June 4, 1865.

Cully, J.–Co.C–PVT, Captured and paroled at Athens, Ga. on May 8, 1865.

Culver, Benjamin C.–Co.K–1st CPL, Appointed 4th SGT in Sept., 1862. Detailed as a Butcher in the Brigade Commissary in 1863. (No later record)

Culver, E.H.–Co.K–PVT, Nov. 7, 1861. Killed at Gettysburg, Pa. on July 3,1863.

Culver, German P.–Co.K–5th SGT, Demoted to Private and Foragemaster in July of 1863. Listed as present in Feb., 1865.

Culver, Henry H.–Co.E–2nd LT, Elected 1st LT on May 13, 1862. Wounded and permanently disabled at 2nd Manassas, Va. on Aug. 30, 1862. Resigned due to disability on Sept. 7, 1863.

Culver, John L.–Co.K–1st LT, Elected CPT on Nov. 1, 1861. Resigned on May 11, 1863.

Culver, Thomas H.–Co.K–2nd SGT, Elected Jr. 2nd LT on July 25, 1862; 2nd LT on May 11, 1863. Wounded in 1863. Killed at Wilderness, Va. on May 6, 1864.

Cummings, John G.–Co.E–PVT, Appointed CPL. Wounded and captured at Gettysburg, Pa. on July 3, 1863. Exchanged prisoner at Point Lookout, Md. on Feb. 18, 1865.

Roster of the Fifteenth Georgia Infantry Regiment 133

Cummings, J. LaFayette–Co.E–PVT, Elected Jr. 2nd LT on May 13, 1862. Killed at 2nd Manassas, Va. on Aug. 30, 1862.

Cummings, W.F.H.–Co.E–PVT, Discharged with disability in Dec., 1861.

Curren, Andrew E.–Co.K–PVT, Deserted at Wilderness, Va. on May 6, 1864.

Curry, William E.–Co.A–PVT, Died of Measles at Culpeper, Va. on April 4, 1862.

Dacres, James, Sr.–Co.E–PVT, June 28, 1864. Surrendered at Appomattox, Va. on Apr. 9, 1865.

Dallas, Thomas N.–Co.G–PVT, Elected Jr. 2nd LT on Dec. 7, 1861. Resigned on Dec. 1, 1862.

Daniel, James W.–Co.F–PVT, Died in a Richmond, Va. hospital on Dec. 14, 1861.

Daniel, John B.–Co.G–PVT, Discharged with disability on Nov. 23, 1861.

Daniel, William J.–Co.F–PVT, Killed at Garnett's Farm, Va. on June 27, 1862.

David, Peter–Co.F–PVT, Wounded at Garnett's Farm, Va. on June 27, 1862. Died of wounds on July 12, 1862.

Davidson, James–Co.G–PVT, Detailed to Charleston Navy Yard as a carpenter in 1862. Transferred to Co. D, 16th GA INF. on Dec. 15, 1864.

Davis, James O.–Co.B–PVT, Surrendered at Appomattox, Va., April 9, 1865.

Davis, James W.–Co.C–PVT, Died of disease on Aug. 13, 1862 in a Liberty, Va. hospital.

Davis, John W.–Co.D–PVT, Mar. 10, 1864. Captured at Petersburg, Va. on Apr. 3, 1865. Took loyalty oath at Harts Island, N.Y. on June 15, 1865. Hair–Dark/ Complexion–Light/ Eyes–Blue/ Height–5'6".

Davis, Mark–Co.C–PVT, Died at Fredericksburg, Va. in Mar., 1863.

Davis, M.L.–Co.B–PVT, Captured and paroled at Greenville, S.C. on May 23, 1865.

Davis, William H.–Co.K–PVT, Feb. 24, 1863. Deserted during the Battle in the Wilderness, Va., on May 6, 1864. Captured and confined in Richmond, Va. Court Martialed in Sept. of 1864. Listed as present in the hospital, with Pneumonia, at Salisbury, N.C. on Jan. 6, 1865.

Dawson, Adam P.–Co.B–PVT, Aug. 23, 1862. Killed at Spotsylvania, Va. on May 10, 1864.

Deadwyler, Joseph L.–Co.I–PVT, Appointed 2nd CPL on May 14, 1862; 4th SGT on Apr. 4, 1863; 2nd SGT on Mar. 9, 1864. Captured at Gettysburg, Pa. on July 3, 1863. Exchanged prisoner on Aug. 1, 1863. Returned to his unit and surrendered at Appomattox Court House, Va. on Apr. 9, 1865.

Deas, Joseph F.–Co.K–4th SGT, Appointed 3rd SGT on July 22, 1861; 1st SGT on May 11, 1863. Surrendered at Appomattox, Va. on Apr. 9, 1865.

Deas, William T.–Co.K–PVT, Transferred to the 15th Georgia in 1862 from the 49th Georgia. Captured at Gettysburg, Pa. on July 2, 1863. Died at Point Lookout, Md. in April 8, 1864. His wife is listed as Mary Jane Deas.

Deerburg, Charles–Co.C–PVT, Transferred to Co. F on May 15, 1862. Appointed COL's orderly, May of 1862. Killed at Chickamauga, Ga. on Sept. 20, 1863.

DeFoor, James–Co.B–PVT, Sept. 22, 1863, Wounded at Petersburg, Va. on June 17, 1864. Present at Winder Hospital in Richmond, Va. in July 1864. (No later record)

DeFoor, Joseph–Co.B–PVT, Captured at Gettysburg, Pa. on July 3, 1863. Listed as an exchanged prisoner in Feb. of 1865.

Denard, William B.–Co.B–PVT, Died in a Richmond, Va. hospital on Oct. 19, 1861.

Dendry, T.–Co.A–SGT, Prisoner–Paroled at Memphis, Tn., U.S. Provost Marshalls Office on June 14, 1865.

Denmand, James L.–Co.B–PVT, Died at Petersburg, Va. on May 14, 1863. Wife listed as Martha Denard of Carnesville, Ga.

Dennard, John A.–Co.C–PVT, Promoted CPL on Jan. 1, 1863. Captured at Gettysburg, Pa. on July 3, 1863. Sent to Ft. Delaware, Del. Present in a U.S. prison hospital in Oct., 1863.

Dennard, Thomas G.–Co.C–PVT, Died on Nov. 7, 1861.

Dent, Anderson.–Co.A–PVT, Died of Typhoid fever in a Richmond, Va. hospital on Sept. 26, 1861.

Dent, John T.–Co.G–PVT, Died in Richmond, Va. on Dec. 6, 1861.

Depuy, John J.–Staff–Assistant Regimental Surgeon–Jan. 1863, Appointed Regimental Surgeon. Surrendered at Appomattox, Va. April 9, 1865.

Dewey, W.S.–Co.C–PVT, Captured and paroled at Athens, Ga. on May 8, 1865.

Dickens, Robert L.–Co.K–PVT, Died in a hospital in 1862.

Dickerson, Charles Y.–Co.F–PVT, Mar. 4, 1862. Transferred to Co.I, June 7, 1862. Wounded on July 1, 1862. Listed as AWOL in Feb. 1865.

Dickerson, James E.–Co.I–PVT, Wounded at Chickamauga, Ga. on Sept. 19, 1863. Died of his wounds on Sept. 26, 1863.

Dickson, David W.–Co.K–PVT, Feb. 24, 1862. Died in Winder Hospital, at Richmond, Va. on Nov. 17, 1862.

Dickson, James C.–Co.K–PVT, Feb. 24, 1862. Surrendered at Appomattox, Va. on Apr. 9, 1865.

Dickson, James L.–Co.B–PVT, Died of Smallpox in Abingdon, Va. on May 15, 1864.

Dickson, John C.–Co.K–PVT, Appointed 3rd CPL in 1862. Surrendered at Appomattox, Va. on Apr. 9, 1865.

Dickson, Joseph C.–Co.K–PVT, Killed at Gettysburg, Pa. on July 3, 1863.

Dickson, Quincy L.–Co.K–PVT, Killed at Chickamauga, Ga. on Sept. 19, 1863.

Dickson, William S. Sr.–Co.K–PVT, Surrendered at Appomattox, Va. on Apr. 9, 1865.

Dickson, William S. Jr.–Co.K–PVT, Wounded in the left shoulder and permanently disabled, at Sharpsburg, Md. on Sept. 17, 1862. Wounded again at Gettysburg, Pa. on July 2, 1863. On detached duty at Corps Hospital on Apr. 9, 1865. Captured and paroled at Athens, Ga. on May 8, 1865.

Dorsey, Lemuel E.–Co.D–PVT, Died at Georgia Hospital in Richmond, Va. on Nov. 1, 1861.

Dorsey, Samuel J.–Co.D–PVT, Discharged and died in 1861.

Downer, William J.–Co.A–PVT, Captured at Dandridge, Tn. on Jan. 22, 1864. Released at Rock Island Ill., June 19, 1865. Took loyalty oath. Eyes–Gray/ Hair–Brown/ Complexion–Fresh/ Height–5'11 & 1/2" / Age–26.

Doyle, William T.–Co.B–PVT, Surrendered at Appomattox, Va., April 9, 1865.

DuBose, Dudley M.–Staff–CPT (Adjutant General); COL (15th Georgia Regimental Commander) in 1864; Brigadier General–Brigade Commander in 1865. Captured at Salems Church, Va. on Apr. 6, 1865.

Dudley, George W.–Co.K–PVT, Died of Pneumonia and Meningitis at Richmond, Va. on Jan. 23, 1862.

Dudley, J.M.–Co.K–PVT, Mar. 26, 1864. Surrendered at Appomattox, Va. on Apr. 9, 1865.

Duggan, Ivy W.–Co.K–PVT–July 15, 1862. Appointed Quartermaster SGT of the 49th Georgia. Described as–Hair–Light/ Complexion–Fair/ Eyes–Blue/ Age–30/ Occupation–Teacher.

Dunaway, John L.–Co.G–PVT, Wounded at Fredericksburg, Va. on Dec. 13, 1862; Gettysburg, Pa. on July 2, 1863; Chickamauga, Ga. on Sept. 19, 1863, and furloughed home. Absent without leave on Feb. 25, 1865.

Dunaway, John M.–Co.A–PVT, Died of Measles in a Richmond, Va. hospital on Sept. 27, 1861.

Dunn, Augustus F.–Co.K–PVT, Discharged in 1861.

Dunn, E.J.–Co.I–CPL, Discharged with disability in Sept. of 1861.

Dunn, George P.–Co.K–PVT, Died of Pneumonia at Chimborazo Hospital in Richmond, Va. on Mar. 11, 1862.

Duran, B.F.–Co.E–PVT, May 18, 1863. Deserted at Petersburg, Va. on July 28, 1864. Captured in DeKalb County, Ga. by U.S. forces. Took loyalty oath at Louisville, Ky. on Oct. 30, 1864.

Durard, A.M.–Co.C–PVT, Captured at Gettysburg, Pa. on July 3, 1865. Taken to Ft. Delaware, Del. on Oct. 15, 1863. Sick at hospital in Oct., 1863.

Dye, B. F.–Co.C–PVT, Mar. 4, 1862, Died of Measles in hospital at Richmond, Va. on Apr. 23, 1862.

Dye, James W.–Co.A–PVT, Wounded at Garnett's Farm, Va. on June 2 27, 1862; Chickamauga, Ga., Sept. 19, 1864. Captured at Chaffins Farm, Va. on 29 Sept. 1864. Released at Point Lookout, Md., June 4, 1865.

Dye, Joseph R.–Co.A–PVT, Mar. 27, 1864. Surrendered at Appomattox, Va. on Apr. 9, 1865.

Eaves, James A.–Co.C–PVT, Transferred to Co. F on July 25, 1862.

Eaves, Jesse–Co.I–PVT, Died on Sept. 12, 1861 at Camp Walker, near Centerville, Va.

Eaves, Joel–Co.C–PVT, Died on Nov. 1, 1861.

Eberhart, J.G.–Co.C–PVT, Discharged with disability in Oct. 1861.

Edwards, Elisha W.–Co.B–PVT, Transferred to Division HQ in 1865.

Edwards, Emory P.–Co.F–Jr. 2nd LT, Wounded at Garnett's Farm, Va. on June 27, 1862. Elected CPT on July 24, 1862. Resigned on Apr. 13, 1863.

Edwards, James A.–Co.F–Elected Jr. 2nd LT on July 24, 1862; 2nd LT Aug. 4, 1862. Seriously wounded in the thigh at Spotsylvania, Va. on May 12, 1864. Resigned on Feb. 5, 1865.

Edwards, William S.–Co.B–PVT, Surrendered at Appomattox, Va. on Apr. 9, 1865.

Elliott, Benjamin–Co.G–PVT, Wounded at Gettysburg, Pa. on July 2, 1863. Detailed as a Division Wagon guard in July of 1864. Surrendered at Appomattox, Va. on Apr. 9, 1865.

Elliott, William W.–Co.G–PVT, Discharged because of Phithisis on June 4, 1862.

English, W.J.–Co.B–PVT, Captured and paroled at Augusta, Ga. on May 8, 1865.

Ensign, W.P.–Co.C–PVT, Captured and paroled at Athens, Ga. on May 8, 1865.

Roster of the Fifteenth Georgia Infantry Regiment

Erlich, Benjamin–Co.D–PVT, Captured near Knoxville, Tn. on Dec. 5, 1863. Enlisted in the U.S. Army for frontier duty on Oct. 13, 1864.

Ertzburger, Robert D.–Co.B–PVT, Died of Measles in a Richmond, Va. hospital on Apr. 29, 1862.

Eskea, Samuel–Co.H–PVT, Discharged with disability at Camp Georgia, near Manassas, Va. on Dec. 9, 1861.

Ester, T.N.–Co.E–PVT, Captured at Gettysburg, Pa. on July 3, 1863. Taken to Ft. Delaware, Del.(No later record)

Estes, J.W.–Co.H–PVT, Discharged with disability at Camp Steiner near Centerville, Va. on Nov. 6, 1861.

Eubanks, Charles H.–Co.K–PVT, Paroled at Farmville, Va. in April, 1865.

Eubanks, James–Co.E–PVT, May 8, 1862. Deserted at Gettysburg, Pa. on July 3, 1863. Captured and sent to Fort Delaware, Del. Joined the Union Army on Sept. 7, 1863.

Evans, E.A.–Co.E–PVT, Listed as present in Dec. of 1861. (No later record)

Evans, Humphrey–Co.G–PVT, Surrendered at Appomattox, Va. on Apr. 9, 1865.

Evans, J.–Co.I–PVT, Died on Sept. 12, 1861 of Typhoid fever.

Evans, James J.–Co.D–PVT, Died at Richmond, Va. on Nov. 24, 1861.

Evans, John D.–Co.D–PVT, Wounded at Thoroughfare Gap, Va. on Aug. 28, 1862. Discharged with disability.

Evans, Russell J.–Co.D–PVT, discharged with disability on Aug. 31, 1864.

Fain, James–Co.H–PVT, May of 1863. Killed at Farmville, Va. on Apr. 6, 1865.(The last battle casualty of the 15th Regiment.)

Fair, Larkin–Co.A–PVT, Jan. 13, 1863. Captured near Knoxville, Tn. on Dec. 18, 1863. Died in Rock Island, Ill. Prison on Apr. 4, 1864 and buried in grave #990.

Farmer, John J.–Co.B–PVT, Listed as AWOL in Feb. 1865.

Farmer, Sylvester J.–Co.D–CPT, Appointed Surgeon on Aug. 1, 1862; Later– Brigade Surgeon. Listed as AWOL in Feb., 1865.

Fauling, William N.–Co.A–PVT, Wounded at Garnett's Farm, Va. on June 27, 1862. Present in Dec. 1863. (No later record)

Faulk, Jared–Co.G–PVT, Died in a Richmond, Va. hospital on Dec. 18, 1861.

Faulkner, Isaac N.–Co.I–PVT, Mar. 1, 1862. Surrendered at Appomattox, Va. on Apr. 9, 1865.

Favors, William W.–Co.A–PVT, Transferred on Dec. 12, 1861 to Co.A, 9th Ga. Inf.

Ferrell, John D.–Co.K–PVT, Died in a Richmond, Va. hospital on Oct. 18, 1864.

Fisher, H.L.–Co.H–PVT, Captured at Gettysburg, Pa. on July 3, 1863. Died at Point Lookout, Md. on Jan. 27, 1864.

Fisher, Thomas–Co.H–2nd SGT, Elected Jr. 2nd LT on July 28, 1862. Wounded in the left leg at Gettysburg, Pa. on July 2, 1863. Retired with disability on Apr. 9, 1864.

Flangue, John–Co.B–PVT, Surrendered at Appomattox, Va. on April 9, 1865.

Flanigan, William A.–Co.G–PVT, Mar. 3, 1862. Surrendered at Appomattox, Va. on Apr. 9, 1865.

Fleming, Absalom F.–Co.G–PVT, Appointed 3rd CPL on Nov. 15, 1862.

Fleming, Leonard–Co.H–PVT, Died in a Richmond, Va. hospital on Nov. 2, 1861.

Fleming, Thomas–Co.H–PVT, Died of Typhoid fever at Camp Walker, near Manassas, Va. on Sept. 13, 1861.

Florence, LaFayette–Co.G–PVT, Feb. 27, 1862. Died in service. Described as having–Hair–Dark / Eyes–Dark / Complexion–Fair / Height–5'8".

Florence, Peyton M.–Co.G–PVT, Severely wounded at Garnett's Farm, Va. on June 27, 1862. Surrendered at Appomattox, Va. on Apr. 9, 1865.

Fluker, Robert H.–Co.D–PVT, Appointed 4th CPL. Surrendered on Apr. 9, 1865 at Appomattox, Va.

Fluker, William T.–Co.D–PVT, Wounded at Garnett's Farm, Va. on June 27, 1862. Surrendered at Appomattox, Va. on Apr. 9, 1865.

Flury, C.H.–Co.K–PVT, Oct. 22, 1863. Surrendered at Appomattox, Va. on Apr. 9, 1865.

Flury, John Joseph–Co.K–PVT, Appointed 1st CPL on Dec. 1, 1864. Wounded at Wilderness, Va. on May 6, 1864. Surrendered at Appomattox, Va. on Apr. 9, 1865.

Flury, William A.–Co.K–PVT, Feb. 24, 1862. Surrendered at Appomattox, Va. on Apr. 9, 1865.

Flynt, Henry H.–Co.D–PVT, Discharged with disability on Jan. 26, 1862.

Flynt, James W.–Co.D–PVT, Transferred on Mar. 12, 1864 to Co. E, 7th CSA Cavalry.

Flynt, Samuel J.–Co.D–2d LT, Wounded at Malvern Hill, Va. on July 1, 1862; 2d Manassas, Va. on Aug. 30, 1862. Elected CPT on Oct. 8, 1862. Wounded at

Gettysburg, Pa. on July 2, 1863; Fort Harrison, Va. on Sept. 29, 1864. Surrendered at Appomattox, Va. on Apr. 9, 1865.

Forbes, H.W.–Staff–CPT, Assistant Quartermaster, Listed as Brigade QM–Present in Mar. 1865, Paroled at Augusta, Ga. on May 20, 1865.

Ford, Jordan R.–Co.I–PVT, Sept. 15, 1862. Wounded at Gettysburg, Pa. on July 2, 1863. Feb. 25, 1865, Absent without leave.

Ford, Joshua A.–Co.I–PVT, Aug. 29, 1862. Wounded at Wilderness, Va. on May 6, 1864. Detailed on duty in a Richmond, Va. hospital on Feb. 28, 1865.

Fortson, Abner T.–Co.I–PVT, Mar. 4, 1862. Died in a Richmond, Va. hospital, (#13), on July 26, 1862.

Fortson, Blanton B.–Co.A–PVT, Discharged with disability in 1861. (Died of disease in 1862.)

Fortson, DeLancey A.–Co.I–PVT, Transferred to 15th Georgia from the 38th Georgia on May 14, 1862. Surrendered at Appomattox, Va. on Apr. 9, 1865.

Fortson, Elijah R.–Co.I–PVT, Surrendered at Appomattox, Va. on Apr. 9, 1865.

Fortson, John–Co.D–PVT, Discharged with disability in Nov. of 1861.

Fortson, John B.–Co.I–PVT, Feb. 28, 1862. Surrendered at Appomattox, Va. on Apr. 9, 1865.

Fortson, John H.–Co.I–PVT, Discharged with disability, at Camp Steiner near Centerville, Va. on Nov. 19, 1861.

Fortson, Moses E.–Co.I–PVT, Surrendered at Appomattox, Va. on Apr. 9, 1865.

Fortson, William–Co.C–PVT, Discharged with disability on Aug.9, 1862.

Fortson, William E.–Co.I–PVT, Appointed 3rd SGT on Mar. 4, 1864. Surrendered at Appomattox, Va. on Apr. 9, 1865.

Fortson, William W.–Co.I–PVT, Apr. 24, 1864. Wounded at Wilderness, Va. on May 6, 1864. Died of his wounds in 1864.

Fowler, S.W.–Co.H–PVT, Died on Oct. 25, 1861.

Fraley, LaFayette I.–Co.E–PVT, Discharged with disability at Richmond, Va. on Sept. 30, 1861.

Franklin, Abraham–Co.I–PVT, Mar. 19, 1862. Substitute for Z.H.C. Mattox. Discharged with disability, at Richmond, Va. on July 15, 1863.

Franklin, Henry–Co.I–PVT, Wounded at New Market Heights, Va. on Aug. 16, 1864. Furloughed home, Sept. 1864. On detached duty at Provost Marshall's Office in Augusta, Ga. on Feb. 28, 1865.

Franklin, Manuel–Co.C–PVT, Appointed duty as Brigade Butcher. Surrendered at Appomattox, Va. on Apr. 9, 1865.

Franklin, Samuel–Co.C–PVT, Appointed 3d SGT on May 17, 1862; Elected 2d LT on July 24, 1862. Captured at Gettysburg, Pa. on July 3, 1863. Exchanged prisoner on Feb. 24, 1865.

Franks, Josephus–Co.E–PVT, Died of disease on May 10, 1864.

Franks, William P.–Co.E–PVT, Captured at Gettysburg, Pa. on July 5, 1863. Exchanged prisoner at Point Lookout, Md. on Feb. 18, 1865.

Freeman, Edward D.–Co.A–PVT, Mar. 4, 1862. Wounded at Wilderness, Va. May 6, 1864. Surrendered at Appomattox, Va. on April 9, 1865.

Freeman, William M.–Co.A–3d CPL, Appointed 4th SGT in Apr. 1862; 2nd SGT in Nov. 1862. Captured at Gettysburg,Pa. on July 2, 1863. Released from Ft. Delaware, Del. on June 16, 1865.

Fuller, Milton–Co.H–PVT, Aug. 22, 1862. Severely wounded in the head at Petersburg, Va. on June 19, 1864. Listed as AWOL on Feb. 25, 1865.

Furgerson, Wilkes W.–Co.G–PVT, Sept. 23, 1862. Surrendered at Appomattox, Va. on Apr. 9, 1865.

Gable, H.F.–Co.H–PVT, Captured at Farmville, Va. on Apr. 6, 1865. Released at Newport News, Va. on June 25, 1865.

Gaines, D.–Co.I–PVT, Taken prisoner and paroled at Warrenton, Va. on Sept. 29, 1862. Listed as a Nurse.

Gaines, Francis–Co.I–PVT, Feb. 28, 1862. Wounded at 2nd Manassas, Va. on Aug. 30, 1862; Gettysburg, Pa. on July 2, 1863. Surrendered at Appomattox, Va. on Apr. 9, 1865.

Gaines, James A.–Co.I–2nd LT, Elected CPT on May 14, 1862. Killed in action at Gettysburg, Pa. on July 2, 1863.

Gaines, James A. Jr.–Co.I–PVT, Died on July 4, 1862, from a head wound received on June 27, 1862.

Gaines, Lindsay A.–Co.F–4th SGT, Appointed 1st SGT on July 24, 1862. Elected 1st LT on Apr. 21, 1863. Surrendered at Appomattox, Va. on Apr. 9, 1865.

Gaines, Livingston J.–Co.I–PVT, Appointed 3rd CPL. Surrendered at Appomattox, Va. on Apr. 9, 1865.

Gaines, Peter C.–Co.I–PVT, Mar. 4, 1862. Surrendered at Appomattox, Va. on Apr. 9, 1865.

Gaines, Thomas S.–Co.I–PVT, Appointed 3rd CPL in May 1862; Sergeant.

Wounded at Sharpsburg, Md. on Sept. 17, 1862. Discharged with disability, Feb. 1, 1864.

Galloway, Richard B.–Co.F–PVT, Detailed as Brigade Commissary SGT in May of 1862. Surrendered at Appomattox, Va. on Apr. 9, 1865.

Garner, Thomas J.–Co.B–PVT, Mar. 4, 1862. Discharged in Oct. of 1864.

Garrett, A.J.–Co.E–PVT, Captured at Gettysburg, Pa. on July 5, 1863. Sent to Ft. Delaware, Del. in Oct. of 1863. Exchanged on Feb. 18, 1865.

Garrett, Herbert E.–Co.E–PVT, Captured at Gettysburg, Pa. on July 2, 1863. Exchanged. Listed as AWOL in Feb. of 1865.

Garret, James V.–Co.A–PVT, Appointed 4th CPL. Wounded at Garnett's Farm, Va. on June 27, 1864. Transferred in May of 1863 to Co.K, 10th Ga. Infantry.

Gaulding, William D.–Co.I–PVT, Discharged with disability, Oct. 31, 1861.

Ghann, Thomas A.–Co.D–PVT, Assigned as Regimental Wagoner. Surrendered at Appomattox, Va. on Apr. 9, 1865.

Gheesling, Virgil A.–Co.D–PVT, Assigned to Division Rear Guard. Surrendered at Appomattox, Va. on Apr. 9, 1865.

Gibson, George W.–Co.D–PVT, Died at Richmond, Va. on Nov. 1, 1861.

Gilbert, M.S.–Co.C–PVT, Captured and paroled at Athens, Ga. on May 8, 1865.

Gill, Isaac M.–Co.A–PVT, Surrendered at Appomattox, Va. on April 9, 1865. **Gill, Jhonathan M.**–Co.A–PVT, Surrendered at Appomattox, Va. on April 9, 1865.

Gill, Micajah A.–Co.A–PVT, Wounded at Spotsylvania, Va. on May 12, 1864. Surrendered at Appomattox, Va. on April 9, 1865.

Gill, William–Co.A–PVT, Discharged on Sept. 21, 1861.

Gillespie, J.M.–Co.B–PVT, Captured and paroled at Hartwell, Ga. on May 19, 1865.

Ginn, James H.–Co.F–2nd CPL, Wounded at Wilderness, Va. on May 6, 1864. Died of wounds in Petersburg, Va., General Hospital on July 13, 1864.

Ginn, Middleton G.–Co.F–PVT, Deserted on Aug. 28, 1862. Took oath of loyalty to the U.S. Govt. and was released on Feb. 12, 1864.

Gladden, S.G.W.–Co.E–PVT, Wounded and disabled at 2nd Manassas, Va. on Aug. 30, 1862. Retired to the Invalid Corps on Sept. 5, 1864.

Glaze, Anderson–Co.G–PVT, July 11, 1862. Substitute for Houston Glaze.

Glaze, Houston–Co.G–PVT, Substituted by Anderson Glaze in 1862.

Gloer, Isaac D.–Co.F–PVT, Sent on wounded furlough in July, 1864. Captured and paroled at Hartwell, Ga. on May 19, 1865.

Gloer, John S.–Co.F–PVT, Captured at Morristown, Tn. on Jan. 18, 1864. Enlisted in the U.S. Army on Oct. 6, 1864.

Golaspy, James W.–Co.A–PVT, Deserted in North Carolina on Apr. 29, 1863. Captured and sent to Ft. Monroe, Va. Released and sent north on May 9, 1863.

Goolsby, Gilbert–Co.G–PVT, Wounded at Gettysburg, Pa. on July 2, 1863; Chickamauga, Ga. on Sept. 19, 1863. Retired with disability on July 27, 1864.

Gothard, Henry C.–Co.C–PVT, Wounded (severely in the foot) at Fredericksburg, Va. on Dec. 13, 1862. Captured at Gettysburg, Pa. on July 2, 1863. Listed as AWOL in Feb., 1865.

Graham, William P.–Co.F–PVT, Mar. 4, 1862. Furloughed for 30 days, Sept. 9, 1864, due to chronic diarrhoea. Feb. 25, 1865, Absent without leave.

Graves, George W.–Co.G–PVT, Captured at Gettysburg, Pa. on July 2, 1863. Released from Ft. Delaware, Del. prison on May 10, 1865.

Gray, Robert–Co.D–PVT, Discharged with disability on Dec. 3, 1861.

Green, John W.–Co.A–Musician, Surrendered at Appomattox, Va. April 9, 1865.

Green, William H.–Co.E–PVT, Transferred to Co.E, 15th Georgia from Co. I, 49th Georgia on Mar. 4, 1862. Discharged due to chronic diarrhoea on Aug. 1, 1862.

Greenway, William M.–Co.F–PVT, Died in a Richmond, Va. hospital in May, 1863.

Gresham, J. Hulbert W.–Co.G–PVT, Surrendered at Appomattox, Va. on Apr. 9, 1865.

Griffin, G.W.–Co.E–PVT, Jan. 21, 1862. Sent to a hospital on Feb. 27, 1862. (No later record)

Griffin, William N.–Co.B–PVT, Wounded (gunshot-thigh) and captured at Gettysburg, Pa. on July 3, 1863. Received treatment at Camp Letterman USA Hospital during Oct. of 1863. Listed as AWOL in Feb. of 1865.

Grimes, Thomas–Co.B–PVT, Captured at Gettysburg, Pa. on Jul. 3, 1863. Sent to Ft. Delaware, Del. on Oct. 22, 1863.

Grubbs, G.W.–Co.H–PVT, Apr. 15, 1862. Killed in action on Aug. 28, 1862.

Grubbs, W.M.–Co.H–PVT, Surrendered at Appomattox, Va. on Apr. 9, 1865.

Gruson, William E.–Co.D–PVT, Discharged on Nov. 1, 1861.

Gudey, W.T.–Co.H–PVT, Mar. 4, 1862. Died of fever at Richmond, Va. on June 22, 1862.

Guest, J.P.–Co.H–PVT, Mar. 4, 1862. Died in a Richmond, Va. hospital on Apr. 1, 1863.

Roster of the Fifteenth Georgia Infantry Regiment   143

Guest, Spencer–Co.H–PVT, Feb. 27, 1863. Deserted at Petersburg, Va. on July 13, 1864.

Gullatt, Absalom–Co.G–PVT, Promoted to 3rd CPL on Aug. 15, 1863; 4th SGT in May 1864. Died at Jackson Hospital in Richmond, Va. of Pneumonia on May 28, 1864.

Gullatt, Henderson–Co.G–PVT, Appointed 1st SGT on Nov. 12, 1861. Died in camp near Orange Court House, Va. on Apr. 6, 1862.

Gullatt, Peter–Co.G–PVT, Elected 1st LT on Dec. 7, 1861. Killed at 2nd Manassas, Va. on Aug. 30, 1862.

Gulley, J.W.–Co.H–PVT, Mar. 4, 1862. Listed as present in 1863. (No later record)

Gully, James M.–Co.F–PVT, Surrendered at Appomattox, Va. on Apr. 9, 1865.

Hackney, Jesse M.–Co.D–PVT, Accidently killed on June 16, 1862.

Hadden, Chalmers C.–Co.I–PVT, Surrendered at Appomattox, Va. on Apr. 9, 1865.

Hagenbaugh, J.–Co.B–PVT,Captured and paroled at Athens, Ga. on May 8, 1865.

Hailey, George W.–Co.I–PVT, Feb. 28, 1862. Died in a Richmond, Va. hospital on June 2, 1862.

Hailey, James–Co.I–PVT, Sent to a Richmond, Va. hospital on Oct. 18, 1861. Died there on Nov. 13, 1861.

Hall, G.W.–Co.H–PVT, Mar. 4, 1862. Died of fever at Richmond, Va. on June 9, 1862.

Hall, William S.–Co.F–Appointed 2nd SGT on Jan. 18, 1862. Transferred to 38th Ga. on Jan. 13, 1863.

Hall, W.M.–Co.H–PVT, Died at Richmond, Va. in Aug., 1862.

Hall, W. W.–Co.A–PVT, Died at Richmond, Va. on July 20, 1862.

Hallow, J.–Co.H–PVT, Captured at Gettysburg, Pa. and exchanged on Feb. 18, 1865.

Hamby, James W.–Co.B–PVT, Died of camp fever at Camp Steiner near Manassas, Va. on Dec. 20, 1861.

Hamby, John P.–Co.B–PVT, Appointed CPL on Oct. 6, 1862.

Hamby, Levi T.–Co.B–PVT, Wounded at Petersburg, Va. on July 12, 1863. Died of wounds on July 15, 1863.

Hamby, Terrel T.–Co.B–PVT, Wounded at Wilderness, Va. on May 6, 1864. Died of wounds on July 25, 1862.

Hamilton, Charles–Co.D–PVT, July 8, 1862. Provided as substitute for Aaron Myers and deserted on July 12, 1862.

Hammock, G.R.–Co.E–PVT, Discharged with disability at Richmond, Va. hospital in Aug., 1862.

Hammock, James M.–Co.D–PVT, Furloughed with disability on Feb. 28, 1865.

Hammock, William H.–Co.D–PVT, Discharged on Jan. 24, 1865.

Hammond, William H.–Co.I–PVT, Deserted on Feb. 20, 1865.

Hamser, D.H.–Staff–Surgeon, Captured at Gettysburg, Pa. on July 5, 1863, Sent to Fortress Monroe, Va. in 1863.

Hancock, M.A.–Co.G–PVT, Captured and paroled in Greenville, S.C. on May 24, 1865.

Harbin, John M.–Co.I–PVT, Wounded at 2nd Manassas, Va. on Aug. 30, 1862. Captured on Sept. 30, 1862. Exchanged prisoner in 1862 and returned to the unit. (No later record)

Harbor, Thomas H.–Co.B–PVT, Died of fever in a Richmond, Va. hospital on Dec. 25, 1861.

Harden, Robert T.–Co.G–PVT, Surrendered at Appomattox, Va. on Apr. 9, 1865.

Hardwick, William H.–Co.K–PVT, Appointed 2nd SGT on July 25, 1862; 1st SGT in 1862. Wounded at Gettysburg, Pa. on July 2, 1863. Died of his wounds on July 25, 1863.

Hardy, Aaron H.–Co.G–PVT, Appointed 1st CPL. Surrendered at Appomattox, Va. on Apr. 9, 1865.

Harland, J.–Co.H–PVT, Captured at Gettysburg, Pa. on July 2, 1863. Sent to Ft. Delaware, Del. in Oct., 1863. Transferred to Point Lookout, Md. (No later record)

Harmon, F. C.–Co.C–PVT, Feb. 25, 1862. Wounded at Wilderness, Va. on May 6, 1864. Died of wounds on May 9, 1864.

Harper, B.–Co.E–PVT, Discharged with disability (hernia) in Dec., 1861.

Harper, Wilkins J.–Co.E–PVT, Discharged with disability on Oct. 28, 1861.

Harper, William M.–Co.A–PVT, Discharged with disability in Sept. 1861.

Harris, A.F.–Staff–Assistant Surgeon, resigned in June of 1862.

Harris, J.D.–Co.H–PVT, Discharged with disability in Oct., 1861.

Harris, Jeptha A.–Co.C–PVT, Died in Orange Court House, Va. hospital on Mar. 29, 1862.

Harris, J.H.–Co.H–PVT, Died at Richmond, Va. Sept. 26, 1862.

Harris, Samuel P.–Co.E–PVT, Appointed CPL; 2nd SGT on Oct. 10, 1862; Assistant Quartermaster. Listed as AWOL in Feb. 1865.

Harris, T.W.–Co.E–PVT, Surrendered at Appomattox, Va. on Apr. 9, 1865.

Harris, William G.–Co.D–PVT, Discharged on Nov. 29, 1861.

Harris, W.P.–Co.H–PVT, Died of fever at Richmond, Va. on June 25, 1862.

Harrison, E.A.–Co.H–PVT, Appointed 2nd CPL on July 1, 1862. Killed at Darbytown Road, Va. on Oct. 7, 1864.

Harrison, John T.–Co.B–PVT, Wounded and captured at Gettysburg, Pa. on July 3, 1863. Died of fever in Ft. Delaware, Del. on Sept. 23, 1863.

Harrison, Montgomery–Co.K–PVT, Killed at Gettysburg, Pa. on July 2, 1863.

Harrison, Thomas J.–Co.B–PVT, Wound resulting in amputation near Richmond, Va., Nov. 11, 1864. Retired in Jan. of 1865.

Harrison, Virgil M.–Co.B–PVT, Died of Typhoid fever in Manassas, Va. on Sept. 14, 1861.

Hatsfield, A.J.–Co.A–PVT, Captured at Gettysburg, Pa. in July 1863 and sent to DeCamp General Hospital at Davids Island, N.Y.

Haverell, Allen–Co.F–PVT, Jan. 18, 1862. Substitute for Dunston Blackwell. Died on Mar. 31, 1863.

Hawes, Thomas D.–Co.G–PVT, Appointed 1st SGT on May 15, 1862. Elected 1st LT on Oct. 11, 1862; CPT on Mar. 4, 1863. Surrendered at Appomattox, Va. on Apr. 9, 1865.

Hawkins, James F.–Co.K–PVT, Wounded and disabled in June of 1864. (No later record)

Haygood, Atticus Green–Staff–Chaplain, Resigned on Nov. 13. 1861.

Haynie, Robert B.–Co.B–PVT, Sent to Staff duty in May 1862. Sick in hospital in July of 1864. (No later record)

Haynie, Smith S.–Co.B–PVT, Aug. 23, 1862. Captured at Gettysburg, Pa. on July 3, 1863.

Heard, George E.–Co.C–SGT, Discharged with disability (Phithisis) on Aug. 1, 1861.

Heard, Mark L.–Co.C–PVT, Surrendered at Appomattox, Va. on Apr. 9, 1865.

Heard, Robert M.–Co.C–1st LT, Elected CPT on May 21, 1862. Resigned on July 11, 1862.

Hearnsberger, Adam–Co.G–PVT, Discharged with disability on Sept. 27, 1861.

Reenlisted on Dec. 1, 1862. Appointed 2nd CPL. Wounded and captured at Gettysburg, Pa. on July 2, 1863. Left arm amputated in 1863. Discharged due to disability in 1863.

Hearnsberger, John T.–Co.G–PVT, Feb. 27, 1862. Listed as present in May of 1862. Records indicate he was–Height–5'10"/ Hair–Dark/ Eyes–Dark/ Complexion–Fair.

Hearnsberger, Stephen Z.–Co.G–1st LT, Elected CPT on Dec. 3, 1861; LT COL on Mar. 4, 1863. Captured at Gettysburg, Pa. on July 3, 1863. Exchanged prisoner on Mar. 22, 1865.

Hembree, Anthony D.–Co.B–PVT, Killed at Wilderness, Va., May 6, 1864.

Hembree, James A.–Co.B–PVT, Surrendered at Appomattox, Va., April 9, 1865.

Henderson, James H.–Co.G–PVT, Discharged with disability at Camp Pine Creek, near Fairfax, Va. on Sept. 27, 1861.

Hendley, John W.–Co.A–4th SGT, Died in a Richmond, Va. hospital on Jan. 3, 1862.

Hendrick, Charles N.–Co.D–PVT, Transferred to Co. D in Oct. 1862. Surrendered at Appomattox, Va. on Apr. 9, 1865.

Hendricks, Isaiah–Co.D–PVT, Wounded at 2d Manassas, Va. on Aug. 30, 1862. Died of disease in a Richmond, Va. hospital on Oct. 4, 1864.

Hendricks, W. W.–Co.D–PVT, Discharged on Nov. 29, 1861.

Henley, James E.–Co.H–PVT, Wounded and captured in 1864. Absent without leave in Feb. 25, 1865.

Herringdine, Joseph R.–Co.E–PVT, Appointed 1st CPL in 1862. Wounded at 2nd Manassas, Va. on Aug. 30, 1862. Appointed 1st SGT on Mar. 24, 1864. Surrendered at Appomattox, Va. on Apr. 9, 1865.

Hester, Thomas–Co.E–PVT, May 8, 1862. Captured at Gettysburg, Pa. on July 3, 1863. Died in prison at Point Lookout, Md. on Dec. 31, 1863.

Hester, Thomas J.–Co.I–1st CPL, Elected 2nd LT on May 14, 1862. Resigned with disability in Mar., 1863.

Higginbotham, Eli–Co.I–PVT, Mar. 4, 1862. Surrendered at Appomattox, Va. on Apr. 9, 1865.

Higginbotham, Nelson R.–Co.F–PVT, Surrendered at Appomattox, Va. on Apr. 9, 1865.

Higginbotham, Willis H.–Co.A–PVT, Died at Staunton, Va., Feb. 31, 1863.

Higgins, C. James A.–Co.H–PVT, Mar. 4, 1862. Died of Typhoid fever in Chimborazo hospital #3, at Richmond, Va. on May 5, 1862.

Roster of the Fifteenth Georgia Infantry Regiment 147

Hill, Kendrick–Co.B–PVT, Surrendered at Appomattox, Va., April 9, 1865.

Hill, Wiley T.–Co.D–PVT, Died in Camp Steiner on Nov. 27, 1861.

Hines, Joseph S.–Co.E–PVT, Wounded at 2nd Manassas, Va. on Aug. 30, 1862. Killed at Wilderness, Va. on May 6, 1864.

Hinton, Jesse H.–Co.A–PVT, Died of Typhoid fever in July, 1862.

Hinton, John T.–Co.A–PVT, Killed at Garnett's Farm, Va., June 27, 1862.

Hinton, Noah–Co.A–PVT, Surrendered at Appomattox, Va., April 9, 1865.

Hodge, Richard–Co.D–PVT, Discharged on Oct. 1, 1861.

Holbrook, Jesse T.–Co.B–2d SGT, Wounded at Wilderness, Va. on May 6, 1864. Surrendered at Appomattox, Va, April 9, 1865.

Holbrook, Nathan J.–Co.B–PVT, Wounded at Petersburg,Va., June 6, 1864. Surrendered at Appomattox, Va., April 9, 1865.

Holbrook, P. C.–Co.C–PVT, Surrendered at Appomattox, Va. on Apr. 9, 1865.

Holbrook, William Y.–Co.B–PVT, Discharged with disability on March 22, 1862.

Holland, B.F.–Co.H–PVT, Discharged with disability on Feb. 20, 1862.

Holland, John T.–Co.H–PVT, Captured at Gettysburg, Pa. on July 3, 1863. Exchanged prisoner on Feb. 20, 1862.

Hollingsworth, Warren T.–Co.I–PVT, Surrendered at Appomattox, Va. on Apr. 9, 1865.

Hollingsworth, William J.–Co.I–4th SGT, Appointed 2nd SGT on May 28, 1862; 1st SGT on Apr. 4, 1863. Wounded and captured at Gettysburg, Pa. on July 2, 1863. Died of wounds in DeCamp General Hospital, David's Island, New York Harbor, July 31, 1863.

Holmes, G.A.–Co.C–PVT, Captured and paroled at Athens, Ga. on May 8, 1865.

Holsey, Marcus M.–Co.E–PVT, Appointed Hospital Steward on Nov. 15, 1861.

Holtzclaw, Timothy–Co.A–PVT, Deserted in North Carolina on April 29, 1863.

Hooks, Green L.–Co.K–PVT, Wounded at Gettysburg, Pa. on July 2, 1863. Listed in Feb. 28, 1865 as AWOL.

Hooks, H.M.–Co.K–PVT, Discharged with disability in 1862.

Hopkins, Martin V.–Co.G–PVT, Died in a Richmond, Va. hospital on Nov. 18, 1861.

House, John W.–Co.A–1st CPL, Died in a Richmond, Va. hospital on Dec. 26, 1861.

House, Leiston–Co.A–PVT, Killed at Garnett's Farm, Va. on June 27, 1862.

Howell, C. A.–Co.D–PVT, Mar. 1, 1862. Surrendered at Appomattox, Va. on Apr. 9, 1865.

Howell, James H.–Co.B–PVT, Died of fever in Richmond, Va. on Dec. 24, 1861.

Howell, Joseph, M.–Co.D–PVT, Wounded and captured at 2d Manassas, Va. on Aug. 30, 1862. Paroled at Warrenton, Va. on Sept. 30, 1862. Died of wounds in a hospital on Dec. 19, 1862.

Howell, Thomas J.–Co.D–PVT, Captured at Gettysburg, Pa. on July 3, 1863. Exchanged prisoner on Apr. 30, 1864. Killed at Ft. Harrison, Va. on Sept. 29, 1864.

Hubbard, John W.–Co.C–PVT, Wounded (severely in the shoulder) at Wilderness, Va. on May 6, 1864. Discharged with disability in July, 1864.

Hubbard, T. P.–Co.C–PVT, Mar. 4, 1862. Died of Typhoid fever in a Richmond, Va. hospital on July 2, 1862.

Hubbard, William D.–Co.C–PVT, Surrendered at Appomattox, Va. on Apr. 9, 1865.

Hudson, David–Co.C–4th SGT, Appointed 1st SGT on May 14, 1862. Wounded at Garnett's Farm, Va. on June 27, 1862. Elected CPT on Sept. 30, 1863. Surrendered at Appomattox, Va. on Apr. 9, 1865.

Hudson, James M.–Co.C–PVT, Appointed 2d SGT on Sept. 30, 1863. Surrendered at Appomattox, Va. on Apr. 9, 1865.

Hudson, J. C.–Co.C–PVT, Died in a Richmond, Va. hospital on July 7, 1862.

Hudson, J.H.–Co.G–PVT, Discharged with disability on Sept. 27, 1861 at Fairfax Court House, VA.

Hudson, John S.–Co.C–4th CPL, Discharged with disability on Nov. 7, 1861.

Hudson, J. S.–Co.C–PVT, Appointed 4th SGT on Aug. 6, 1862. Killed at Sharpsburg, Md. on Sept. 17, 1862.

Hudson, T. J.–Co.C–PVT, Died of Typhoid fever near Richmond, Va. on Sept. 18, 1861.

Hudson, William D.–Co.C–PVT, Appointed 4th SGT in Oct. 1862. Captured at Gettysburg, Pa. on July 3, 1863. Exchanged prisoner on Feb. 25, 1865.

Hulme, Easton LaFayette–Co.F–3rd SGT, Wounded at Garnett's Farm, Va. on June 27, 1862. Captured at Gettysburg, Pa. on July 3, 1863. Paroled at Point Lookout, Md. on Feb. 18, 1865.

Hulme, G.W.–Co.F–PVT, Mar. 4, 1862. Died in a Richmond, Va. hospital on Apr. 25, 1862.

Hulme, John D.–Co.C–PVT in 1861. Discharged. Re-enlisted in Co. F. on Aug. 28, 1862. Surrendered at Appomattox, Va. on Apr. 9, 1865.

Hulme, John H.–Co.F–PVT, Transferred to 15th Georgia from 38th Georgia on Oct. 10, 1862. Captured at Dandridge, Tn. on Jan. 22, 1864. Died of Variola at Rock Island, Ill. prison on Mar. 24, 1864.

Humphrey, James M.–Co.D–PVT, Promoted to 1st CPL on July 24, 1862. Wounded on Sept. 29, 1864 at Ft. Harrison, Va. Died of wounds on Sept. 30, 1864 in Richmond, Va.

Humphrey, N. M.–Co.D–PVT–Jan. 29, 1864. Present in Feb. of 1865. (No later record)

Hunbun, James–Co.C–PVT, Took a loyalty oath at Ft. Delaware, Del. on Aug. 2, 1862.

Hungerford, Thomas–Co.K–PVT, Captured at Dumfries, Va. on Sept. 14, 1863. Sent to Old Capitol Prison, Washington D.C., Released and sent to Philadelphia, Pa. on Sept. 23, 1863 where he took a loyalty oath. Captured and paroled again in Augusta, Ga. in 1865. Described as–Hair–Light/ Complexion–Light/ Height–5' 8 1/4".

Hunt, Elijah–Co.B–PVT, Died of chronic diarrhoea, Nov. 5, 1863.

Hunt, Sion W.H.–Co.F–1st CPL, Wounded at Garnett's Farm, Va. on June 27, 1862. Died of wounds in July, 1862.

Hunt, W.J.C.–Co.H–PVT, Discharged with disability on Mar. 27, 1863.

Hyman, Abram–Co.A–PVT, Discharged with substitute, Nov. 20, 1862.

Hyman, Henry–Co.A–PVT, Appointed 3d CPL. Killed at Garnett's Farm, Va. on June 27, 1862.

Isbell, Robert G.–Co.B–4th CPL, Captured at Ft. Harrison, Va. on Sept. 30, 1864. Died in a Union prison on December 10, 1864.

Ivey, John W.–Co.D–PVT, Died of Typhoid fever at Camp Walker, near Manassas, Va. on Sept. 19, 1861.

Ivey, Myrick–Co.D–Jr. 2d LT. Killed at Garnett's Farm, Va. on June, 27, 1862.

Jackson, Frederick–Co.E–PVT. Listed as AWOL in Feb. 1865. (No later record).

Jackson, John W.–Co.A–PVT, Wounded and permanently disabled at Garnett's Farm, Va. on June 27, 1862. (No later record)

Jackson, Joseph–Co.H–PVT–Mar. 4, 1862. Wounded in 1864. Surrendered at Appomattox, Va. on Apr. 9, 1865.

Jackson, Matthew G.–Co.A–PVT, Captured at Gettysburg, Pa. on July 3, 1863. Paroled at Point Lookout, Md. on Feb. 18, 1865.

Jackson, Thomas H.–Co.H–1st SGT, Elected 1st LT on Feb. 29, 1862; CPT on Apr. 25, 1862. Captured at Ft. Harrison, Va. on Sept. 29, 1864. Released on June 17, 1865.

Jackson, William H.–Co.E–PVT, Wounded at Gettysburg, Pa. on July 2, 1863. Surrendered at Appomattox, Va. on Apr. 9, 1865.

James, Alvin A.–Co.I–PVT, Detailed as a Regimental Teamster in 1862. Surrendered at Appomattox, Va. on Apr. 9, 1865.

James, John–Co.B–PVT, Surrendered at Appomattox, Va. on Apr. 9, 1865.

Jenkins, E.P.–Co.F–PVT, Discharged with disability on Oct. 22, 1861.

Jennings, James A.–Co.G–PVT, Discharged with disability on May 30, 1862.

Jesse, Thomas H.–Co.A–PVT, Permanently disabled, (Leg Amputated) at Garnett's Farm, Va. on June 27, 1862.

Johnson, C.C.–Co.B–PVT, Captured and paroled in Athens, Ga., on May 8, 1865.

Johnson, F.W.S.–Co.E–PVT, Surrendered at Appomattox, Va. on Apr. 9, 1865.

Johnson, James H.–Co.A–PVT, Deserted on Aug. 29, 1862.

Johnson, James W.–Co.D–PVT, Furloughed to Crawfordsville, Ga. on Sept. 17, 1864. Captured and paroled at Newton, N.C. on Apr. 19, 1865.

Johnson, James W.–Co.E–PVT, Deserted in Tennessee on Feb. 12, 1864.

Johnson, John J.–Co.D–PVT, Elected 2d LT on Oct. 8, 1862. Wounded at Wilderness, Va. on June 6, 1864. Surrendered at Appomattox, Va. on Apr. 9, 1865.

Johnson, Michael–Co.H–2nd LT, Resigned on Sept. 10, 1861.

Johnson, Robert H.–Co.C–PVT, Captured at Gettysburg, Pa. on July 3, 1863. Exchanged prisoner on Feb. 10, 1865.

Johnson, Tapley B.–Co.C–PVT, Wounded at Chickamauga, Ga. on Sept. 19, 1863. Retired from service on July 20, 1864.

Johnson, Theophilus J.–Co.D–PVT, Died in Richmond, Va. on Dec. 3, 1861.

Johnson, William–Co.D–PVT, Jan. 29, 1864. Wounded at Spotsylvania, Va. on May 10, 1864, and died later the same day at a field hospital.

Jones, Benjamin Jr.–Co.D–PVT, Wounded at Wilderness, Va. on May 6, 1864. Surrendered at Appomattox, Va. on Apr. 9, 1865.

Jones, James–Co.K–PVT, Discharged in Sept., 1861.

Jones, James A.–Co.C–PVT, Died of Typhoid on Aug. 25, 1861.

Jones, James W., Jr.–Co.F–PVT, Surrendered at Appomattox, Va. on Apr. 9, 1865.

Roster of the Fifteenth Georgia Infantry Regiment 151

Jones, John H.–Co.I–PVT, Wounded at Malvern Hill, Va. on July 1, 1862. Captured at Mossy Creek, Tn. on Jan. 10, 1864. Took loyalty oath at Rock Island Ill. prison and was released on June 21, 1865.

Jones, John M.–Co.E–PVT, Appointed 3rd SGT on Apr. 15, 1862. Wounded at Thoroughfare Gap, Va. on Aug. 28, 1862. Surrendered at Appomattox, Va. on Apr. 9, 1865.

Jones, John P.–Co.D–PVT, Died at Richmond, Va. in 1865.

Jones, John S.–Co.B–PVT, Surrendered at Appomattox, Va., April 9, 1865.

Jones, Joshua H.–Co.G–PVT, Discharged with disability on Nov. 5, 1861. Reenlisted Feb. 27, 1862. Killed at Gettysburg, Pa. on July 3, 1863.

Jones, J.W.–Co.F–PVT, Appointed 5th SGT. Surrendered at Appomattox, Va. on Apr. 9, 1865.

Jones, Martin–Co.F–PVT, Mar. 18, 1863. Detailed to Engineer Corps in 1863. Captured and paroled at Athens, Ga. on May 8, 1865.

Jones, Moses J.–Co.G–PVT, Died of Typhoid fever in a Richmond, Va. hospital, Sept. 9, 1861.

Jones, R.W.–Co.K–PVT, Died in April, 1862.

Jones, William–Co.F–PVT, Died on Oct. 5, 1861. (No later record)

Jones, William L.–Co.D–PVT, Unit Blacksmith. Listed as present in Feb., 1865.

Jordan, Aaron–Co.H–PVT, Mar. 4, 1862. Severely wounded in the arm, June 4, 1864. At home, absent without leave, Feb. 25, 1864.

Junkin, James–Co.A–PVT, Elected 2d LT; 1st LT; Wounded at Chickamauga, Ga. on Sept. 19, 1863. Surrendered at Appomattox, Va. Apr. 9, 1865.

Justice, Preston–Co.F–PVT, Captured at Gettysburg, Pa. on July 2, 1863. Taken to Ft. Delaware, Del. (No later record)

Keels, J.–Co.H–PVT, Wounded (Shot in the throat) at Gettysburg, Pa. Died of his wounds on July 4, 1863.

Kendall, Levi–Co.G–PVT, Discharged with disability in Dec. of 1862.

Kendall, William R.–Co.A–3rd SGT, Appointed 2nd SGT in Apr. 1862; Appointed Regimental Commissary SGT in May of 1862. Surrendered at Appomattox, Va. on April 9, 1865.

Kerlin, David S.–Co.C–PVT, Aug. 27, 1862. Wounded (severely in the groin) at Spotsylvania, Va. on May 10, 1864.

Kesler, Phillip J.–Co.B–PVT, Deserted in Dec. 1864.

King, John H.–Co.D–PVT, Wounded at Chickamauga, Ga. on Sept. 19, 1863. Discharged with disability, Feb. 1, 1865.

King, John M.–Co.I–PVT, Mar. 20, 1863. Died of Dysentery in Jackson Hospital at Richmond, Va., Oct. 15, 1864.

King, Rufus–Co.I–PVT, Mar. 4, 1862. Captured at Mud Tavern, Va. on May 23, 1864. Exchanged prisoner on Jan. 21, 1865. Listed as Absent without leave on Feb. 28, 1865.

King, William B.–Co.I–PVT, Transferred to 15th Georgia from the 38th Georgia, Sept. 10, 1862. Deserted near Knoxville, Tn. in Jan. 1864. (No later record)

Kinnebrew, Edward N.–Co.C–PVT, Appointed 4th CPL in June, 1862. Wounded at Spotsylvania, Va. on May 10, 1864. Appointed 5th SGT on Mar. 18, 1864. Listed as AWOL in Feb. 1865.

Kinnebrew, William H.–Co.C–PVT, Discharged with disability on Oct. 6, 1862.

Kirkpatrick, John K.–Co.D–PVT, Wounded at Malvern Hill, Va. on July, 1, 1862. Appointed 4th SGT on July 24, 1862. Wounded in the face, Feb., 1865. Released on furlough. (No later record)

Knight, Andrew,–Co.B–PVT, AWOL in Feb. 1865.

Knight, Downs–Co.B–PVT, Surrendered at Appomattox, Va., April 9, 1865.

Knight, Marcus A.–Co.C–PVT, Transferred to Co. F on June 12, 1862. Captured at U.S. Ford, Va. on Sept. 1, 1863. Paroled at Elmira, N.Y. on Feb. 25, 1865.

Knox, Michael–Co.H–Jr. 2nd LT, Resigned on Oct. 17, 1861.

Laird, J.P.–Co.H–PVT, Mar. 1, 1863. Killed at Chickamauga, Ga. on Sept. 19, 1863.

Lamar, LaFayette–Co.G–CPT, Died at Warrenton, Va. in Nov., 1861.

Lamar, Lavoiscia L.–Co.E–Jr. 2nd LT, Resigned on Sept. 15, 1861.

Landers, B.L.–Co.E–PVT, Mar. 4, 1862. Surrendered at Appomattox, Va. on Apr. 9, 1865.

Lane, John A.–Co.G–2nd LT, Elected CPT in 1863. Captured at Gettysburg, Pa. on July 2, 1863. Exchanged prisoner on Feb. 24, 1865.

Langston, Junius C.–Co.B–PVT, Died at home of disease, Sept. 21, 1862.

Langston, Shannon A.–Co.B–PVT, Appointed CPL. Wounded at New Market, Va. in 1864.

Lary, James H.–Co.D–PVT, Wounded at Malvern Hill, Va. on July 1, 1862. Appointed 3d CPL on July 24, 1862. Surrendered at Appomattox, Va. on Apr. 9, 1865.

Lary, John–Co.E–PVT, Mar. 1862. Surrendered at Appomattox, Va. on Apr. 9, 1865.

Latimer, G.R.–Co.E–PVT, Discharged with disability on Oct. 18, 1861.

Latimer, Mark–Co.K–2nd LT, Elected 1st LT on Nov. 1, 1861; CPT on May 11, 1863. Retired to Invalid Corps in Nov., 1864.

Latimer, Thomas H.–Co.K–CPT, Resigned on Nov. 1, 1861.

Latimer, T.W.–Co.E–PVT, Discharged with disability on Nov. 30, 1861.

Lauglin, John–Co.K–PVT, Killed at Gettysburg, Pa. on July 3, 1863.

Lawrence, J.R.–Co.E–1st SGT, Discharged with disability on Oct. 23, 1861 at Camp Rocky Run in Virginia.

Layfield, John–Co.K–PVT, Died at Camp Pine Creek, Va. on Sept. 27, 1861.

Leach, James W.–Co.B–PVT, Discharged with disability, Dec. 17, 1861.

Leach, W. C.–Co.B–PVT, Wounded arm resulting in amputation at Sharpsburg, Md. on Sept. 17, 1862.

Leuth, J.S.–Co.G–PVT, Captured at South Mountain, Va. on July 4, 1863. Paroled at Baltimore, Md. and sent to City Point, Va. on Aug. 24, 1863. (No later record)

Leverett, Elijah–Co.G–PVT, Discharged with disability in June, 1862.

Leverett, Hardy–Co.G–PVT, Captured at Dandridge, Tn. on Jan. 22, 1864. Enlisted in the U.S. Army at Rock Island, Ill. on Oct. 13, 1864.

Lewis, Hamlin–Co.K–PVT, Elected 2nd LT on Nov. 1, 1861. Resigned with disability, July 3, 1863.

Linder, John–Co.H–1st LT, Resigned on Feb. 29, 1862.

Linder, Lee–Co.H–PVT, Transferred to the 7th South Carolina Cavalry on Oct. 29, 1863.

Lindsey, Joseph S.–Co.B–PVT, Mar. 4, 1862. Captured at Gettysburg, Pa., July 3, 1863. Exchanged prisoner in Feb. of 1865.

Lindsey, W.–Co.B–PVT, Captured at Blackwater, Va. Paroled at Ft. Monroe, Va. on May 13, 1863.

Linn, Joseph C.–Co.D–PVT, Discharged on Jan. 19, 1865.

Little, Frank L.–Co.E–PVT, Discharged with disability on July 12, 1862.

Little, J. Wilber F.–Co.E–PVT, Appointed ensign of the 20th GA Regiment. Surrendered at Appomattox, Va. on Apr. 9, 1865.

Lockart, Asa G.–Co.G–PVT, Killed at Chickamauga, Ga. on Sept. 19, 1863.

Loehr, George–Co.I–PVT, Discharged with disability on Aug. 11, 1862.

Loflin, James A.–Co.G–PVT, Wounded at Chickamauga, Ga. on Sept. 19, 1863. (No later record)

Loftin, James B.A.–Co.G–PVT, Discharged with disability on Nov. 5, 1861. Reenlisted on Mar. 1, 1862. Wounded and captured at Gettysburg, Pa. on July 2, 1863. (No later record)

Lofton, Bedford H.–Co.C–3d SGT, Elected Ordnance SGT; Adjutant. Listed as present in June of 1863.

Lofton, James H.–Co.C–Jr. 2d LT, Resigned on Oct. 30, 1861.

Lotheridge, John H.–Co.B–PVT, Died in a Richmond, Va. hospital on Nov. 18, 1861.

Lovett, W.J.–Co.K–PVT, Discharged in Jan. of 1862.

Lovingood, George W.–Co.C–PVT, Wounded at Thoroughfare Gap, Va. on Aug. 27, 1862. Surrendered at Appomattox, Va. on Apr. 9, 1865.

Lovingood, Samuel J.–Co.C–PVT, Appointed 3d CPL in June 1862. Wounded at 2nd Manassas, Va. on Aug. 30, 1862. Captured at Mossy Creek, Tn. on Jan. 22, 1864. Exchanged prisoner at James River Va. on Feb. 15, 1865.

Lovingood, William L.–Co.C–PVT, Wounded at Gettysburg, Pa. on July 2, 1863. Captured and paroled at Hartwell, Ga. on May 5, 1865.

Lovit, James A.–Co.K–PVT, Paroled at Augusta, Ga. on May 19, 1865.

Lucas, William–Co.I–PVT, Paroled at Goldsboro, N.C. on May 1, 1865.

Lucroy, Jesse M.–Co.H–PVT, Killed at Sharpsburg, Md. on Sept. 17, 1862.

Lumpkin, Samuel J.–Co.I–PVT, Aug. 7, 1862. Substitute for T. Biggs. Absent without leave, Mar. 18, 1863. Dropped from the rolls on Dec. 1, 1863. (No later record)

Lunceford, Thomas W.–Co.A–PVT, Surrendered at Appomattox, Va. April 9, 1865.

Lunsford, William P.–Co.F–PVT, Deserted and took an oath of loyalty to the U.S. Govt. at Knoxville, Tn. on Feb. 12, 1864.

Lyles, James–Co.D–PVT, Oct. 9, 1863. Wounded and captured at Ft. Harrison, Va. on Sept. 29, 1864. Died of wounds in a Union hospital on Oct. 5, 1864.

Lyons, B.F.–Co.E–PVT, Jan. 18, 1863. Killed at Gettysburg, Pa. on July 2, 1863.

Madden, J.T.–Co.H–PVT, Killed at Sharpsburg, Md. on Sept. 17, 1862.

Mahoney, Micajah L.–Co.A–PVT, Furloughed on Aug. 21, 1864.

Mailey, J.M.–Co.I–PVT, Appointed CPL. Died in a Richmond, Va. hospital on Nov. 13, 1861.

Mailey, Joseph R.–Co.I–PVT, Feb. 28, 1862. Died of fever in a Richmond, Va. hospital on July 28, 1862.

Mailey, Martin V.–Co.I–PVT, Appointed 1st SGT. Wounded at Gettysburg, Pa. on July 2, 1863; Spotsylvania, Va. on May 12, 1864. Listed as absent without leave on Feb. 28, 1865.

Mailey, W. D.–Co.C–PVT, Died in a Liberty, Va. hospital on July 20, 1862.

Marchman, William L.–Co.E–PVT, Appointed 2nd CPL in 1862. Died of Smallpox at Richmond, Va. on Feb. 10, 1862.

Marcus, Madison A.–Co.I–2nd SGT, Elected 1st LT on May 5, 1862; CPT on Aug. 2, 1863. Wounded at Chickamauga, Ga. on Sept. 19, 1863. Killed near Darbytown Road, Va. on Oct. 13, 1864.

Marcus, Madison J.–Co.C–2d CPL, Appointed Musician on Apr. 2, 1862. Present in Jan. 1865.

Marshall, Daniel P.–Co.G–PVT, Dec. 19, 1862. Wounded at Darbytown Road, Va. on Oct. 7, 1864. Discharged from Jackson Hospital at Richmond, Va. on Nov. 27, 1864.

Martin, Benjamin T.–Co.E–PVT, Surrendered at Appomattox, Va. on Apr. 9, 1865.

Martin, Luther H.–Co.C–CPT, Resigned on Feb. 21, 1862.

Martin, W.G.–Co.C–CPL, Captured at Gettysburg, Pa. on July 3, 1863.Taken to Pt. Lookout, Md. in Nov., 1863. (No later record)

Martin, W.B.–Co.D–PVT, Captured and paroled at Athens, Ga. on May 8, 1865.

Martin, William Q.–Co.G–PVT, Mar. 4, 1862. Appointed 2nd CPL. Captured at Gettysburg, Pa. on July 2, 1863. Died in a Union hospital on May 1, 1864.

Martin, William T.–Co.E–1st SGT, Appointed LT and Drill Master, P.A.C.S. at Macon, Ga. Listed as present in Feb. of 1865.

Mason, Alfred–Co.I–PVT, Wounded at Wilderness, Va. on May 6, 1864. Surrendered at Appomattox, Va. on Apr. 9, 1865.

Mason, James J.–Co.K–PVT, Severely wounded in the right arm at Chickamauga, Ga. on Sept. 19, 1863. Furloughed for an extended period. Listed in Feb., 1865 as AWOL.

Mason, J.D.–Co.K–PVT, Died in Richmond, Va., Dec., 1861.

Mason, Thomas K.–Co.K–PVT, Killed in action at Sharpsburg, Md. on Sept. 17, 1862.

Mathews, James F.–Co.K–PVT, Mar. 20, 1862. Captured at Gettysburg, Pa. on July 2, 1863. Exchanged prisoner and returned to unit. Surrendered at Appomattox, Va. on Apr. 9, 1865.

Mathews, William H.–Co.K–PVT, April 8, 1864. Wounded in the left wrist and permanently disabled at Petersburg, Va. on July 18, 1864. Listed as AWOL on Feb. 28, 1864.

Matthews, A.C.–Staff–Assistant Surgeon, resigned in Nov. of 1861.

Matthews, George B.–Co.I–PVT, Captured at Gettysburg, Pa. on July 2, 1863. Died of chronic diarrhoea at Fortress Monroe, Va. on Nov. 3, 1864.

Matthews, J.F.–Co.E–PVT, Discharged with disability on Dec. 18, 1861.

Mattox, Hosea B.–Co.I–PVT, Wounded and captured at Gettysburg, Pa. on July 2, 1863. Exchanged. Surrendered at Appomattox, Va. on Apr. 9, 1865.

Mattox, Nathan M.–Co.I–2nd CPL, Appointed 3rd SGT on May 14, 1862; 2nd SGT on Apr. 4, 1863; Ordnance SGT on July 1, 1863. Wounded at Gettysburg, Pa. on July 2, 1863. AWOL on Feb. 25, 1865.

Mattox, William H.–Co.I–Jr. 2nd LT, Elected 2nd LT on Oct. 13, 1861; CPT on Dec. 25, 1861. Resigned on Apr. 9, 1862.

Mattox, Z.H. Clark–Co.I–PVT, Discharged, furnished Abraham Franklin as substitute, Mar. 19, 1862. Reenlisted May 15, 1862. Discharged, furnished Elbert C. McDaniel as his substitute on Sept. 10, 1862.

Mauldin, Benjamin W.–Co.B–PVT, Wounded at Gettysburg, Pa. on July 2, 1863. Surrendered at Appomattox, Va. on Apr. 9, 1865.

Mauldin, Isaac N.–Co.B–PVT, Killed at Spotsylvania, Va., May 10, 1864.

Mauldin, James F.–Co.B–PVT, Died in a Richmond, Va. hospital on June 9, 1862.

Maxwell, James K.–Co.A–PVT, Furloughed home in Aug. 1864.

McCall, John P.–Co.B–PVT, Wounded at Gettysburg, Pa. on July 3, 1863. Paroled at Hartwell, Ga. on May 23, 1865.

McCarty, John T.–Co.C–2d SGT, Transferred to Co. F, May 15, 1862.

McClellan, Thorntotine P.–Co.I–PVT, Transferred to the South Carolina Inf. on Mar. 18, 1863.

McClendon, William E.–Co.A–PVT, Appointed 2d SGT; 1st SGT. Died at Garnett's Farm, Va. on June 28, 1862.

McCluskey, John–Co.D–PVT, Wounded at Garnett's Farm, Va. on June 27, 1862. Died of wounds in a hospital on July 29, 1862.

McCook, B. Franklin–Co.E–PVT, Wounded at Malvern Hill, Va. on July 1, 1862. Captured at Gettysburg, Pa. on July 3, 1863. Died of Smallpox in Point Lookout, Md. hospital on Dec. 4, 1863.

McCook, Dawson–Co.K–PVT, Captured near Knoxville, Tn. on Dec. 3, 1863. Released at Rock Island, Ill. prison on June 19, 1865.

McCord, Elisha A.–Co.G–PVT, Feb. 27, 1862. Surrendered at Appomattox, Va. on Apr. 9, 1865.

McCord, James A.–Co.G–PVT, Appointed 3rd SGT on Oct. 11, 1862; 2nd SGT on Dec. 6, 1862. Surrendered at Appomattox, Va. on Apr. 9, 1865.

McCord, John W.–Co.G–PVT, Killed at Ft. Harrison, Va. on Sept. 29, 1864.

McCormigh, S.–Co.H–PVT, Captured and paroled at Farmville, Va. in Apr., 1865.

McCullum, A. Cyrus–Co.B–PVT, Aug. 30, 1862, Captured at Gettysburg, Pa. on July, 3, 1863. Died in a Union prison on Mar. 22, 1864.

McDaniel, Elbert C.–Co.I–PVT, Sept. 10, 1862. Substitute for Z.H. Clark Mattox. Captured at Gettysburg, Pa. on July 3, 1863. Exchanged prisoner, Mar. 12, 1865.

McDaniel, Solomon G.–Co.E–PVT, Died in Orange Court House, Va. hospital on Apr. 15, 1862.

McDonald, John W.–Co.B–PVT, Mar. 4, 1862. Wounded at Malvern Hill, Va. on July 1, 1862. Died of disease, July 13, 1864.

McDougald, William M.–Co.B–PVT, Discharged with disability, on Dec. 30, 1861.

McFarland, D.S.–Co.B–PVT, Later promoted to CPL. Captured and paroled at Hartwell, Ga. on May 18, 1865.

McFarland, James–Co.B–PVT, Elected 2d LT; 1st LT on May 14, 1862, Wounded at Petersburg, Va. on June 9, 1864. Retired from service on Jan. 11, 1865.

McFarland, Thomas A.–Co.B–PVT, Wounded at Petersburg, Va. on June 9, 1864. Surrendered at Appomattox, Va. on Apr. 9, 1865.

McFarland, William–Co.B–PVT, Wounded at Gettysburg, Pa., July 2, 1863. (No later record)

McGregor, Adolphus–Co.B–PVT, Captured at Gettysburg, Pa. on July 3, 1863. Died in a Union prison on Oct. 22, 1863.

McGregor, William L.–Co.B–PVT, Deserted in Dec. of 1864.

McIntosh, William M.–Staff–MAJ; LTC; COL in 1862. Killed at Garnett's Farm, Va., June 27, 1862 while leading the attack. Brevetted Brigadier General for gallantry in action by order of General Robert Toombs.

McLanahan, J.W.–Co.C–PVT, Mar. 4, 1862. Surrendered at Appomattox, Va. on Apr. 9, 1865.

McLendon, Isaac A.–Co.A–2d LT, Elected 1st LT in Oct. 1861; CPT, Feb. 1862. Resigned with disability in Feb. of 1863.

McMurray, Madison M.–Co.B–PVT, Discharged with disability, on Dec. 14, 1861.

McWhorter, Jesse–Co.E–PVT, Died in Richmond, Va. on Sept. 22, 1861.

Meadows, William T.–Co.E–PVT, Died of Meningitis in a hospital at Petersburg, Va. on Apr. 20, 1863.

Medlock, George B.–Co.K–PVT, Appointed 5th SGT in 1863. Wounded in 1864. Died from gunshot wound in the right lung, at Receiving and Wayside Hospital, Richmond, Va. on Sept. 29, 1864.

Medlock, James E.–Co.K–PVT, June 3, 1863. Surrendered at Appomattox, Va. on Apr. 9, 1865.

Michie, Junius–Staff–Assistant Surgeon. (No later record)

Middlebrooks, George C.–Co.K–2nd CPL, Discharged with disability, Mar. 27, 1862.

Middlebrooks, Henry C.–Co.E–PVT, Transferred to Co.K, Sept. 21, 1861. Appointed Sergeant Major on Mar. 1, 1863. Surrendered at Appomattox, Va. on Apr. 9, 1865.

Middlebrooks, J.T.–Co.K–PVT, Feb. 24, 1862. Captured at Gettysburg, Pa. on July 3, 1863. Paroled from Point Lookout, Md. on Feb. 18, 1865. (No later record)

Millican, William T.–Co.B–CPT, Elected LTC; Elected COL, July, 1862. Wounded, captured, and died at Sharpsburg, Md. on Sept. 17, 1862.

Mitchell, James A.–Co.B–PVT, Deserted in Dec. of 1864.

Mitchell, D.J.–Co.B–PVT, Captured and paroled at Hartwell, Ga. on May 18, 1865.

Mitchell, Ephraim–Co.B–PVT, Deserted in Dec., 1864.

Mitchell, James H.–Co.E–PVT, Wounded at Sharpsburg, Md. on Sept. 17, 1862. Surrendered at Appomattox, Va. on Apr. 9, 1865.

Mitchell, Roland–Co.B–PVT, Died of Typhoid fever in a Williamsburg, Va. hospital on July 3, 1862.

Mitchell, Wiley T.–Co.B–PVT, Surrendered at Appomattox, Va. on Apr. 9, 1865.

Mitchell, William E.–Co.B–PVT, Died of disease in a Orange Court House, Va. hospital on Aug. 21, 1862.

Mobley, Isaac M.–Co.I–PVT, Transferred to 38th Georgia on Jan. 1, 1863.

Monk, R. A.–Co.D–PVT, Died of Typhoid fever at Richmond, Va. on Oct. 20, 1861.

Moon, John S.–Co.I–PVT, Discharged with disability, Oct. 25, 1861.

Moon, Joseph M.–Co.C–PVT, Surrendered at Appomattox, Va. on Apr. 9, 1865.

Moon, William H.–Co.C–PVT, Died in camp on June 17, 1862.

Moon, William P.–Co.I–PVT, Discharged with disability on Oct. 26, 1861.

Moore, Albert–Co.A–PVT, Captured in Scott County, Va. on Apr. 3, 1864. Paroled at Military Prison in Louisville, Kentucky, May of 1864.

Moore, Charles R.–Co.A–PVT, Died of Typhoid fever in Manassas, Va. on Aug. 31, 1861.

Moore, Ebenezer I.–Co.A–PVT, Died of Pneumonia in Richmond, Va. on Apr. 18, 1862.

Moore, James A.–Co.D–PVT, Sent to Mr. Wright's near camp in Sept. 1861. Sick with Typhoid fever. (No later record)

Moore, Lucius A.–Co.K–PVT, Appointed Hospital Steward and detached on duty in hospital service throughout the war.

Moore, R.F.–Co.H–PVT, Mar. 1, 1863. Wounded in 1864. Surrendered at Appomattox, Va. on Apr. 9, 1865.

Moore, Thomas P.–Co.A–PVT, Died in Richmond, Va. on Apr. 23, 1862.

Moore, William M.–Co.F–PVT, Captured at Dandridge, Tn. on Jan. 22, 1864. Exchanged prisoner on Mar. 2, 1865. (No later record)

Moore, W. P.–Co.D–PVT, Jan. 29, 1864. Surrendered at Appomattox, Va. on Apr. 9, 1865.

Moran, William B.–Co.E–PVT, Died at Camp Walker on Sept. 17, 1861.

Morris, James F.–Co.B–PVT, Mar., 1862. Wounded at Malvern Hill, Va. on July 1, 1862. Surrendered at Appomattox, Va. on Apr. 9, 1865.

Morris, Peter–Co.K–PVT, Captured at Dumfries, Va. on Sept. 14, 1863. Took loyalty oath and went north in 1865. Described as–Hair–Brown/ Complexion–Light/ Eyes–Gray/ Height–5' 9".

Moulder, William J.–Co.B–PVT, Mar. 1862. Wounded at Gettysburg, Pa. on July 2, 1863.

Mullally, John T.–Co.E–2nd SGT, Elected Jr. 2nd LT on Oct. 10, 1862; CPT, Mar. 30, 1863. Absent without leave on Feb. 28, 1865.

Mullikin, Felix L.–Co.A–PVT, Died at Fussells Mill, Va., July 17, 1864.

Mumford, Daniel R.–Co.G–PVT, Surrendered at Appomattox, Va. on Apr. 9, 1865.

Mumford, Robert D.–Co.G–PVT, Surrendered at Appomattox, Va. on Apr. 9, 1865.

Murden, John M.–Co.D–PVT, Captured at Ft. Harrison, Va. on Sept. 30, 1864. Exchanged prisoner on Mar. 17, 1865.

Murden, Mack H.–Co.D–PVT, Wounded in 1862 and died near Fredericksburg, Va. on Feb. 4, 1863.

Murden, Redmon S.–Co.D–PVT, Furloughed on Feb. 28, 1865.

Murrah, Benjamin–Co.C–PVT, Transferred to Co. F, May 15, 1862.

Murrah, John W.–Co.C–PVT, Appointed 4th SGT in June, 1862. Elected 2d LT on July 19, 1862. Killed at Gettysburg, Pa. on July 2, 1863.

Murray, William T.–Co.G–PVT, Surrendered at Appomattox, Va. on Apr. 9, 1865.

Musgrove, Joseph E.–Co.G–PVT, Mar. 1, 1863. Captured at Russellville, Tn. on Apr. 16, 1864. Exchanged prisoner on Mar. 23, 1865.

Myers, Aaron–Co.D–3d SGT, Discharged, furnished Charles Hamilton as substitute on July 8, 1862.

Nash, Henry H.–Co.C–PVT, Mar. 29, 1864. Listed as AWOL in Nov. 1864.

Nash, J. B.–Co.C–PVT, Captured at Gettysburg, Pa. on July 3, 1863. Exchanged prisoner on Apr. 30, 1864.

Nash, J. C.–Co.C–PVT, Died in a Richmond, Va. hospital on July 6, 1862.

Neel, Charles M.–Co.K–PVT, Surrendered at Appomattox, Va. on Apr. 9, 1865.

Neel, J.H.–Co.K–PVT, Discharged with disability on Oct. 28, 1861.

Neel, William S.–Co.K–PVT, Captured at Ft. Harrison, Va. on Sept. 30, 1864. Exchanged prisoner on Mar. 17, 1865. (No later record)

Nelms, David L.–Co.F–PVT, Wounded at Garnett's Farm, Va. on June 27, 1862. Died of wounds in 1862.

Nelms, Vandiver C.–Co.F–4th CPL, Discharged in Nov. 1861. Re-enlisted on Sept. 19, 1862 and joined the 7th Ga. Cavalry. Surrendered at Appomattox, Va. on Apr. 9, 1865.

Nelson, George W.–Co.K–PVT, Wounded at Wilderness, Va. on May 6, 1864. Died of his wounds on June 19, 1864.

Nelson, John W.–Co.K–PVT, Listed as AWOL in Feb., 1865.

Newsom, G.B.–Co.E–PVT, Jan. 1, 1863. Deserted at Petersburg, Va. on July 28, 1864.

Nichols, George T.–Co.F–PVT, Wounded at Ft. Harrison, Va. on June 29, 1864. Left arm was amputated at Jackson Hospital on Oct. 4, 1864. Furloughed for 60 days on Oct. 27, 1864. (No later record)

Roster of the Fifteenth Georgia Infantry Regiment 161

Norman, Elijah B.–Co.I–PVT, Aug. 29, 1862. Discharged, furnished Nathan Pulliam as substitute, Mar. 26, 1863. Reenlisted Aug. 24, 1863 as substitute for Nathan Pulliam. Surrendered at Appomattox, Va. on Apr. 9, 1865.

Norman, George W.–Co.G–PVT, Feb. 27, 1862. Wounded at Sharpsburg, Md. on Sept. 17, 1862. Captured at Gettysburg, Pa. on July 3, 1863. Released at Ft. Delaware, Del. on June 16, 1865.

Norman, Isaac W.–Co.A–PVT, Died at Garnett's Farm, Va. on June 28, 1862.

Norman, James J.–Co.I–3rd SGT, Appointed 1st SGT on May 14, 1862. Elected Jr. 2nd LT on Apr. 4, 1863; 1st LT on Aug. 2, 1863. Killed at Ft. Harrison, Va. on Sept. 29, 1864.

Norman, John H.–Co.A–PVT, Feb. 22, 1862. Captured at Gettysburg, Pa. on July 3, 1863.

Norman, John L.–Co.A–2d SGT, Died at Manassas, Va. in Oct. 1861.

Norman, John L.–Co.C–PVT, Surrendered at Appomattox, Va. on Apr. 9, 1865.

Norman, John S.–Co.G–PVT, Feb. 27, 1862. Surrendered at Appomattox, Va. on Apr. 9, 1865.

Norman, Peyton S.–Co.G–PVT, May 16, 1862. Skull fractured at 2nd Manassas, Va. on Aug. 30, 1862. Captured at Gettysburg, Pa. on July 3, 1863. Exchanged prisoner on Feb. 18, 1865.

Norman, Thomas B.–Co.A–PVT, Died of Measles in Richmond, Va. on Sept. 17, 1861.

Norman, William L.–Co.A–PVT, Wounded at 2d Manassas, Va. on Aug. 30, 1862 and died Sept. 3, 1862.

Norwood, Levi M.–Co.B–PVT, Captured at Dandridge, Tn. on Jan. 26, 1864. Released from Rock Island, Ill. prison on June 17, 1865.

Nunn, Uriah W.–Co.D–PVT, Died at Front Royal, Va. on Dec. 31, 1861.

Obarr, J. Hezekiah–Co.H–PVT, Mar. 1, 1863. Captured at Carrsville, Va. in May, 1863. Exchanged prisoner on May 23, 1863. Died of chronic diarrhoea in General Hospital at Lynchburg, Va. on July 3, 1863.

Obarr, Whitner–Co.H–PVT, Wounded at Sharpsburg, Md. on Sept. 17, 1862. Captured at Gettysburg, Pa. on July 2, 1863. Exchanged prisoner. Killed at Wilderness, Va. on May 6, 1864.

Ogilvie, James S.–Co.A–PVT, Captured near Knoxville, Tn. on Dec. 14, 1863. Sent to Camp Chase, Ohio on Dec. 12, 1863. (No later record)

Oglesby, Jefferson C.–Co.A–PVT, Wounded at Garnett's Farm, Va. on June 27, 1862, and died in a Richmond, Va. hospital on July 12, 1862.

Oliver, J.D.–Co.F–PVT, Appointed Colonel's Orderly in Sept., 1861. (No later record)

Oliver, John A.–Co.F–PVT, Furloughed in Nov., 1861. (No later record)

Orrie, Louis–Co.D–PVT, Wounded at Malvern Hill, Va. on July 1, 1862, resulting in the amputation of his left arm. Released from Army to work in C.S. Powder Works in Augusta, Ga. until the end of the war.

Owens, Asher L.–Co.A–PVT, Died in Richmond, Va. on May 1, 1862.

Owens, Francis E.–Co.A–PVT, Wounded at 2d Manassas, Va. on Aug. 30, 1862. Captured in Virginia, Apr. 1865.

Owens, William D.–Co.A–PVT, Deserted and joined Union forces at Knoxville, Tn. in Dec. 1863.

Pace, George A.–Co.B–2d LT, Elected 1st LT; Elected CPT on May 14, 1862. Surrendered at Appomattox, Va on April 9, 1865.

Page, John O.–Co.F–PVT, Died in Lynchburg, Va., June, 1862.

Pannell, Abraham–Co.F–PVT, Sent to a hospital in Richmond, Va. in Sept., 1861. (No later record)

Parker, James P.–Co.B–PVT, Discharged with disability, Dec. 28, 1861.

Parker, Joseph H.–Co.E–PVT, Wounded at Garnett's Farm, Va. on June 27, 1862. Deserted at Gettysburg, Pa. on July 3, 1863. Surrendered to Union forces at Williamsport, Md. on July 12, 1863. Sent to Fort Delaware, Del. in 1863. Enlisted in the Union Army on Oct. 5, 1863.

Parker, Mason E.–Co.K–PVT, Feb. 24, 1864. Wounded at Wilderness, Va. on May 6, 1864. Died of his wounds on May 26, 1864.

Parker, William T.–Co.E–PVT, Died in camp near Richmond, Va. on May 23, 1862.

Parks, John K.–Co.G–2nd CPL, Appointed 2nd SGT on Apr. 7, 1862. Elected Jr. 2nd LT on Dec. 6, 1862; 1st LT. Wounded at Gettysburg, Pa. on July 3, 1863. Died of wounds on July 5, 1863.

Parks, Lewis–Co.G–PVT, Feb. 27, 1862. Sick on July 17, 1862. (No later record)

Parnell, A.–Co.F–PVT, Discharged with disability on Oct. 4, 1861.

Parnell, John R.–Co.K–PVT, Discharged in April, 1862.

Parrott, A.B.–Co.K–PVT, Listed as Present in Feb., 1863. (No later record)

Partridge, William J.–Co.A–PVT, Surrendered at Appomattox, Va. on Apr. 9, 1865.

Pascal, William Cobb–Co.G–PVT, Discharged with disability at Richmond, Va. on Dec. 4, 1861.

Pascal, William O.–Co.G–Jr. 2nd LT, Resigned with disability on Nov. 25, 1861.

Pasnett, H.H.–Co.E–PVT, Discharged with disability on Sept. 26, 1861.

Patterson, Wiley W.–Co.I–PVT, Died in a Richmond, Va. hospital on Nov. 21, 1861.

Payne, Asa S.–Co.B–PVT, Feb. 24, 1862. Discharged with disability, Aug. 11, 1862.

Payne, James M.–Co.B–PVT. Captured and paroled at Hartwell, Ga. on May 18, 1865.

Payne, John B.–Co.B–PVT, Wounded at Petersburg, Va. on June 9, 1864. Surrendered at Appomattox, Va., April 9, 1865.

Payne, John W.–Co.B–PVT, Detailed to Division Commissary Guard in Sept. 1864. Listed as AWOL in Feb. of 1865.

Peak, G. A.–Co.B–Musician, Present for duty in Feb. of 1865.

Pearman, C.C.–Co.H–PVT, Captured at Gettysburg, Pa. on July 2, 1863. Died in General Hospital at Point Lookout, Md. on Dec. 20, 1863.

Pearman, Weldon C.–Co.H–PVT, Mar. 4, 1862. Died of Typhoid fever in a Petersburg, Va. hospital on Apr. 13, 1863.

Pearson, George W.–Co.I–PVT, Sent to a Richmond, Va. hospital on Mar. 8, 1863. (No later record)

Peck, Josiah S.–Co.D–PVT, Wounded at Chickamauga, Ga. on Sept. 19, 1863. Died of wounds in a field hospital on Sept. 26, 1863.

Peeler, G.R.–Co.K–PVT, Died of camp fever on Dec. 3, 1861.

Pegg, Leander M.–Co.C–PVT, Discharged with disability on July 25, 1862.

Pendley, J.H.–Co.E–PVT, June 21, 1864. Listed as AWOL in Feb. 1865.

Perrin, William B.–Co.F–PVT, Died in a Richmond, Va. hospital on Feb. 11, 1862.

Perryman, J.A.–Co.I–PVT, Deserted on Feb. 19, 1865.

Pickens, John–Co.C–PVT–Nov. 3, 1862, Substitute for George M. Bell.

Pierce, Lovick, Jr.–Co.E–PVT, Appointed Adjutant on Aug. 1, 1862. Wounded at Gettysburg, Pa. on July 3, 1863. Surrendered at Appomattox, Va. on Apr. 9, 1865.

Pinkston, H.B.–Co.K–PVT, Surrendered at Appomattox, Va. on Apr. 9, 1865.

Pinkston, William T.–Co.D–PVT, Surrendered at Appomattox, Va. on Apr. 9, 1865.

Pledger, Simeon L.–Co.I–PVT, Mar. 4, 1862. Surrendered at Appomattox, Va. on Apr. 9, 1865.

Pledger, William P.–Co.I–PVT, Mar. 4, 1862. Appointed as a Regimental Teamster in June of 1862. Listed in Jan. of 1865 as reassigned to the Corps.

Pool, William R.–Co.H–CPT, Resigned on Apr. 5, 1862.

Powers, John–Co.K–PVT, Died in Jan., 1862, at Moore Hospital in Danville, Va.

Prather, Thomas Z.–Co.A–PVT, Wounded at Chickamauga, Ga. on Sept. 19, 1863. Surrendered at Appomattox, Va. on Apr. 9, 1865.

Prescott, William H.–Co.E–PVT, Jan. 18, 1863. Detailed for light duty because of disability at Richmond, Va. in Nov., 1864. Captured at Richmond, Va. on Apr. 3, 1865. Paroled on Apr. 20, 1865.

Prewitt, W.H.–Co.H–PVT, Mar. 10, 1864. At home, absent without leave, Feb. 25, 1865.

Price, Laneston H.–Co.H–PVT, Mar. 4, 1862. Died of fever at Richmond, Va. on May 10, 1864.

Psalmonds, Thomas H.–Co.A–PVT, Appointed 4th SGT. Wounded at Gettysburg, Pa. on July 2, 1863. Surrendered at Appomattox, Va. on Apr. 9, 1865.

Pullen, E. B.–Co.A–PVT, Discharged with disability at Richmond, Va. on Nov. 1, 1861.

Pullen, Elijah B.–Co.A–PVT, Wounded at Garnett's Farm, Va. on June 27, 1862. Died on Aug. 1, 1862.

Pullen, J.D.–Co.A–PVT, Wounded and captured at Petersburg, Va. on Apr. 3, 1865.

Pullen, John M.–Co.A–PVT, Home on sick furlough. Died of disease on Oct. 9, 1864.

Pullen, John T.–Co.A–PVT, Discharged with disability, June 15, 1862.

Pullen, William G.–Co.A–PVT, Wounded at Chickamauga, Ga. on Sept. 19, 1863. Captured at Dandridge, Tn. on Jan. 22, 1864. Released at Rock Island, Ill. prison on June 18, 1865.

Pulliam, Francis M.–Co.C–PVT, Transferred from Co. I on May 15, 1862. Wounded at Sharpsburg, Md. on Sept. 17, 1862. Taken prisoner in East Tn. on Jan. 22, 1864. Sent to Rock Island, Ill. prison. He took a loyalty oath and was released on June 21, 1865.

Pulliam, John–Co.I–PVT, Discharged with disability at Camp Steiner, near Centerville, Va. on Nov. 30, 1861.

Pulliam, Mathew E.–Co.I–PVT, Mar. 4, 1862. Furloughed for illness, 60 days, Jan. 29, 1865. (No later record)

Pulliam, Nathan B.–Co.I–PVT, Mar. 26, 1863. Discharged, furnished Elijah Norman as substitute, Aug. 24, 1863.

Quinn, Leonidas W.–Co.A–PVT, Appointed 1st CPL. Wounded at Spotsylvania, Va. on May 12, 1864. Permanently disabled in the back.

Quinn, William A. Jr.–Co.A–2d LT, Elected 1st LT Oct. 1861. Resigned in Mar. of 1862.

Rachels, John L.–Co.K–PVT, Died in 1862.

Ray, A. J.–Co.B–PVT, Sept. 1862. Discharged with disability on Dec. 12, 1862.

Ray, James A.–Co.C–PVT, Captured and paroled at Andersonville, S.C. on May 3, 1865.

Ray, James A.–Co.K–PVT, Captured at Gettysburg, Pa. on July 3, 1863. Released from Ft. Delaware, Del. prison on June 22, 1865.

Ray, John T.–Co.D–PVT, Assigned as Regimental Teamster in July, 1862. Absent in consequence of the movements of the enemy on Feb. 25, 1865.

Ray, William R.–Co.K–PVT, Surrendered at Appomattox, Va. on Apr. 9, 1865.

Redfiern, E.W.–Co.K–PVT, Surrendered at Appomattox, Va. on Apr. 9, 1865.

Redfiern, James–Co.K–PVT, Captured at Gettysburg, Pa. on July 2, 1863. Exchanged prisoner and returned to unit. Surrendered at Appomattox, Va. on Apr. 9, 1865.

Redfiern, W. Andrew–Co.K–PVT, Surrendered at Appomattox, Va. on Apr. 9, 1865.

Reed, W.A.P.–Co.H–PVT, Discharged with disability on Oct. 25, 1861.

Reese, Columbus–Co.E–PVT, Discharged on Jan. 13, 1862. (No later record)

Reeves, Jesse–Co.E–PVT, Captured at Falling Waters, Md. on July 14, 1862. Exchanged prisoner at City Point, Va. on Mar. 16, 1864. Surrendered at Appomattox, Va. on Apr. 9, 1865.

Reid, Felix C.–Co.D–2d CPL, Wounded at Malvern Hill, Va. on July 1, 1862. Appointed 1st SGT on Oct. 25, 1864. Surrendered at Appomattox, Va. on Apr. 9, 1865.

Reid, Jabez M.–Co.G–PVT, Captured at Gettysburg, Pa. on July 2, 1863. Died of Smallpox at Fort Delaware, Del. on Oct. 27, 1863.

Reid, William W.–Co.D–PVT, Died at Richmond, Va. in 1861.

Remsen, James B.–Co.G–PVT, Mar. 4, 1862. Wounded at Garnett's Farm, Va. on June 27, 1862. Appointed 4th SGT on Oct. 11, 1862; 1st SGT on Mar. 4, 1863. Captured at Gettysburg, Pa. on July 2, 1863. Exchanged prisoner on Sept. 18, 1864. Surrendered at Appomattox, Va. on Apr. 9, 1865.

Remsen, Rem–Co.G–4th CPL, Severely wounded at Garnett's Farm, Va. on June 27, 1862. Detailed as a clerk in the Commissary Dept. in 1862. Surrendered at Appomattox, Va. on Apr. 9, 1865.

Remsen, Thomas H.–Co.C–PVT, Appointed CPL in 1862. Elected 2d LT of Co. G in Mar. 1863. Surrendered at Appomattox, Va. on Apr. 9, 1865.

Reynolds, James R.–Co.D–PVT, Transferred to Co. A on Oct. 2, 1862.

Reynolds, David S.–Co.K–PVT, Died in a Richmond, Va. hospital on Apr. 20, 1862.

Reynolds, James R.–Co.E–PVT, May 12, 1864. Surrendered at Appomattox, Va. on Apr. 9, 1865.

Reynolds, James R.–Co.K–PVT, Wounded and captured at Gettysburg, Pa. in July, 1863. Left arm amputated above the elbow in a Gettysburg, Pa. hospital, July of 1863. Exchanged prisoner on Aug. 24, 1863.

Reynolds, John–Co.G–PVT, Died in a Richmond, Va. hospital on Nov. 24, 1861.

Reynolds, William James–Co.K–PVT, Aug. 1, 1862. Captured at Gettysburg, Pa. on July 2, 1863. Exchanged prisoner and returned to his unit. Surrendered at Appomattox, Va. on Apr. 9, 1865.

Rhodes, Greenberry B.–Co.A–PVT, Mar. 23, 1863. Surrendered at Appomattox, Va. on Apr. 9, 1865.

Rhodes, Robert M.–Co.D–PVT, Discharged with disability on Nov. 20, 1861.

Rhodes, Simeon–Co.A–PVT, Captured at Ft. Harrison. Va., Sept. 29, 1864.

Rhodes, William H.–Co.D–PVT, Wounded at Wilderness, Va. on May 6, 1864. Died of wounds on May 20, 1864.

Richardson, J.M.–Co.H–PVT, Discharged with disability on Nov. 9, 1861.

Ricketson, William S.–Co.D–PVT, Elected Jr. 2d LT on Oct. 8, 1862. Wounded at Fredericksburg, Va. on Dec. 13, 1862. Died of Pneumonia on May 27, 1864.

Rigsby, William–Co.I–PVT, Captured at West Point, Ga. in April of 1865. (No later record)

Ritchie, A. C.–Co.B–PVT, Died of Typhoid fever in a Richmond, Va. hospital in Dec. of 1861.

Roberson, J.A.P.–Co.K–1st SGT, Discharged in Jan. of 1862.

Roberson, William F.–Co.K–PVT, Appointed 4th CPL on Mar. 27, 1862; Chaplain on Nov. 30, 1862. Surrendered at Appomattox, Va. on Apr. 9, 1865.

Roberson, Wingfield–Co.K–PVT, Elected 1st LT on Nov. 17, 1864. Surrendered at Appomattox, Va. on Apr. 9, 1865.

Roberts, Edward M.–Co.C–PVT, Surrendered at Appomattox, Va. on Apr. 9, 1865.

Roberts, T.E.–Co.E–PVT, Discharged with disability on Oct. 17, 1861.

Roberts, William H.–Co.I–PVT, Discharged with disability at Camp Steiner, near Centerville, Va. on Nov. 12, 1861.

Robertson, G.C.–Co.H–PVT, Discharged with disability on Dec. 31, 1861.

Rocker, Charles J.–Co.K–PVT, Appointed 1st CPL on May 11, 1863; 3rd SGT on Dec. 1, 1864. Wounded and detached on hospital duty in Richmond, Va. throughout the remainder of the war.

Roe, C.W.G.–Co.H–PVT, Killed at Chickamauga, Ga. on Sept. 20, 1863.

Roe, Samuel L.–Co.H–lst CPL, Killed at Petersburg, Va. on June 20, 1864.

Roebuck, Robert C.C.–Co.F–PVT, Discharged. Furnished Alexander Stratton as a substitute on Feb. 18, 1862.

Rogers, J.C.–Co.E–PVT, Feb. 5, 1864. Surrendered at Appomattox, Va. on Apr. 9, 1865.

Rose, A. J.–Co.C–PVT, Mar. 4, 1862. Listed as absent and sick in Feb. of 1865.

Rowland, G.M.–Co.H PVT, Discharged with disability on Oct. 19, 1861.

Rowland, W.–Co.B–PVT, Listed serving as a teamster at Morristown, Tu. in Jan. of 1864.

Rowland, W.H.–Co.H–PVT, Killed at 2nd Manassas, Va. on Aug. 30, 1862.

Rowland, William–Co.H–PVT, Captured at Dandridge, Tn. on Jan. 22, 1864. (No later record)

Rowzee, Theodore F.–Co.F–PVT, Appointed 4th SGT on May 29, 1864. Surrendered at Appomattox, Va. on Apr. 9, 1865.

Rucker, Alexander–Co.K–PVT, Sent to a Richmond, Va. hospital in Sept., 1861. Died there in Jan. of 1862.

Ruff, James C.–Co.C–PVT, Deserted on Feb. 20, 1865.

Ruff, Martin–Co.C–PVT, Surrendered at Appomattox, Va. on Apr. 9, 1865.

Rumbley, William R.–Co.G–PVT, Wounded at Darbytown Road, Va. on Oct. 7, 1864. Surrendered at Augusta, Ga. on May 18, 1865.

Ruskin, J.G.–Co.E–PVT, Died on Nov. 19, 1861 at Charlottsville, Virginia.

Russell, David A.–Co.A–PVT, Wounded at Garnett's Farm, Va. on June 27, 1862. Appointed Courier in 1863. Surrendered at Appomattox, Va. on Apr. 9, 1865.

Sale, Hickerson M.–Co.G–PVT, Discharged, due to consumption at Camp Walker, near Manassas, Va. on Aug. 30, 1861.

Sale, Thomas S.–Co.G–3rd. SGT, Appointed Ensign. Killed at Sharpsburg, Md. on Sept. 17, 1862.

Sammons, Benjamin, F.–Co.B–PVT, Wounded at 2d Manassas, Va. on Aug. 30, 1862; Again at Fredericksburg, Va. on Dec. 13, 1862 and surrendered at Appomattox, Va. on Apr. 9, 1865.

Sasnett, H. H.–Co.E–PVT, Discharged with disability on Sept. 26, 1861.

Sasnett, William Pembroke–Co.E–1st CPL, Appointed 4th SGT in 1862. Died of disease on Dec. 30, 1864.

Saunders, S.D.–Co.K–PVT, Mar. 26, 1864. Died at home in Georgia on Sept. 1, 1864.

Scarborough, Frederick B.–Co.F–PVT, Wounded in the right shoulder and permanently disabled at Garnett's Farm, Va. on June 27, 1862.

Scarborough, William B.–Co.F–PVT, Captured at Gettysburg, Pa. on July 3, 1863. Exchanged prisoner in Feb. of 1865.

Scott, Hartwell G.–Co.E–PVT, Transferred to Co.E, 15th Georgia from Co.G, 8th Georgia Regiment on May 16, 1861. Wounded at Malvern Hill, Va. on July 1, 1862. Appointed CPL. Killed at Chickamauga, Ga. on Sept. 19, 1863.

Scott, J.A.–Co.K–PVT, Surrendered at Appomattox, Va. on Apr. 9, 1865.

Scott, Noah–Co.A–PVT, Mar. 4, 1862. Captured at Gettysburg, Pa. on July 2, 1863. Exchanged prisoner. Surrendered at Appomattox, Va. on Apr. 9, 1865.

Scott, Oscar D.–Co.K–PVT, Feb. 24, 1862. Appointed Drum Major in Dec. 1862. Surrendered at Appomattox, Va. on Apr. 9, 1865.

Seals, Henry B.–Co.K–PVT, Killed at Sharpsburg, Md. on Sept. 17, 1862.

Seals, William D.–Co.K–PVT, Appointed 4th SGT in 1863. Wounded at Wilderness, Va. on May 6, 1864. Detached on hospital duty, Feb. 28, 1865.

Seidel, Charles W.–Co.C–PVT, Captured at Gettysburg, Pa. on July 2, 1863. Paroled at Augusta, Ga. on May 24, 1865.

Sewell, Spencer–Co.B–PVT, Died of disease in a Richmond, Va. hospital, Nov. 4, 1862.

Sewell, William F.–Co.B–PVT, Wounded at Fredericksburg, Va. on Dec. 13, 1862. Surrendered at Appomattox, Va. on Apr. 9, 1865.

Seymour, Marshall M.–Co.I–PVT, Mar. 4, 1862. Transferred to 38th Georgia in 1863.

Shannon, James D.–Co.B–2d CPL, Captured at Gettysburg, Pa. on July 3, 1863. Exchanged prisoner, Apr. 27, 1864.

Shannon, John H.–Co.B–1st SGT, Demoted to PVT being unable to perform duties. Sent home sick and returned to duty in 1864. Captured and exchanged on Jan. 17, 1865. Paroled at Augusta, Ga. on May 18, 1865.

Shannon, John L.–Co.B–PVT, May 10, 1862. Captured at Gettysburg, Pa. on July 3, 1863. Released from a Union prison on June 16, 1865.

Shannon, John M.–Co.B–PVT, Died in Richmond, Va. on Dec. 5, 1861.

Shannon, Peter J.–Co.I–1st LT, Resigned his commission on Dec. 19, 1861. Appointed Regimental Adjutant on Feb. 9, 1862. Elected MAJ on Aug. 1, 1862. Surrendered at Appomattox, Va., as the Commander of the Regiment, on Apr. 9, 1865.

Shannon, Thomas E.–Co.B–PVT, Mar. 10, 1862. Died of Pneumonia near Fredericksburg, Va. on Dec. 1, 1862.

Shannon, William D.–Co.B–PVT, May 10, 1862. Died of disease at Petersburg, Va. on May 15, 1863.

Shannon, William J.–Co.B–PVT, Wounded and captured at Gettysburg Pa. on July 3, 1863. Released from a Union prison on May 18, 1865. Paroled at Augusta, Ga. on May 18, 1865.

Sharp, A.D.–Co.K–PVT, Appointed Sergeant Major on Aug. 5, 1862; 1st LT and Drillmaster on Mar. 11, 1864. (No later record)

Sharp, J.H.–Co.K–PVT, Discharged in Jan. of 1862.

Sharp, Levi L.–Co.D–PVT, Mar. 1, 1862. Died of disease in a Danville, Va. hospital in Jan. of 1863.

Sharp, Thomas J.–Co.D–PVT, Wounded at Ft. Harrison, Va on Sept. 29, Died of wounds at Richmond, Va. on Sept. 30, 1864.

Shirley, J.D.–Co.H–3rd CPL, Died of fever at Richmond, Va. on May 25, 1862.

Shirley, Joel M.–Co.H–3rd SGT, Captured at Gettysburg, Pa. on July 3, 1863. Enlisted in the U.S. Army at Point Lookout, Md. on Oct. 15, 1864.

Shirley, William M.–Co.H–PVT, Died of Typhoid fever at Richmond, Va. on May 25, 1862.

Shoemodder. W.–Co.G–PVT, Admitted to the Smallpox hospital at Pt. Lookout, Md. prison on Nov. 12, 1863. (No later record)

Shumate, John D.–Co.A–PVT, Discharged with disability on Sept. 26, 1861.

Simmons, Charles, E.–Co.E–3rd CPL, Elected 2nd LT on Sept. 17, 1863. Killed at Chickamauga, Ga. on Sept. 19, 1863.

Simmons. J. Clarence–Co.E–PVT, Appointed Quartermaster SGT in Nov., 1861. Surrendered at Appomattox, Va. on Apr. 9, 1865.

Simmons. Marcellus A.–Co.E–PVT, Wounded in the eye which resulted in the loss of sight. Also, left leg disabled at 2nd Manassas, Va. on Aug. 30, 1862. Paroled at Warrenton, Va. on Sept. 29, 1862.

Simmons, William H.–Co.E–PVT, Captured at Malvern Hill, Va. on July 1, 1862. Exchanged. Surrendered at Appomattox, Va. on Apr. 9, 1865.

Simpson, Edward–Staff–Assistant Surgeon, Died of Typhoid in Charlottsville, Va. on Oct. 23, 1861.

Simpson, E.W.–Co.K–PVT, Wounded at Wilderness, Va. on May 6, 1864. Died of his wounds in a Richmond, Va. hospital on July 6, 1864.

Simpson, Leonard K–Co.C–PVT, Died in Smallpox Hospital at Petersburg, Va. on June 4, 1863.

Sims, James R.–Co.A–PVT, Died in Richmond, Va. on May 12, 1862.

Sims, John J.–Co.A–PVT, Discharged with disability on Nov. 11, 1861.

Sims, William B.–Co.G–PVT, Died at White Mills, N.C. in 1863.

Sink, W.A.–Co.F–PVT, Captured at Smith Mountain, Va. on Sept. 14, 1862. Exchanged prisoner in Nov. of 1862. (No later record)

Skrine, Eugene A.–Co.E–PVT, Died of disease in June of 1863.

Slack, Luke R.–Co.A–PVT, Appointed 3rd CPL. Surrendered at Appomattox, Va. on Apr. 9, 1865.

Slay, G. F.–Co.C–PVT, Discharged with disability on July 28, 1862.

Slay, James T.–Co.C–PVT, Wounded in Va. on May 31, 1864. Died of wounds on June 1, 1864.

Smith, A.J.–Co.E–PVT, Discharged with disability on Oct. 28, 1861.

Smith, Andrew–Co.A–PVT, Discharged because he was overage on June 17, 1862. (Age–61)

Smith, Daniel C.–Co.A–PVT, Captured at Ft. Harrison, Va. on Sept. 30, 1864. Exchanged on Mar. 17, 1865. (No later record)

Smith, Franklin–Co.F–PVT, Present in Feb. of 1865. (No later record)

Smith, Francis W.–Co.I–1st SGT, Elected Jr. 2nd LT on May 14, 1862. Wounded at 2nd Manassas, Va. on Aug. 30, 1862. Elected 2nd LT on Apr. 4, 1863. Captured and paroled at Hartwell, Ga. on May 18, 1865.

Smith, Franklin–Co.A–PVT, Deserted on Nov. 20, 1862.

Smith, George–Co.B–PVT, Mar. 4, 1862. Wounded at Spotsylvania, Va. on May 10, 1864; again at Petersburg, Va., Sept. of 1864.

Smith, G.W.–Co.E–PVT, Jan. 18, 1863. Died of disease in Jackson Hospital, Richmond, Va. on Aug. 6, 1864.

Smith, Henley G.–Co.I–PVT, Deserted on Feb. 19, 1865.

Smith, Henry F.–Co.B–PVT, Wounded at Thoroughfare Gap, Va., Aug. 28, 1862. (No later record)

Smith, I.T.–Co.D–PVT, Surrendered at Appomattox, Va. on Apr. 9, 1865.

Smith, James W.–Co.C–PVT, Surrendered at Appomattox, Va. on Apr. 9, 1865.

Smith, John H.–Co.F–PVT, July 18, 1862. Killed near New Market, Va. on Aug. 16, 1864.

Smith, John L.–Co.A–PVT, Oct. 1862. Transferred on July 1, 1863.

Smith, Joseph T.–Co.I–CPT, Elected MAJ on Dec. 23, 1861. Resigned on Mar. 5, 1862.

Smith, T. B.–Co.C–PVT, Captured at Gettysburg, Pa. on July 4, 1863. Released from a Union prison on June 16, 1865.

Smith, Theophilus J.–Co.E–CPT, Elected MAJ on May 1, 1862. Resigned on July 25, 1862.

Smith, Thomas S.–Co.D–PVT, June 11, 1862. Surrendered at Appomattox, Va. on Apr. 9, 1865.

Smith, William–Co.H–PVT, Discharged at Richmond, Va. on Dec. 17, 1861.

Smith, William P.–Co.I–PVT, Discharged because of Dropsy at Richmond, Va. hospital on Nov. 15, 1862.

Smith, William T.–Co.C–PVT, Surrendered at Appomattox, Va. on Apr. 9, 1865.

Smith, William W.–Co.B–PVT, Died of Typhoid fever in a Richmond, Va. hospital on Dec. 10, 1861.

Snellings, George W.–Co.C–Musician, Discharged with disability on Dec. 12, 1861.

Snellings, Peter P.–Co.C–PVT, Mar. 4, 1862. Wounded at Malvern Hill, Va. on July 1, 1862. (No later record)

Snellinos, William H.–Co.C–PVT, Discharged with disability on Dec. 28, 1861.

Snipes. L.G.–Co.E–PVT, Discharged with disability on Dec. 4, 1861.

Snipes, W.W.–Co.E–PVT, Discharged with disability on Dec. 14, 1861.

Sorrow, McKenzie–Co.C–PVT, Discharged with disability on Nov. 12, 1861.

Sorrow, M.H.–Co.C–PVT, Discharged with disability on Nov. 1, 1861.

Sorrow, Stinson P.–Co.C–PVT, Died in a Culpeper, Va. hospital on Nov. 27, 1861.

Sorrow, Terrell T.–Co.C–PVT, Mar. 9, 1863. Wounded at Cold Harbor, Va. on June 3, 1864. Died of wounds in a Richmond, Va. hospital on June 8, 1864.

Spratling, James M.–Co.A–PVT. (No later record)

Spratling, Johnson M.–Co.A–PVT, Died at Richmond, Va. in May 1862.

Spratling, Henry E.–Co.A–PVT, Mar. of 1862. Appointed 1st SGT. Surrendered at Appomattox, Va. on April 9, 1865.

Spratling, Henry G.–Co.A–PVT. (No later record)

Spratling, William J.–Co.A–PVT, Discharged in July of 1862.

Stafford, John–Co.E–PVT, Feb. 25, 1863. On detached duty in hospital. (No later record)

Starr, Alfred N.–Co.B–PVT, Aug. 30, 1862. Deserted near Petersburg, Va. on July, 28, 1864.

Starr, James–Co.B–PVT, Aug. 30, 1862. Deserted. (No later record)

Starrett, Benjamin F.–Co.B–PVT, Died of fever in a Richmond, Va. hospital on Nov. 19, 1861.

Starrett, William S.–Co.B–PVT, Died of fever in a Richmond, Va. hospital on May 31, 1862.

Steadman, Levi–Co.I–PVT, Died on Oct. 26, 1861.

Steed, Adoniram J.–Co.G–PVT, Feb. 27, 1862. Surrendered at Appomattox, Va. on Apr. 9, 1865.

Stephens. John A.–Co.D–PVT, Appointed 2d CPL. Elected 2d LT of Co. G, 1st Ga. Regiment on Sept. 12, 1861.

Stephens, Linton–Staff–LTC, Resigned on Dec. 19, 1861. Brother of Alexander Stephens, Vice President of the Confederacy.

Stephenson, Alexander W.–Co.B–PVT, Wounded and captured at Chaffin's Farm, Va. on Sept. 29, 1864. Released from a Union prison hospital on Jan. 13, 1865.

Roster of the Fifteenth Georgia Infantry Regiment 173

Stephenson, David L.–Co.A–PVT, Wounded at Garnett's Farm, Va. on June 27, 1862. Transferred to Co. G. Captured at Gettysburg, PA on July 2, 1863. Exchanged prisoner in Nov. of 1863. Discharged with disability on Aug. 14, 1864.

Stephenson, Joseph W.–Co.B–3d CPL, Elected 2d LT, May 1862. Captured at Gettysburg, Pa. on July 3, 1863. Exchanged prisoner, Mar. 14, 1865.

Stephenson, Newton W.–Co.G–PVT, Feb. 27, 1862. Appointed 3rd CPL. Surrendered at Appomattox, Va. on Apr. 9, 1865.

Stewart, G.M.–Staff–Nurse, Captured at Seminary Hospital, Hagerstown, Md. (No later record)

Stewart, Thomas J.–Co.D–PVT, Discharged with disability on Nov. 13, 1861.

Stokes, J. S.–Co.A–PVT, Deserted in July of 1863.

Stone, Jesse David–Co.G–PVT, Feb. 13, 1863. Captured in a Richmond, Va. hospital on Apr. 3, 1865. Released at Newport News, Va. on June 26, 1865.

Stone, Robert G.–Co.K–PVT, Appointed Drum Major and Chief Musician of the 15th Regimental Band, June 9, 1863. Surrendered at Appomattox, Va. on Apr. 9, 1865.

Stone, W.H.–Co.A–PVT, Captured at Strasburg, Va. on Oct. 19, 1864. Released from Pt. Lookout, Md. on June 19, 1865.

Story, Lewellyn–Co.F–SGT, Captured near Knoxville, Tn. on Dec. 3, 1863. Taken to Rock Island, Ill. prison. (No later record)

Stovall, George M.–Co.C–PVT, Transferred to Co. F on May 15, 1862.

Stovall, J.B.–Co.C–PVT, Wounded (left leg amputated) on May 18 and died on May 29, 1864.

Stovall, J. C.–Co.B–PVT, Surrendered at Appomattox, Va., April 9, 1865.

Stovall, Job H.–Co.C–PVT, Discharged with disability on Jan. 27, 1862.

Stovall, Josiah T.–Co.B–PVT, AWOL Feb. 1865.

Stratten, Alexander H.–Co.F–PVT, Feb. 18, 1862. Substitute for Robert C.C. Roebuck. Discharged with disability on Nov. 12, 1862.

Stribling, Francis H.–Co.A–PVT, Died in Richmond, Va. on April 22, 1864.

Stribling, Isaac N.–Co.A–PVT, Wounded at 2d Manassas, Va. on Aug. 30. 1862. Appointed 3rd SGT. Surrendered at Appomattox, Va. on Apr. 9, 1865.

Stribling, J.M.–Co.A–PVT, Died in a hospital on Dec. 22, 1864.

Stribling, Micajah L.–Co.A–PVT, Surrendered at Appomattox, Va. on Apr. 9, 1865.

Stribling, Thomas M.–Co.A–PVT, Sent to Huguenot Springs, Va., on May 21, 1864.

Sullivan, James–Co.H–PVT, Wounded at Sharpsburg, Md. on Sept. 17, 1862. Listed as AWOL on Feb. 25, 1865.

Sutton, Moses G.–Co.A–PVT. (No later record)

Swint, Edmund–Co.E–PVT, Appointed 2nd CPL on Feb. 10, 1862. Surrendered at Appomattox, Va. on Apr. 9, 1865.

Sykes, William A. Epps–Co.E–PVT, Discharged with disability on Mar. 28, 1862.

Tate, Edmund B., Jr.–Co.C–3d CPL, Appointed 2d SGT in June, 1862. Wounded at Chickamauga, Ga. on Sept. 19, 1863. Appointed 1st SGT, Sept. 30, 1863. (No later record)

Tate, Enos R.–Co.C–PVT, Wounded at Gettysburg, Pa. on July 3, 1863. Died of wounds on July 5, 1863.

Tate, Jasper S.–Co.C–PVT, Discharged but re-enlisted on Mar. 3, 1863. Appointed 4th CPL. Surrendered at Appomattox, Va. on Apr. 9, 1865.

Tate, W. T.–Co.C–PVT, Captured at Gettysburg, Pa. on July 3, 1863. Died of disease in a Union hospital on Sept. 20, 1863.

Tatum, William P.–Co.G–PVT, Feb. 27, 1862. Surrendered at Appomattox, Va. on Apr. 9, 1865.

Taylor, Columbus W.–Co.D–PVT, Captured at Gettysburg, Pa. on July 3, 1863. Died in a Union prison hospital of disease on Oct. 14, 1863.

Taylor, J.J.–Co.F–PVT, Mar. 4, 1862. Died in a Richmond, Va. hospital in July of 1862.

Taylor, James L.–Co.D–PVT, Killed at Wilderness, Va. on May 6, 1864.

Taylor, James M.–Co.F–PVT, Mar. 4, 1862. Captured at Gettysburg, Pa. on July 3, 1863. Enlisted in the U.S. Army on May 1, 1864.

Taylor, John H.C.–Co.F–PVT, Mar. 4, 1862. Transferred to Co.I on Jan. 1, 1863. Captured at Dandridge, Tn. on Jan. 22, 1864. Released at Knoxville, Tn. on May 1, 1865.

Taylor, William C.–Co.D–PVT, Surrendered at Appomattox, Va. on Apr. 9, 1865.

Taylor, William T.–Co.D–PVT, Transferred to Co. F on May 15, 1862. Detailed as Wardmaster in a Richmond, Va. hospital in Apr., 1864. Listed as present in Jan. 1865.

Taylor, Zachary B.–Co.F–PVT, Mar. 4, 1862. Wounded at Malvern Hill, Va. on July 1, 1862. Surrendered at Appomattox, Va. on Apr. 9, 1865.

Teague, John–Co.B–PVT, Mar. 4, 1862. Surrendered at Appomattox, Va. on Apr. 9, 1865.

Teasley, Alfred J.–Co.I–PVT, June 15, 1862. Elected Jr. 2nd LT on Aug. 2, 1863. Surrendered at Appomattox, Va. on Apr. 9, 1865.

Tebow, John–Co.G–PVT, Died of Typhoid fever in a Richmond, Va. hospital on Sept. 8, 1861.

Tennent, Henry A.–Co.I–PVT, Captured at Gettysburg, Pa. on July 2, 1863. Exchanged prisoner in Mar., 1865. (No later record)

Tennent, Orville T.–Co.I–PVT, Appointed CPL on July 1, 1863; Sergeant, in 1864. Deserted on Feb. 19, 1865.

Tennent, William C.–Co.I–PVT, Apr. 25, 1864. Surrendered at Appomattox, Va. on Apr. 9, 1865.

Terry, James J.–Co.F–PVT, Died near Manassas, Va. on Nov. 16, 1861.

Terry, John W.–Co.F–PVT, Mar. 4, 1862. On detached duty to hospital due to disability on Feb. 25, 1865. (No later record)

Terry, W.A.J.–Co.F–PVT, Mar. 4, 1862. Discharged with disability on July 28, 1862.

Terry. William T.–Co.F–PVT, Died in a Mt. Jackson, Va. hospital on Oct. 29, 1862.

Thomas, Henry–Co.B–PVT, Discharged with disability on May 14, 1862.

Thomas, Thomas W.–Staff–COL, Resigned with disability on Mar. 26, 1862.

Thomas, William A.–Co.K–PVT, Appointed 3rd CPL on May 10, 1863. Captured near Mine Run, Va. on May 10, 1864. Exchanged prisoner in March, 1865.

Thomas, William M.–Staff–Assistant QM, resigned on Sept. 27, 1861.

Thomasson, James C.–Co.B–PVT, Died of Dysentery in Feb. of 1863.

Thomasson, John F.–Co.B–PVT, Died in a hospital, 1864.

Thomaston, Matthew D.–Co.F–PVT, Died in a Richmond, Va. hospital on Dec. 10, 1861.

Thompson, Frederick T.–Co.G–2nd SGT, Appointed 1st SGT in 1862. Died in a Richmond, Va. hospital on July 14, 1862.

Thompson, J.M.–Co.C–PVT, Captured and paroled in Athens, Ga. on May 8, 1865.

Thompson, John P.–Co.K–PVT, Present in Dec. of 1862. (No later record)

Thornton, Mallory J.–Co.I–PVT, Captured at Mossy Creek, Tn. on Jan. 22, 1864. Released at Rock Island, Ill. prison on May 18, 1865.

Thrasher, Clark Tvrell–Co.H–PVT, Died in a Richmond, Va. hospital on Sept. 23, 1861.

Thrasher, H.–Co.H–PVT, Captured and paroled at Andersonville, S.C. on May 3, 1865.

Thrasher, L. H.–Co.H–PVT, Mar. 4, 1862. Died of Pneumonia at Montgomery Springs, Va. on June 5, 1863.

Thrasher, T.J.–Co.H–PVT, Wounded at Malvern Hill, Va. on July 1, 1862. (No later record)

Thrasher, Tyrrel–Co.H–PVT, Died of Typhoid at Richmond, Va. on Sept. 23, 1861.

Tilley, John M.–Co.D–1st LT, Killed at Garnett's Farm, Va. on June 27, 1862.

Tollard, William A.–Co.C–PVT, Captured and paroled at Athens, Ga. on May 8, 1865.

Tolly, H.–Co.C–PVT, Captured and paroled at Athens, Ga. on May 8, 1865.

Treadwell, Terry–Co.I–PVT, Wounded at Sharpsburg, Md. on Sept. 17, 1862. Paroled at Farmville, Va. in Apr. of 1865.

Trout, J.M.–Co.C–PVT, Captured and paroled at Athens, Ga. on May 8, 1865.

Turman, George E.–Co.C–PVT, Transferred to Co. F on May 15, 1862. Captured at Gettysburg, Pa. on July 3, 1863. Sent to Ft. Delaware, Del. prison. (No later record)

Turman. Thomas M.–Co.C–PVT, Transferred to Co. F on May 15, 1862. Captured at Gettysburg, Pa. on July 3, 1863. Sent to Ft. Delaware, Del. prison. Exchanged on Feb. 20, 1865.

Ussery, H.–Co.H–PVT, Promoted to 4th CPL in May, 1864; 3rd CPL in July, 1864. Received a severe facial wound on Mar. 22, 1865.

Vasser, George L.–Co.F–PVT, Transferred to the 38th Georgia Inf. on July 15, 1863.

Vaughn, A.W.–Co.C–PVT, Discharged with disability on Sept. 22, 1861.

Vaughn, James P.–Co.B–PVT, Captured and paroled at Andersonville, S.C. on May 3, 1865.

Vaughn, Joshua–Co.B–PVT, Killed at Gettysburg, Pa. July 2, 1863.

Vaughn, Peter D.–Co.C–PVT, Died in a Richmond, Va. hospital on Apr. 19, 1862.

Vaughn, Samuel–Co.B–PVT, Deserted near Petersburg, Va., July 28, 1864.

Veal, J.M.–Co.A–SGT, Captured at Mine Run, Va. on May 4, 1864. Exchanged at Pt. Lookout, Md. on Sept. 18, 1864.

Veazey, Prior G.–Co.D–2d SGT, Elected Jr. 2d LT on July 24, 1862; 1st LT on Oct. 8, 1862. Wounded at Chickamauga, Ga. on Sept. 20, 1863. Surrendered at Appomattox, Va. on Apr. 9, 1865.

Vest, Alfred W.–Co.B–Musician, Discharged with disability in Dec. of 1861.

Vickery, Charles E.–Co.H–PVT, Appointed 2nd CPL on Dec. 10, 1861. Wounded in the cheek at Darbytown Road, Va. on Oct. 7, 1864. At home on wounded furlough at the end of the war.

Vickery, James P.–Co.H–PVT, Appointed 1st SGT in Apr., 1862. Surrendered at Appomattox, Va. on Apr. 9, 1865.

Vickery, James Percy–Co.H–PVT, Appointed 4th CPL in 1862. Died at Richmond, Va. on July 7, 1862.

Wade, J.A.C.–Co.H–PVT, Sept. 13, 1863. At home without leave, Feb. 25, 1865.

Wade, W.G.–Co.H–PVT, Sept. 17, 1862. Died in an Edray, W.Va. hospital, May 5, 1864.

Wagner, Joseph–Co.D–PVT, Feb. 17, 1864. Captured at Cold Harbor, Va. on June 4, 1864. Paroled on Mar. 2, 1865. Captured in a Richmond, Va. hospital on Apr. 3, 1865.

Walker, L.–Co.F–PVT, Listed as sick and sent to the hospital in Sept. of 1861. (No later record)

Wall, John T.–Co.D–PVT, Listed as present in Feb. of 1865.

Waller, Benjamin–Co.E–PVT, Discharged with disability on Oct. 10, 1861.

Waller, George L.–Co.K–4th CPL, Appointed 2nd CPL on Mar. 27, 1862; 3rd SGT May 10, 1863. Wounded at Ft. Harrison, Va. on Sept. 29, 1864. Died of wounds in a Richmond, Va. hospital on Sept. 30, 1864.

Waller, William A.–Co.E–PVT, Surrendered at Appomattox, Va. on Apr. 9, 1865.

Walseman, William–Co.F–PVT, Wounded at Sharpsburg, Md. on Sept. 17, 1862. Surrendered at Appomattox, Va. on Apr. 9, 1865.

Walters, B.W.–Co.H–PVT, Discharged at Richmond, Va., Nov. 5, 1861.

Walters, Dean W.–Co.H–PVT, Died at Richmond, Va. on Dec. 5, 1861.

Walters. Franklin–Co.H–PVT, Mar. 4, 1862. Captured at Gettysburg, Pa. on July 3, 1863. Released at Ft. Delaware, Del. on June 7, 1865.

Walters, Henry Freeman–Co.H–PVT, Mar. 4, 1862. Discharged with disability on Dec. 26, 1862.

Walters, J.G.–Co.H–PVT, May 1, 1862. Died of fever at Richmond, Va. on June 27, 1862.

Walters, John F.–Co.H–PVT, Wounded at Wilderness, Va. on May 6, 1864. Died of wounds in 1864.

Walters, Joseph Charles–Co.H–PVT, Listed as at home, absent without leave, Feb. 25, 1865.

Walters, William R.–Co.H–PVT, Elected 2nd LT on Dec. 4, 1862. Killed at Petersburg, Va. on June 19, 1864.

Wanslev, William J.–Co.I–PVT, Captured at Mud Tavern, Va. on May 23, 1864. Exchanged prisoner, Mar. 14, 1865.

Ward, Thomas–Co.K–PVT, Captured at Dumfries, Va. on Sept. 14, 1863. Taken to Old Capitol prison, Washington, D.C., Took a loyalty oath on Sept. 27, 1863. Described as–Hair–Brown/ Complexion–Dark/ Eyes–Blue/ Height–5' 5 1/2".

Ware, Robert Andrews–Co.G–PVT, Transferred to the 15th Georgia from the 6th Alabama Inf. in 1862. Captured at Gettysburg, Pa. on July 3, 1863. Exchanged prisoner on Feb. 18, 1865. Furloughed home on Feb. 21, 1865.

Ware, Thomas L.–Co.G–PVT, Appointed 2nd SGT on Dec. 6, 1862. Killed at Gettysburg, Pa. on July 2, 1863.

Ware, William S.–Co.G–PVT, Sept. 28, 1863. Surrendered at Appomattox, Va. on Apr. 9, 1865.

Warren, Epps–Co.E–PVT, Discharged with disability on Nov. 1, 1861.

Warren, H.G.–Co.E–PVT, Jan. 18, 1863. Accidentally wounded while guarding baggage. Roll for Jan.–Feb. 1865, states–"No doubt unfit for duty."

Warren, Thomas J.–Co.E–PVT, Surrendered at Appomattox, Va. on Apr. 9, 1865.

Warthen, David D.–Co.K–PVT, Appointed 2nd CPL on May 11, 1863. Wounded at Gettysburg, Pa. on July 2, 1863; Promoted to 5th SGT on Sept. 29, 1864. Surrendered at Appomattox, Va. on Apr. 9, 1865.

Warthen, George W.–Co.K–3rd SGT, Appointed 5th SGT in the 28th Georgia Regiment.

Warthen, William T.–Co.K–PVT, Missing at Gettysburg, Pa. on July 3, 1863. (No later record)

Washington, A.–Co.I–PVT, Captured and paroled at Athens, Ga. on May 8, 1865.

Watkins, John R.–Co.G–Discharged with disability on Dec. 20, 1861. Reenlisted on Aug. 12, 1862. On detached duty as a guard in Charleston, S.C. in 1863. Discharged with disability again on Sept. 20, 1863.

Weaver, Henry C.–Co.B–PVT, Aug. 30, 1862. (No later record)

Webb, Andrew J.–Co.F–PVT, Transferred to Co.F, 15th Georgia from 38th Geor-

Roster of the Fifteenth Georgia Infantry Regiment 179

gia in Sept. 1862; Co.I, 15th Georgia in Jan. 1863. Surrendered at Appomattox, Va. on Apr. 9, 1865.

Webb, John C.–Co.I–PVT, Wounded at Gettysburg, Pa. on July 3, 1863. Captured at Mud Tavern, Va. on May 23, 1864. Exchanged prisoner, Feb. 10, 1865.

Webb, Martin–Co.I–PVT, Discharged in 1861. Reenlisted on Mar. 1, 1863. Surrendered at Appomattox, Va. on Apr. 9, 1865.

Welban, Elijah J.–Co.D–PVT, Discharged on Nov. 1, 1861.

Wells, Jeremiah S.–Co.D–PVT, Captured at Petersburg, Va. on Apr. 3, 1865. Released on June 15, 1865.

Wells, William–Co.E–PVT, Died in a Richmond, Va. hospital on Apr. 15, 1862.

West, A.A.–Staff–Adjutant, Resigned on Sept. 13, 1861.

West, William H.–Co.B–PVT, Captured at Gettysburg, Pa., July 2, 1863. (No later record)

Westbrook, Samuel D.–Co.B–PVT, Mar. 10, 1862, Captured at a Gettysburg, Pa. on July 3, 1863. Died in a Union prison hospital of smallpox on Dec. 12, 1863.

Westbrook. Thomas S.–Co.B–Musician, Captured at Gettysburg, Pa. on July 3, 1863. Exchanged prisoner in Feb., 1865.

Wharton, T.R.–Co.K–PVT, Died at Camp Douglas, Ill. on Feb. 13, 1865.

Wheatley, Ezra–Co.A–PVT, Died at Richmond, Va. on Dec. 22, 1861.

Wheatley, Greenberry–Co.A–PVT, Died at Richmond, Va. of Typhoid fever on May 9, 1862.

Wheatley, Leonard, P.–Co.A–PVT, Surrendered at Appomattox, Va. on Apr. 9, 1865.

Wheatley, O.–Co.A–PVT, Nov. of 1863. Died of Typhoid at Lynchburg, Va. on June 25, 1864.

Wheatley, Timothy–Co.A–PVT, Died of Typhoid Pneumonia in a Richmond, Va. hospital on May 19, 1862.

Wheelis, David M.–Co.C–PVT, Mar. 4, 1862. Wounded at Malvern Hill, Va. on July 1, 1862. Absent, sick in Feb. 1865.

Wheland, John–Co.K–PVT, Surrendered at Appomattox, Va. on Apr. 9, 1865.

White, Alexander–Co.B–PVT, May 12, 1862. Transferred. (No later record)

White, Archibald L.–Co.F–PVT, Appointed 1st CPL in July, 1862. Captured at Gettysburg, Pa. on July 3, 1863. Died at Point Lookout, Md. prison on Nov. 19, 1863.

White, George–Co.E–PVT, Surrendered at Appomattox, Va. on Apr. 9, 1865.

White, J.–Co.K–PVT, Discharged with disability on Oct. 15, 1861.

White, Luke H.–Co.F–PVT, Appointed 5th SGT in Apr., 1863. Captured at Gettysburg, Pa. on July 3, 1863. Exchanged prisoner in Feb., 1865.

White, M.D.–Co.H–PVT, Wounded at Sharpsburg, Md. on Sept. 17, 1862. Captured at Greenville, S.C. on May 23, 1865.

White, N.A.–Co.F–PVT, Sent to a Richmond, Va. hospital in Sept. of 1861. Discharged with disability on Oct. 17, 1861.

White, T.–Co.G–PVT, Captured and paroled at Athens, Ga. on May 8, 1865.

White, Tinsley R.–Co.I–PVT, Wounded at Garnett's Farm, Va. on June 27, 1862. Surrendered at Appomattox, Va. on Apr. 9, 1865.

White, William B.–Co.F–3rd CPL, Wounded at Garnett's Farm, Va. on June 27, 1862. Died of wounds on Aug. 12, 1862.

Wiley, Samuel H.–Co.E–PVT, Appointed clerk for Brigade Quartermaster on Oct. 10, 1862. Surrendered at Appomattox, Va. on Apr. 9, 1865.

Wiley, Sylvanus G.–Co.F–PVT, Sick in a hospital on Feb. 25, 1865. (No later record)

Wilkins, F. M.–Co.C–PVT, Died in a hospital on May 3, 1862.

Wilkins, Judas L.–Co.C–PVT, Transferred to Co. F on May 15, 1862. Killed at Chickamauga, Ga. on Sept. 20, 1863.

Williams, George T.–Co.I–PVT, Feb. 28, 1862. Transferred to the Regimental Band on Apr. 3, 1862. Surrendered at Appomattox, Va. on Apr. 9, 1865.

Williams, J.–Co.C–PVT, Captured and paroled at Athens, Ga. on May 8, 1865.

Williams, William W.–Co.I–PVT, Appointed Drum Major on Dec. 2, 1861. Sick in Richmond, Va. hospitals during 1862. (No later record)

Willingham, John C.–Co.G–PVT, Died in a Richmond, Va. hospital on Oct. 29, 1861.

Willis, Ennis–Co.A–PVT, Surrendered at Appomattox, Va., April 9, 1865.

Willis, James H.–Co.A–PVT, Appointed CPT. Discharged with disability on Nov. 20, 1861.

Willis, J.H.–Co.C–PVT, Died on Sept. 22, 1861.

Willis, Richard M.M.–Co.C–PVT, Severely wounded in the leg at Wilderness, Va. on May 6, 1865. Wounded again at North Anna River on May 23, 1864. Wounds resulted in leg amputation and he was furloughed home.

Willis, Thomas B.–Co.C–PVT, Captured at Gettysburg, Pa. on July 4, 1863. Exchanged prisoner on Jan. 17, 1865.

Willis, William–Co.A–PVT, Feb. 25, 1862. Killed at Fredericksburg, Va. on Dec. 13, 1862.

Willis, William J.–Co.C–PVT, Elected 2d LT in Jan. 1862; Elected CPT on July 13, 1862. Wounded at Chickamauga, Ga. on Sept. 20, 1863. Died of wounds in Sept. of 1863.

Willis, William W.–Co.B–PVT, Deserted near Bull's Gap, Tn., March 3, 1864.

Wilson, Benjamin C.–Co.E–PVT, Captured at Gettysburg, Pa. on July 3, 1863. Died on Nov. 5, 1864.

Wood, William R.–Co.A–PVT, Captured and paroled at Salisbury, N.C. on Apr. 12, 1865.

Woodruff, James W.–Co.A–PVT, Feb. 27, 1862. Wounded at Chickamauga, Ga. on Sept. 19, 1863. Surrendered at Appomattox, Va., April 9, 1865.

Woodruff, J. W.–Co.D–PVT, Wounded at Richmond, Va. on June 20, 1864. Surrendered at Appomattox, Va. on Apr. 9, 1865.

Wright, A.–Co.E–PVT, Captured at Gettysburg, Pa. on July 3, 1863. (No later record)

Wright, Francis M.–Co.G–1st SGT, Discharged with disability on Nov. 12, 1861.

Wright, James–Co.G–1st CPL, Captured at Ft. Harrison, Va. on Sept. 30, 1864. Released at Point Lookout, Md. on July 25, 1865.

Wright, John T.–Co.D–PVT, Discharged with disability on Nov. 4, 1861.

Wright, Joseph–Co.E–PVT, Wounded at Wilderness, Va. on May 6, 1864. Died of wounds on May 9, 1864.

Wright, Joseph B.–Co.K–PVT, Feb. 24, 1862. Surrendered at Appomattox, Va. on Apr. 9, 1865.

Wright, S. B. H.–Co.B–PVT, Died in a Richmond, Va. hospital on Dec. 19, 1861.

Wright, T. G.–Co.H–PVT, Mar. 4, 1862. Captured at Gettysburg, Pa. on July 2, 1863. Exchanged prisoner and rejoined the unit. Surrendered at Appomattox, Va. on Apr. 9, 1865.

Wvnn, Samuel–Co.A–PVT, Discharged with disability on Sept. 26, 1861.

Yarborough, J.J.–Co.K–PVT, Captured at Gettysburg, Pa. on July 2, 1863. Took oath of allegiance to the U.S. and was released at Point Lookout, Md. on Jan. 26, 1864.

Yates, Elisha–Co.H–PVT, Deserted at Petersburg, Va. on July 13, 1864.

Yow, Thomas Anderson–Co.H–PVT, Died of Typhoid fever in Chimborazo Hospital #4, at Richmond, Va. on Nov. 1, 1861.

Zellars, Peter–Co.G–PVT, Feb. 27, 1862. Died in a Richmond, Va. hospital in June of 1862.

Roster of Men
Assigned to the Fifteenth Georgia
Captured or Surrendered and Paroled at the End of the War
(Company Assignment not listed)

Athens, Georgia—May 8, 1865

Barnett, S.J.	Hawkins, A.	Roberts, J.B.
Bittman, J.F.	Hawkins, William	Rogers, William
Blackman, J.	Holmes, B.J.	Sane, W.
Blackman, W.S.	Hoyler, C.	Sawyer, J.
Blackwell, J.A.	Johnson, M.	Shoe, J.C.
Bowels, F.V.	Lester, T.	Williams, Y.
Bray, C.B.	Marther, E.	Williamson, T.J.
Bromand, J.J.	McArther, J.S.	Willis, J.H.
Chapman, W.A.	McConnel, J.P.	Windle, S.N.
Clark, G.N.	Mibbard, W.P.	Wood, J.
Cromich, P.T.	Moody, D.M.	Youngblood, C.J.
Evens, William M.	Price, B.G.	

Augusta, Georgia—May 2, 1865
Demay, James—SGT, Described as: Hair- Dark/ Complexion- Light/ Eyes- Blue/ Height—5' 10 1/2".
Quincy, Florida—1865
Sands, S.W.
Memphis, Tennessee—May 27, 1865
White, Alfred
Washington, D.C.—August 5, 1865
Massey, P.B.
Captured in 1862, Company assignment unknown
Smith, I.W.—LT, Captured and paroled in Warrenton, Va. on Sept. 29, 1862.
Herdin, W.R.—PVT, Captured and paroled by the 6th U.S. Army Corps, on Sept. 26, 1862.

Notes

Abbreviations

AP   Edward Porter Alexander Papers, Southern Historical Society Collection, Wilson Library, University of North Carolina, Chapel Hill, N.C.

BP   Henry Lewis Benning Papers, Southern Historical Society Collection, Wilson Library, University of North Carolina, Chapel Hill, N.C.

B&L   Johnson, Robert Underwood and Clarence Buel, eds. *Battles and Leaders of the Civil War.* 4 vols., New York, N.Y., 1887-1888.

CMH   General Clement A. Evans, Editor, *Confederate Military History, Georgia*, Vol. 6, Atlanta, Ga., 1899.

L&L   Helen D. Longstreet, *Lee & Longstreet at High Tide*, Gainesville, Ga., 1904.

LONG   James Longstreet, *From Manassas to Appomattox*, Philadelphia, Pa., 1896.

NA   Archives of the 15th Georgia Regiment (CSA), Record Group 109, National Archives, Washington, D.C.

OR   U.S. War Department. *The War of the Rebellion: A Compilation of the Official Records of the Union and Confederate Armies.* 127 Vols., index and atlas. Washington, D.C., 1880-1901.

Ware   Thomas L. Ware Diary, Southern Historical Collection, Wilson Library, University of North Carolina, Chapel Hill, N.C.

Wiley   Samuel H. Wiley Diary, Southern Historical Collection, Wilson Library, University of North Carolina, Chapel Hill, N.C.

SHSP   Jones, J. William, et al., eds. *Southern Historical Society Papers.* 52 Vols. 1876-1959. Reprint with 2-vol. index. New York, N.Y., 1977-1980.

Introduction

1. SHSP, Vol. 7, *Notes on the Final Campaign of April, 1865*, General H.L. Benning, pp. 193-195; LONG, page 606; Vol. XIV, Field, Charles, *The Campaign of 1864 and 1865*, 1886, pp. 560-61.

2. OR, Vol. XLVII, part 1, Report of General Gregg; OR, Vol. XLII, part 1; NA, Company Returns: Oct. 1864.

3. LONG, page 161; BP, papers concerning transfer of command from Toombs to Benning; CMH, pp. 190-191; SHSP, Vol. 16, *Notes by General H.L. Benning on the Battle of Sharpsburg*, pp. 393-94.

4. OR, Vol. XIX, part 1, pp. 888-93; LONG, pp. 256-59.

5. *Confederate Veteran*, "Longstreet's Forces at Chickamauga," Vol. 20, # 12,

Dec. 1912, Captain J.H. Martin, Hawkinsville, Georgia, page 564; LONG, page 448.
    6. B&L, Vol. IV, Law, E.M., "From the Wilderness to Cold Harbor," pp. 118-144; SHSP, Vol. XIV, Field, Charles, "The Campaign of 1864 and 1865," 1886, pp. 542-46; NA, Company Returns: April-May, 1864; LONG, page 568 and 570.
    7. OR, Vol. XLVII, part 1, Report of General Gregg.
    8. AP, Letter from Dudley DuBose to E.P. Alexander, dated Aug. 23, 1866; *Confederate Veteran*, Articles concerning the Battle of Ft. Gilmer: Vol. 12, No. 12 (1904), pp. 587-88; Vol. 13, No. 6, (1905), pp. 269-70.

Chapter 1

    1. CMH, pp. 9-17.; NA (15th Georgia Company Returns (Aug.-Sept. 1861) and Compiled Service Roster.
    2. NA, Microfilm Rolls 290-296 (Muster Rolls).
    3. BP, Letter to Edward Porter Alexander, 1866.
    4. Wiley, pp. 1-2 (July, 1861); LONG, pp. 81-112; Ware, Vol. 1, 1-10.
    5. Ware, Vol.1 (July-Aug. 1861), pp. 1-48; LONG, pp. 112-140.
    6. NA, Microfilm Rolls 290-296 (Aug.-Nov. 1861).
    7. Ware, Vol.1 (Dec. 1861-Jan. 1862), pp. 49-74; Rozier, John, Ed., *The Granite Farm Letters, The Civil War Correspondence of Edgeworth & Sallie Bird*, Athens & London, 1988, pp. 42-47, letters dated: Nov. 19 & 21, 1861. (The compiled war time letters contained in this book were extracted and edited from the Special Collections of the University of Georgia at Athens. They provide detailed insight of life back home in Georgia, and at the front, with the Army of Northern Virginia. Edgeworth Bird began the war in Company E, 15th Georgia, but he was transferred to the Brigade Q.M. Department after being severely wounded at the battle of 2nd. Manassas.)
    8. BP, Letter to Edward Porter Alexander, 1866; NA, Microfilm Rolls 290-296 (Aug.-Nov. 1861.)
    9. Southern Historical Society Collection, Stephens, Alexander Hamilton, Correspondence with his brother, Judge Linton Stephens, 15th Georgia Regiment, 1861, Wilson Library, Chapel Hill, N.C.; Ware (Dec. 1861-Jan. 1862), Vol.1, pp. 49-74; NA (Muster Rolls)
    10. NA (Company Returns: (Dec. 1861-Jan. 1862); Ware, Vol.1, pp. 60-61; Rozier, John, Ed.,*The Granite Farm Letters, The Civil War Correspondence of Edgeworth & Sallie Bird*, Athens & London, 1988, pp. 51-53, letter dated: Jan. 10, 1862; LONG, pp. 59-63.
    11. Ware, Vol.1, pp. 61-77; *The Granite Farm Letters, The Civil War Correspondence of Edgeworth & Sallie Bird*, Athens & London, 1988, pp. 57-58, letter dated: Jan. 12, 1862.
    12. NA (Company Returns & Muster Rolls, Jan. 1862.)

Chapter 2

1. Ware, Vol.2 (March 8 & 9, 1862), pp. 87 & 88; NA (Company Returns: Mar.–May 1862); LONG, page 64.
2. OR, Vol.II, Part 1, pp. 943-946; Vol.XI, part 3, pp. 444-445; Ware, Vol.2 (April 17-20, 1862), pp. 120-125.
3. Ware, Vol.2 (May 1862), pp. 135-163; B&L, Johnston, Joseph E., Gen.(CSA), "Manassas to Seven Pines," Vol.2, pp. 202-219; LONG, pp. 68-71.
4. Ware, Vol.2 (March-April 1862), pp. 81-134; SHSP, Vol. 1, Alexander, E.P., Gen. Chief of Artillery, Records of Longstreet's Corps, A.N.V., "The Seven Days Battle," Jan. to June 1876, pp. 61–65.
5. OR, Vol. XXIII; B&L, Longstreet, James, Lt.Gen. (CSA), "The Seven Days," Including Fraysers Farm, Vol.2, pp. 396-405; Fluker, W.T., papers, 1861-1865, Special Collections Library, Durham, N.C., pp. 4 & 5.
6. Fluker, W.T., papers, 1861-1865, Special Collections Library, Durham, N.C., pp. 4 & 5.
7. CMH, Battles of Garnetts Farm and Malvern Hill, pp. 172-176.
8. Ware, Vol.2 (June 1862), pp. 155-182; OR, Vol. XXIII, pp. 701–704.
9. NA (Company Returns: June–August 1862); OR, Vol. XII (part 2), pp. 586-589; Ware, Vol.3, pp. 183-187.
10. BP & AP (Various papers concerning events leading up to 2nd Manassas); Ware, Vol.3 (Aug. 12, 1862), page 211; LONG, page 158.
11. LONG, page 161; BP (Various papers concerning replacement of Toombs with Benning.)
12. NA (Company Returns, July 1862); CMH, 2nd. Manassas, page 182.
13. B&L, Longstreet, James, Lt. Gen. (CSA), "Our March Against Pope," Vol.2, pp. 512-526; LONG, pp. 174-175.
14. OR, Vol. XII, part 2, pp. 588-595; CMH, 2nd Manassas, p. 182.
15. OR, Vol. XII, part 2, page 600; LONG, page 189.
16. NA (Company Returns: July-August 1862); OR, Vol. XII, part 2.

Chapter 3

1. Ware, Vol. 3 (July 1-3), 1862, pp. 183-187; B&L, Longstreet, James, Lt. Gen. (CSA), "The Invasion of Maryland," Vol.2, pp. 662–665; LONG, pp. 201-205; NA (Company Returns, Sept. 1862).
2. OR, Vol. LI, part 1, pp. 160-168; LONG, pp. 239-254.
3. CMH, Engagement at Burnsides Bridge, pp. 190-191; BP, Memoirs of events at the Battle of Antietam. Benning noted that Gen. A.P. Hill has always received credit for saving the day at Burnsides Bridge, but he notes that it was his brigade with the aid of the 11th Georgia that performed this task, and they even rescued elements of Hill's units, as further stated in the report of the 17th Virginia Regiment in OR, Vol. XIX, part 1; SHSP, Vol.16, "Notes by Gen. H.L. Benning on the Battle of Sharpsburg," pp. 393 & 394.

4. OR, Vol. XIX, part 1, pp. 888-893.
5. LONG, pp. 256-259. (On page 257, Longstreet commends Benning and Toombs for their work at the Battle of Sharpsburg.)
6. NA (Company Returns: Aug.–Sept. 1862); B&L, "With Burnside at Antietam," D.L. Thompson, Co.G, 7th New York Volunteers, page 662.

Chapter 4

1. NA (Company Returns/ Muster Rolls: Aug.–Sept. 1862); CMH, Biographical sketch of Robert Toombs and Dudley M. DuBose, CSA, pp. 446-448 & 414-415; LONG, pp. 113 & 161.
2. B&L, Irwin, Richard B., Col. (U.S.), "The Removal of McClellan," pp.102-104.
3. NA (Company Returns: Oct.1862); Ware, Vol.4 (Oct. 30 & 31, 1862), pp. 1&2; CMH, pp. 194-195.
4. OR, Vol. XXI; B&L, Longstreet, James, Lt. Gen. (CSA), "Burnside at Fredericksburg," pp.70-85.
5. NA (Company Returns: Oct. 1862).
6. OR, Vol. XXI, p. 173; Ware, Vol.4 (Dec. 13, 1862), page 24.
7. Ware, Vol.4 (Dec. 16 & 17, 1862), pp. 27&28; CMH, p. 198.
8. Ibid. (Dec. 28, 1862), pp. 32&33; NA (Company Returns: Dec. 1862.)
9. Ibid. (Jan. 1-2, 1863), pp. 35&36; NA, Company Returns: Jan. 1863.
10. Ibid. (Jan. 2-25, 1863), pp. 36-44; NA, Company Returns: Jan. 1863.
11. Ibid. (Jan. 26– Feb. 15, 1863), pp. 45-54; NA, Company Returns: Feb. 1863.
12. Ibid. (Feb. 16– Mar. 11, 1863), pp. 54-65; NA, Company Returns: Mar. 1863).
13. *Confederate Veteran*, "Accurate Historic Records," by John H. Martin, pp. 114-115; Ware, Vol.4 (March 6, 1863), page 66.
14. CMH, Biographical sketch of Henry L. Benning,(CSA), pp. 395-396.
15. NA, Company Returns: Apr. 1863); Ware, Vol. 5 (April 13-16, 1863), pp. 69-72; LONG, pp. 323-324.
16. BP (Various papers concerning details of his brigade during the Suffolk Campaign); AP (Various papers concerning the 1st Corps events during the Suffolk Campaign); Ware, Vol.5 (May 3, 1863), pp. 85 & 86.
17. Ware, Vol. 5 (May 4, 1863), page 87.
18. Ibid., Vol.5 (May 10, 1863), page 89; OR, Vol. XXV, parts 1&2.
19. Ware, Vol. 5 (May 27, 1863), pp. 98 & 99.
20. OR, Vol. XXV, part 2; NA (Company Returns: May-June 1863);

Chapter 5

1. Ware, Vol. 5 (15-30 June, 1863),pp. 110-127; NA (Company Returns: June and July 1863); OR, Vol. XXVII, parts 1-3.

End Notes   *189*

    2. B&L, Hunt, Henry J., Brevet Maj. Gen. (U.S.), "The First Day at Gettysburg," Vol. 3, pp. 255-290.
    3. L&L, Chapter II, pp. 40-49; B&L, Law, E.W., Maj. Gen. (CSA), "The Struggle for Round Top"; OR, Vol. XXVII, part 2, pp. 392-395.
    4. OR, Vol. XXVII, part 2, pp. 420-426.
    5. Ware, Vol. 5 (30 June, 1863), page 128.6. OR, Vol. XXVII, part 2, pp. 420-426; Norton, Oliver Willcox, "The Attack and Defense of Little Round Top, Gettysburg, July 2, 1863," pp. 167-171 and 227-233, New York, 1913; BP, Benning mentioned in his memoirs that his units fought in the Devils Den and in the Plum Run Valley and that although they never received any special recognition for their efforts, his men had captured the only Federal artillery pieces north of the Potomac River. (It is also important to note that place names such as the "Devils Den" were unknown to the southern soldiers at the time of the engagement, they were simply a "high, wooded, rocky hill."
    6. OR, Vol. XXVII, part 2, pp. 421-424, Report number 460. (Col. D.M. DuBose, July 27, 1863.)
    7. OR, Series 3, Vol. IV, p. 817, entry 5; *Confederate Veteran*, "Account of How Some Flags Were Captured," Flanagan, W.A., Lincolnton, Georgia, page 250.
    8. CMH, Chapter IX, pp. 228-229.
    9. Ware, Vol. 5 (2 July 1863), pp. 128 & 129; B&L, Hunt, Henry, J., Brevet Maj. Gen. (U.S.), "The Second Day at Gettysburg," Vol. 3, pp. 290-312.
    10. B&L, Hunt, Henry J., Brevet Maj. Gen. (U.S.), "The Third Day at Gettysburg," Vol.3, pp. 369-384; OR, Vol. XXVII, parts 1-3, A compilation of the dead at Gettysburg is staggering. In the aftermath of the battle, there were approximately 60,000 men and an almost equal number of horses which littered the fields surrounding Gettysburg.
    11. Ibid.
    12. NA (Company Returns: July-August, 1863).

Chapter 6

    1. OR, Vol. XXX, pp. 260-261 and 517-520. L&L, pp.191-194; NA (Company Returns: Aug.–Sept. 1863).
    2. CMH, p.252, Hoods wound was originally believed to be mortal, however, he survived.
    3. L&L, p. 194; B&L, Vol. III, Hill, Daniel H., Gen. (CSA), "Chickamauga, The Great Battle in the West," pp. 638-661.
    4. OR, Vol. XXX, pp. 260-261 & 517-520.
    5. *Confederate Veteran*, "Longstreet's Forces at Chickamauga," Vol. 20, #12, Dec. 1912, Captain J.H. Martin, Hawkinsville, Georgia, page 564; LONG, page 448.
    6. AP, Notes concerning events leading up to Battle at Wauhatchie. (Later published as *Military Memoirs of a Confederate* by Edward Porter Alexander, pp.

467-473, New York, 1907, Reprinted by the De Capo Press, Inc., New York, 1993. Alexander was the Artillery Commander of the 1st Corps. His detailed memoirs contain valuable insight into why certain events occurred as they did, including his personal feelings about key members of the command and their actions.)
    7. OR, Vol. LXIV, pp. 89-90.
    8. NA (Company Returns: Sept.–Oct. 1863); AP (Notes concerning occurrences between the Battle of Chickamauga and Knoxville.)

Chapter 7

    1. NA (Company Returns: Oct.–Nov. 1863); B&L, Vol. III, Alexander, E.P., Gen. (CSA), "Longstreet at Knoxville," pp. 745–752.
    2. OR, Vol. XLIII, pp. 440-443, Vol. XXXI, part 2, Vol. XXXV, part 1; AP, Notes concerning events at Knoxville and East Tennessee Campaign, Vol. 42 and 51.
    3. L&L, pp. 195-204; CMH, Chapter 14, pp. 264-268; LONG, pp. 504, 511 and 521.
    4. NA (Company Returns: April 1864); CMH, pp. 395-396; LONG, pp. 512-516.
    5. L&L, pp. 205-208; CMH, Chapter 15, pp. 290-293; OR, Vol. XXXIII, XXXVI, parts 1&2.
    6. L&L, page 208.
    7. NA (Company Returns: March-April 1864)
    8. B&L, Vol. IV, Law, E.M., "From the Wilderness to Cold Harbor," pp. 118-144; SHSP, Vol. XIV, Field, Charles, "The Campaign of 1864 and 1865," 1886, pp. 542-546.
    9. NA (Company Returns: Apr.–May 1864); AP (Notes concerning the Battles of the Wilderness and Spotsylvania.)
    10. LONG, page 568.
    11. Ibid., page 570 (Longstreet survived his wound, but he was incapacitated for the next six months.); SHSP, Vol. XIV, Field, Charles, "The Campaign of 1864 and 1865," 1886, pp. 545.
    12. NA (Company Returns & Muster Rolls: May 1864).
    13. AP (Notes concerning the 1st. Corps data, commanded by Gen. R.H. Anderson, dates: June 12-19, 1864.)
    14. NA (Company Returns & Muster Rolls: June 1864).
    15. AP (Notes concerning the battle of Cold Harbor and the Union movements toward Richmond & Petersburg, Va.); SHSP, Vol. XIV, Field, Charles, "The Campaign of 1864 and 1865," 1886, pp. 548–549.

Chapter 8

    1. B&L, Vol. IV, Grant, U.S., Gen. (U.S.), "General Grant on the Siege of Petersburg," pp. 574-579; AP (Letter from Dudley M. DuBose to E.P. Alexander, dated Aug. 23, 1866 and 1st Corps data, June 12-19, 1864.)

2. NA (Company Returns: June-July 1864).
3. AP (Notes concerning life in the breastworks during the siege of 1864.); *The Granite Farm Letters, The Civil War Correspondence of Edgeworth & Sallie Bird*, Athens & London, 1988, page 176, letter dated: July 17, 1864; LONG, pp. 580-581.
4. OR, Vol. XLII,part 1, pp. 761, 764-765; SHSP, Vol. XIV, Field, Charles, "The Campaign of 1864 and 1865," 1886, pp. 552-554.
5. *Richmond Enquirer*, Article entitled "Field's Division," August 31, 1864.
6. OR, Vol. XL, parts 1-3, Vol. XLII, parts 1-3.
7. CMH, Chapter 27, p.353; NA (Company Returns: Sept. 1864).
8. OR, Vol. XL, pp. 474-478; AP (Notes concerning the Fall of 1864.) SHSP, Vol. XIV, Field, Charles, "The Campaign of 1864 and 1865," 1886, pp. 552-555.
9. SHSP, Articles appearing in: Vol. XIV, Field, Charles, "The Campaign of 1864 and 1865," 1886, page 556; Vol. II, McCabe, W. Gordon, "Defense of Petersburg," 1876, pp. 257-306.
10. AP, Notes concerning the Fall of 1864; NA (Company Returns: Sept. 1864.); *Confederate Veteran* Magazine, Articles appearing in: Vol. 13, No. 9, Moore, James B., "The Attack of Fort Harrison," 1905, pp. 418-420; Allen, Cornelious Tacitus, "Fight at Chaffin's Farm, Fort Harrison."
11. *Confederate Veteran* Magazine, Articles appearing in: Vol. 12, No.12, May, T.J., "The Fight at Fort Gilmer," 1904, pp. 587-588; Vol. 13, No. 6, Martin J.H., "The Assault on Fort Gilmer," 1905, pp. 269-270; Vol. 13, No. 9, Granberry, J.A.H., "That Ft. Gilmer Fight," 1904, pp. 587-588.
12. Ibid.
13. AP (Letter from Dudley M. DuBose to E.P. Alexander, dated Aug. 23, 1866 and 1st Corps data, Sept. 1864.)
14. AP, Notes concerning the Fall of 1864. Published in *Fighting for the Confederacy*, Chapel Hill & London, 1989, page 478, edited by Gary W. Gallagher.
15. OR, Vol. XLVII, part 1, Report of General Gregg.
16. OR, Vol. XLII, part 1; NA (Company Returns: Oct. 1864).

Chapter 9

1. SHSP, Field, Charles, Vol. XIV, "The Campaign of 1864 and 1865," page 558; AP (Notes concerning 1st Corps data, Oct. 1864.)
2. AP (Notes concerning the fall of 1864 and letter: D.M. DuBose to E.P. Alexander, dated 1866.)
3. NA (Company Returns: Sept.-Oct. 1864).
4. Ibid., Nov. 1864; B&L, Vol. IV, Sherman, William T., Gen. (U.S.), "The Grand Strategy of the Last Year of the War," pp. 247-259.
5. *The Granite Farm Letters, The Civil War Correspondence of Edgeworth & Sallie Bird*, Athens & London, 1988, pp. 194-196, letter dated: Sept. 3, 1864; Wiley, Letter to his parents, dated Nov. 26, 1864.
6. Wiley, letter to his parents, dated Nov. 26, 1864.

7. NA, Microfilm, copy 331, No. 60, Military service record of Dudley M. DuBose (CSA). (DuBose was appointed to the position of Brigadier-General in Nov. of 1864, but officially promoted in Jan. of 1865.)

8. NA (Company Returns: Jan.–Feb. 1865); B&L, Vol. IV, Slocum, Henry W., "Sherman's March From Savannah to Bentonville," pp. 681–700; *The Granite Farm Letters, The Civil War Correspondence of Edgeworth & Sallie Bird*, Athens & London, 1988, pp. 203-206, letter dated: Sept. 22, 1864.

9. SHSP, Vol. 7, "Notes on the Final Campaign of April, 1865," Gen. H.L. Benning, pp. 193-195; LONG, page 606; Vol. XIV, Field, Charles, "The Campaign of 1864 and 1865," 1886, pp. 560-561.

10. Booklet entitled, "Thirty-Six Hours Before Appomattox: April 6 and 7, 1865," Christopher M. Calkins, 1980, Chapter 3 (Farmville & Cumberland Church; B&L, Vol. IV, Porter, Horace, Gen. (U.S.), "Five Forks and the Pursuit of Lee," pp. 708-722; OR, Vol. XLVI, Chapter 58, "Lee's Report of the Appomattox Campaign," pp. 1264-1270.

11. L&L, pp. 209-210.

12. AP, Notes concerning The Fall of 1864 (Which include the retreat and surrender in 1865.); The Century Illustrated Monthly Magazine, Vol. LXIII, Alexander, E.P., "Lee at Appomattox," pp. 921-931.

13. NA (Compiled Military Service Records, Co.H, PVT James Fain.)

14. SHSP, Vol.XX, Perry, Herman H., Col. (CSA), "Account of the Surrender of the Confederate States of America, April 9, 1865," 1892.

15. NA (Company Returns: Jan.–Apr. 1865); OR Vol. XLVI, LVIII, pp. 1268-1269; SHSP, List—"Paroles of the Army of Northern Virginia," 15th Georgia Regiment, pp. 113-115. (*This list is inaccurate. See–Vol. XIV, Field, Charles, "The Campaign of 1864 and 1865," 1886, page 562.)

16. NA (Compiled Military Service Records, Co.H, SGT James C. Brown); Brown Family Genealogy Papers, Private Collection, Huntsville, Alabama, Mr. Harold E. Brown.

17. NA (Compiled Military Service Records, Co.G, Robert A. Ware)

18. *The Granite Farm Letters, The Civil War Correspondence of Edgeworth & Sallie Bird*, Athens & London, 1988, pp. 218-220, letter dated: Nov. 30, 1864, See editors note #1.

19. CMH, Biographical data of Robert Toombs (CSA), pp. 446-448.

20. CMH, Biographical data of Dudley M. DuBose (CSA), pp. 414–415; NA, Military Service Record of Dudley M. DuBose (CSA).

21. CMH, Biographical data of Henry L. Benning (CSA), pp. 395–396; BP, Personal letters of Henry L. Benning; Fort Benning, Infantry Museum, biographical data of General Benning and the military post, Fort Benning.

BIBLIOGRAPHY

Allen, Cornelious Tacitus. "Fight at Chaffin's Farm, Fort Harrison," *Confederate Veteran*, Vol. XIII, No.9 (1905), p.418.

Alexander, Edward Porter, Papers, Southern Historical Society Collection, Wilson Library, University of North Carolina, Chapel Hill.

Alexander, Edward Porter, *Military Memoirs of a Confederate*. Bloomington: Indiana University Press, 1962. Reprint Edition, New York, New York, DeCapo Press, 1993.

Benning, Henry Lewis, Papers, Southern Historical Society Collection, Wilson Library, University of North Carolina, Chapel Hill.

Bowman, John S., Executive Editor, *The Civil War Almanac*. New York, New York, World Almanac Publications, 1983.

Evans, General Clement A., Editor, *Confederate Military History*, Georgia, Vol. 6, Atlanta, Ga, 1899.

Field, Charles W. "The Campaign of 1864 and 1865: The Narrative of Major General C.W. Field," *Southern Historical Society Papers*. Vol. XIV (1886), pp. 542-563.

Flanigan, W.A. "That Fight at Fort Gilmer," *Confederate Veteran*, Vol. XIII, No.3 (1905), p. 123.

Freeman, Douglas Southall. *Lee's Lieutenants: A Study in Command*. New York: Charles Scribner's Sons, 1944.

Gallagher, Gary W., ed. *Fighting for the Confederacy*, The Personal Recollections of General Edward Porter Alexander. Chapel Hill: The University of North Carolina Press.

Granberry, J.A.H. "That Fort Gilmer Fight," *Confederate Veteran*. (1904), pp. 587-588.

Hood, John Bell, General. *Advance and Retreat*, Philadelphia, Pennsylvania, Burk & M'Fetridge Press, 1880.

Howard, James McHenry. "Closing Scenes of the War About Richmond," *Southern Historical Society Papers*. Vol. XXXI (1903), pp. 129-145.

Johnson, Robert Underwood and Clarence Buel, eds. *Battles and Leaders of the Civil War*. 4 vols., New York, 1887-1888.

Johnston, Charles. "Attack on Fort Gilmer, September 29th, 1864," *Southern Historical Society Papers*. Vol. 1 (1876), pp. 438-442.

Longstreet, Helen D. *Lee & Longstreet at High Tide*, Gainsville, Ga, 1904.

Martin, J.H. "The Assault on Fort Gilmer," Confederate Veteran, Vol. XIII, No. 6 (1905), pp. 269-270.

May, T.J. "The Fight at Fort Gilmer," Confederate Veteran, Vol. XII, No. 12 (1904), pp. 587-588.

Moore, James B. "The Attack of Fort Harrison," *Confederate Veteran*, Vol. XIII, No. 9 (1905), pp. 418-420.

Norton, Oliver Wilcox. *The Attack and Defense of Little Round Top, Gettysburg, Jul 2, 1863*, New York, The Neale Publishing Company, 1913.

Perry, Herman H. "Assault on Fort Gilmer," *Confederate Veteran*, Vol. XIII, No. 9 (1905), pp. 413-415.

Perry, Herman H., Colonel (CSA). "Account of the Surrender of the Confederate States of America, April 9, 1865, *Southern Historical Society Papers*, Vol. XX, 1892.

Pickens, J.D. "Fort Harrison," *Confederate Veteran*, Vol. XXI, No. 10 (1913), p. 484.

Polley, J.B. *Hood's Texas Brigade*, Reprint Edition, Dayton, Ohio, Morningside Bookshop, 1976.

Regimental Records & Muster Rolls, 15th Georgia (CSA), Record Group 109, National Archives, Washington, D.C.

Richmond Enquirer. Richmond, Virginia, 1861-1865.

Sommers, Richard J. *Richmond Redeemed*, Garden City, New York, Doubleday & Company, 1981.

U.S. War Department. *The War of the Rebellion: A Compilation of the Official Records of the Union and Confederate Armies*. 127 Vols., index and atlas. Washington, D.C., 1880-1901.

Ware, Thomas L. Unpublished diary, Southern Historical Collection, Wilson Library, University of North Carolina, Chapel Hill.

Wiley, Samuel H. Unpublished diary, Southern Historical Collection, Wilson Library, University of North Carolina, Chapel Hill.

Winder, J.R. "Judge Martin's Report Approved," *Confederate Veteran*, Vol. XIII, No. 9 (1905), p. 417.

INDEX

Abbie, H., 115
Adams, Ausburn G., 115
Adams, G., 115
Adams, J.D. (Cpl.), 113
Adams, James, 115
Adams, James A., 115
Adams, John D., 115
Adams, Jonathan, 110, 115
Adams, Richard C., 115
Adams, Rueben M., 115
Adams, William C., 115
Adams, William H., 115
Adderhold, A. C., 116
Adderhold, J.H.P., 116
Adoms, J.A., 116
Aiken's Landing, 80
Alabama Brigade, 40
Alabama regiments, 78, 79
Albea, Cyrus P., 116
Albea, Thomas H., 116
Albea, William H., 116
Alexander, Dunston, 112
Alexander, Dunston B., 116
Alexander, Gaines T., 116
Alexander, George W., 116
Alexander, Guilford, 110
Alexander, Guilford L., 116
Alexander, Henry C., 116
Alexander, J.H., 116
Alexander, James H., 116
Alexandria pike, 41
Alford, James T., 116
Alford, Owen, 116
Alfriend, Alfred H., 116
Alfriend, Benjamin A., 116
Alfriend, Dudley, 111
Alfriend, E. Dudley, 116
Alfriend, E.W., 2, 117
Alfriend, J.A., 117
Algood, Elijah, 117
Allen, Elisha, 117
Almand, Thomas F., 117
Almand, William U., 117

Almond, George M., 117
Amelia Court House, 91
Anderson, George T. (Gen.), 74, 78, 87
Anderson, John, 110
Anderson, John L., 117
Anderson, William, 113
Anderson, William G., 117
Anderson, Zacharia W., 117
Anderson's Brigade, 17, 42
Anderson's Corps, 40, 42, 75
Andrews, Andrew J., 117
Andrews, Michael L., 117
Anesloy, L.O., 117
Antietam Creek, 21, 22, 25, 27
Applebee, J.H., 117
Appomattox Courthouse, Virginia, 92, 94, 109
Appomattox River, 91
Ariail, William J., 117
Armor, Claiborne R., 117
Armor, James N., 117
Armor, Newton D., 117
Army of Northern Virginia, 11, 16, 21, 31, 32, 34, 39, 40, 41, 43, 49, 50, 55, 71, 72, 74, 75, 77, 91, 92, 93, 94
Army of Tennessee, 55, 56, 61, 62
Army of the Cumberland, 55, 56
Army of the Potomac, 9, 21, 32, 37, 39, 49
Army of the Potomac C.S.A., 3, 9
Arnold, Juluis B.D., 117
Asbell, James E., 118
Asbell, William P.F., 118
Ash, John S., 118
Ashby's Gap, 41
Ashmore, Thomas L., 118
Ashworth, Robert W., 118
Askea, Martial, 118
Askew, F.J., 118
Athens, Georgia, 38, 183
Atlanta, 1, 2, 56, 80, 88, 94
Augusta, 1, 56, 89, 183
Aycock, Drury J., 118
Ayers, Asa, 110

Ayers, Asa C., 118
Ayers, John R., 118
Ayers, Obediah W., 118
Ayers, Thomas J., 118
Ayers, William R., 118
Ayres, John W., 118

Babb, J.B., 118
Bagwell, William A., 118
Bailey, Fernando O., 112, 118
Bailey, J.A., 118
Bailey, Pascal, 119
Bailey, Rueben, J., 119
Bailey, Samuel, 119
Bailey, W.J., 119
Bailey, William, 113, 119
Balchin, Thomas, 119
Barger, W.D., 119
Barnes, J.J., 119
Barnes, James K., 119
Barnes, John T., 119
Barnes, W.H., 119
Barnes, W.W., 119
Barnett, S.J., 183
Barr, George I., 119
Bass, A. Sidney, 119
Bass, Benjamin S., 119
Bass, Frederick S. (Col.), 79, 80
Bass, G.J., 119
Bass, George E., 119
Bass, J.E., 119
Bass, Sidney (Sgt.), 113
Bass, Simeon (Cpl.), 113
Bass, Simeon D., 119
Bates, E., 120
Battery Harrison, 81
Battle, C. F., 120
Battle, G.W. (Cpl.), 111
Battle, George W., 120
Battle, Thomas A., 120
Battle, William J., 120
Battle of Antietam, 21-27
Battle of Cedar Mountain, 16
Battle of Chancellorsville, 40
Battle of Chickamauga, 56, 65
Battle of Cold Harbor, 76
Battle of Five Forks, 91
Battle of Fredericksburg, 33
Battle of Garnett's Farm, 11
Battle of Gettysburg, 51, 55, 93
Battle of Sayler's Creek, 94

Battle of Seven Pines, 11
Battle of Seven Pines/Fair Oaks, 11, 88
Battle of Sharpsburg, 21-27, 32
Battle of Spotsylvania Court House, 75
Battle of the Wilderness, 72, 74, 88
Baxter, Richard B., 120
Beall, Robert A., 120
Beard, Henry W., 120
Beauregard, P.G.T. (Gen.), 2, 77
Bell, George S., 120
Bell, Harmon L., 120
Bell, J.B., 120
Bellamy, John, 120
Bellamy, Thomas J., 120
Bellamy, William P., 120
Beman, Thomas S., 120
Benning, Henry L. (Brig. Gen.), 1, 17, 19, 22, 27, 33, 38, 39, 40, 45, 47, 56, 61, 62, 65, 71, 74, 88, 94
Benning, Mary, 94
Benning's Georgia Brigade, 17, 32, 33, 39, 41, 44, 50, 56, 62, 65, 74, 79, 80, 82, 84, 87, 88, 91, 92
Bentley, Charles M., 120
Bermuda Hundred, 77
Berry, George, 120
Bethune, Joseph D., 58
Big Round Top, 44
Biggs, Thomas D., 120
Binns, Enoch G., 120
Binns, George S., 120
Binns, Isaiah M., 121
Binns, Joseph A., 121
Binns, Mitchell, 109, 121
Binns, William Lee, 121
Bins, J.C., 121
Bird, William Edgeworth (Maj.), 4, 88, 93, 121
Birney, William (Gen.), 82, 83
Birney's troops, 80, 81
Bittman, J.F., 183
Black, J.M., 121
Black, Thomas J., 121
Blackman, J., 183
Blackman, W.S., 183
Blackwell, Dunston R., 121
Blackwell, J.A., 183
Blackwell, L. L., 121
Blankman, Dr., 36
Bledsoe, John N., 121
Bloody Angle, 75

Index

Blue Ridge Mountains, 17, 43
Boggs, Joseph R., 121
Bohler, John T., 121
Bolton, Miles J., 121
Bolton, William M., 121
Bolton, William T., 121
Bond, Francis K., 121
Bond, J.A., 121
Bond, John B., 121
Bond, Martin R., 113, 122
Bond, Willis H., 113, 122
Bonds, Joseph M., 122
Bonds, William, 122
Bonner, John F., 122
Booth, James C., 122
Boren, Clark, 122
Boston, 94
Bourne, Powhatan B., 122
Bowels, F.V., 183
Bowers, Noah W., 122
Bowie, J.J., 122
Boyer, Americus V., 111, 122
Boyer, Jasper J., 122
Bradford, Daniel W., 110, 122
Bradford, Junius B., 122
Bradford, Nathaniel M., 122
Bradley, George M., 122
Brady, James R., 122
Bragg, Braxton (Gen.), 55, 56, 61, 62, 69, 70
Brake, Charles I., 111, 122
Brake, Daniel C., 123
Brake, John W., 123
Branklin, J., 123
Brantley, James A. (Cpl.), 113, 123
Brantley, Lewis, 114, 123
Bratton, John (Col.), 62, 63, 64, 79
Brawner, J. K., 123
Brawner, William M., 123
Brawner, William T., 123
Bray, C.B., 183
Breedlove, Jesse M., 123
Brewer, John M., 123
Bridges, Jeremiah, 123
Briggs, John W., 123
Brinn, Nathan, 123
Bristol, Tennessee, 3, 70, 71
Brock, Francis J., 123
Brock road, 74
Bromand, J.J., 183
Brooke, C.C., 123

Brooke, Joseph G., 123
Broom, Cicero, 123
Broom, Marion, 123
Broom, Nathaniel, 124
Broom, W.C., 124
Brown, A. Ruffin, 93, 124
Brown, Andrew F., 124
Brown, C., 124
Brown, Clement C., 124
Brown, George T., 110, 124
Brown, James, 111
Brown, James Clayburn (Sgt.), 93, 124
Brown, James M., 124
Brown, John M., 124
Brown, L. M., 124
Brown, Mary Matilda, 93
Brown, Rebecca, 93
Brown, S.C., 124
Brown, Samuel, 93
Brown, Samuel F., 124
Brown, Solomon, 113
Brown, Solomon W., 124
Brown, T. J., 124
Brown, Willis H., 124
Bruce, James A., 124
Bryan, Ephraim O., 124
Bryant, Joseph, 125
Buckner, Simon Bolivar (Gen.), 56
Buffington, J.W., 125
Buffington, John H., 125
Buffington, Reuben T., 125
Buffington, William R., 125
Buffington, Willis W., 125
Bull Run, 19
Bull Run Mountains, 17
Bullard, G. F., 125
Bullard, J.B., 125
Bullard, Jeptha R., 125
Bullard, William H., 110, 125
Bunch, Edward A., 125
Bunch, Gideon B., 109, 125
Bunch, William A., 109, 125
Burch, James J. (Capt.), 112, 125
Burch, John C. (Capt.), 2, 12, 125
Burdett, George M., 125
Burnley, James T., 111, 126
Burnley, John D., 126
Burnley, R. Henry, 126
Burns, E.G., 126
Burnside, Ambrose (Gen.), 22, 24, 27, 32, 39, 61, 69, 70, 74

Burnside's Bridge, 21-27
Burnside's Corps, 22, 24, 27, 61
Burroughs, Fred W.A., 126
Burroughs, John, 109
Burroughs, John E., 126
Burton, Joseph J., 126
Bush, W.G., 126
Bush, William F., 126
Butler, Benjamin (Gen.), 77
Butler, E. A., 126
Butler, Martin T., 126
Butler, Robert, 126
Butler, William P., 126
Butler, William S., 126
Butts, Jesse G. (Sgt.), 111, 126
Butts, Winfield S., 126
Byce, William A., 126
Byrom, Samuel D., 126

Cade, Drury B. (Capt.), 2, 126
Cade, J.S., 110, 126
Cade, Robert B., 126
Cade, Samuel R., 110, 127
Cade, William B., 127
Callaway, John B., 127
Callaway, John S.1, 127
Callaway, Joseph, 127
Camp, Sims S., 127
Camp Georgia, 5
Camp Pine Creek, 4
Camp Walker, 4
Campbell, James C., 127
Cane, Levi, 127
Carey, Thomas, 110, 127
Carpenter, Thomas J., 127
Carroll, A.J., 127
Carroll, Clement, 127
Carroll, G.W., 113, 127
Carroll, Larkin, 127
Carroll, Nelson, 127
Carroll, Thomas, 127
Carson, Alfred P. (Sgt.), 110, 127
Carson, Augustus, 110
Carson, Augustus L., 127
Carson, James M., 127
Carson, Robert H., 127
Carter, Charles T., 127
Carter, Francis, 110
Carter, Francis M., 128
Carter, James M., 128
Cartledge, James J. (Sgt.), 112, 128

Cartledge, Walton, 128
Cartledge, William H., 128
Cary, Thomas, 110, 128
Cashtown, PA, 49
Catharpin Road, 72
Cato, James J., 128
Catoosa Station, 56
Cauley, Clem, 128
Cauley, Henry, 128
Cauley, Luke, 128
Cauthern, John G., 128
Caver, Henry A., 112, 128
Caver, James H., 128
Cawthorn, Thomas J. (Sgt.), 110, 128
Cemetery Ridge, 44
Centreville, 3, 17, 19
Chaffin's Farm, 78, 80
Chafin, Thomas P., 128
Chambersburg, Pennsylvania, 43
Chancellorsville, Virginia, 51, 72
Chandler, Howard M., 128
Chapman, James S. (Sgt.), 111, 128
Chapman, W.A., 183
Chappelear, Henry S. (Lt.), 110, 128
Charlottesville, Virginia, 3, 71
Charlton, William W. (Maj.), 58
Chattanooga, 2, 55, 56, 61, 65, 69
Chattanooga road, 57
Chattanooga Valley, 61
Cheek, James M., 129
Cheek, John, 129
Cheek, Patterson F., 129
Cheek, Welborn D., 129
Chickamauga, 5, 56, 61, 62
Childs, Hugh, 110
Childs, Hugh M., 129
Chinn Ridge, 17
Chowan County, 39
City Point, Virginia, 78, 93
Civil War, 1
Clark, Benjamin J., 111, 129
Clark, G.N., 183
Clark, George W., 129
Clark, J. R., 129
Clark, Larkin L., 129
Clark, Urbin W., 129
Clark, W.H. (Sgt.), 111
Clark, W.J., 129
Clark, W.T. (Cpl.), 110
Clark, Warren H., 129
Clark, William B., 129

Index

Clark, William T., 129
Clary, James M., 112, 129
Clary, Sebron Jonah, 129
Clary, Thomas, L. 112, 129
Clemons, William G., 111, 130
Cleveland, Daniel E., 130
Cleveland, Reuben (Sgt.), 113, 130
Cleveland, William L., 130
Cobb, Howell (Gen.), 33
Coffee, C., 130
Cohen, Aaron, 109, 130
Cohron, George W., 109, 130
Coker, Burgess P., 130
Cold Harbor, 5, 75
Coleman, James M., 111, 130
Collins, John, 130
Collins, Richard, 130
Colson, S. D., 130
Columbus, Georgia, 94
Colvin, Leviticus L., 112, 130
Colvin, Preston L., 130
Colwell, A.V., 110, 130
Colwell, Edmond, 110, 130
Colwell, Henry, 110, 130
Company A, 1
Company B, 1, 12, 13, 19, 110
Company C, 1, 65, 110
Company Commanders, 2
Company D, 1, 11, 111
Company E, 1, 2, 4, 10, 111
Company F, 1, 12, 112
Company G, 1, 2, 12, 19, 20, 81, 112
Company G, First Pennsylvania Rifles, 49
Company H, 1, 36, 65, 78, 92, 93, 113
Company I, 1
Company K, 1, 19, 20, 113
Cone, Jonathan B. (Pvt.), 10, 130
Confederate artillery, 87
Confederate cemeteries, 93
Confederate Cavalry, 12
Confederate defenses, 76, 78, 82, 88
Connel, E.B., 130
Connell, Daniel (Capt.), 113, 131
Conwir, J., 131
Cook, Eldridge W. (Cpl.), 111, 131
Cook, G., 131
Cooper, Joseph P., 131
Cornelius Creek, 88
Cosby, David C., 110, 131
Cosby, John H., 110, 131
Cosby, Napoleon Bonaparte, 110, 131

Coward, A. (Col., commander 5th South Carolina), 79
Craft, David L., 131
Craft, E.L., 131
Craft, Jasper E., 131
Craft, John F., 131
Craft, William A., 112, 131
Craft, William M., 131
Crawford, Benjamin S., 112, 131
Crawford, George H., 131
Crawford, J.J., 114, 132
Crawford, J.M., 112
Crawford, Jabez M., 131
Crawford, James C., 131
Crawford, James J., 131
Crawford, Jerry, 112, 132
Crawford, John, 132
Crawford, Thomas W., 132
Cromer, Thomas N., 132
Cromich, P.T., 183
Crow, James A., 132
Crow, P.M., 132
Crowley, John, 132
Crymes, Thomas, 132
Cullars, James M., 132
Cullars, Robert T., 132
Cully, J., 132
Culpeper Court House, 40
Culps Hill, 44
Culver, Benjamin C., 132
Culver, E.H., 132
Culver, German P., 132
Culver, Henry H., 132
Culver, John L., 132
Culver, Thomas H., 132
Culvers, 90
Cumberland Church, 92
Cumming, John B. (Col.), 22, 24, 25, 26
Cummings, J. LaFayette, 133
Cummings, John G., 132
Cummings, W.F.H., 133
Curren, Andrew E., 133
Curry, William E., 133
Custer, 92

Dacres, James, Sr., 111, 133
Dallas, Thomas N., 133
Dalton, Georgia, 2, 70
Daniel, James W., 133
Daniel, John B., 133
Daniel, William J., 133

Darbytown, 88
Darbytown road, 78, 79, 87, 88
David, Peter, 133
Davidson, James, 133
Davis, James O., 110, 133
Davis, James W., 133
Davis, Jefferson, 2, 5, 11, 31, 37, 55, 61, 69
Davis, John W., 133
Davis, M.L., 133
Davis, Mark, 133
Davis, William H., 133
Dawson, Adam P., 133
Deadwyler, Joseph L. (Sgt.), 113, 133
Deas, Joseph F. (Sgt.), 113, 134
Deas, William T., 134
Deep Bottom, 78, 79
Deerburg, Charles, 134
DeFoor, James, 134
DeFoor, Joseph, 134
Demay, James, 183
Denard, William B., 134
Dendry, T., 134
Denmand, James L., 134
Dennard, John A., 134
Dennard, Thomas G., 134
Dent, Anderson., 134
Dent, John T., 134
Depuy, John J., 109, 134
Devil's Den, 41, 50
Dewey, W.S., 134
Dick, R. (Cpl., USCT), 83
Dickens, Robert L., 134
Dickerson, Charles Y., 134
Dickerson, James E., 134
Dickson, David W., 134
Dickson, James C., 114, 135
Dickson, James L., 135
Dickson, John, 114
Dickson, John C., 135
Dickson, Joseph C., 135
Dickson, Quincy L., 135
Dickson, William, 114
Dickson, William S. Jr., 135
Dickson, William S. Sr., 135
Dorsey, Lemuel E., 135
Dorsey, Samuel J., 135
Downer, William J., 135
Doyle, William T., 110, 135
DuBose, Dudley M. (Col.), 1, 31, 34, 36, 37, 39, 45, 49, 55, 58, 71, 74, 78, 79, 80, 82, 83, 90, 91, 94, 135

Dudley, George W., 135
Dudley, J.M., 114, 135
Duggan, Ivy W., 135
Dunaway, John L., 135
Dunaway, John M., 135
Dunn, Augustus F., 136
Dunn, E.J., 136
Dunn, George P., 136
Duran, B.F., 136
Durard, A.M., 136
Dye, B. F., 136
Dye, James W., 136
Dye, Joseph R., 110, 136

East Tennessee, 3, 70, 72
Eaves, James A., 136
Eaves, Jesse, 136
Eaves, Joel, 136
Eberhart, J.G., 136
Edwards, 34, 35
Edwards, Elisha W., 136
Edwards, Emory P., 34, 136
Edwards, James A., 136
Edwards, William S., 110, 136
Eighth Georgia Regiment, 13
Eighth USCT Regiment, 83
Elbert County, 1
Eleventh Georgia, 25
Elliott, Benjamin, 112, 136
Elliott, William W., 136
Ely's Ford, 72
Emmitsburg Road, 44
English, W.J., 136
Ensign, W.P., 136
Erlich, Benjamin, 137
Ertzburger, Robert D., 137
Eskea, Samuel, 137
Ester, T.N., 137
Estes, J.W., 137
Eubank, Captain, CSA Artillery, 23
Eubanks, Charles H., 137
Eubanks, James, 137
Evans, E.A., 137
Evans, Humphrey, 112, 137
Evans, J., 137
Evans, James J., 137
Evans, John D., 137
Evans, Russell J., 137
Evens, William M., 183
Ewell, Richard S. (Gen.), 82

Index 201

Fain, James (Pvt.), 92, 137
Fair, Larkin, 137
Fairfax Courthouse, Virginia, 4
Farmer, John J., 137
Farmer, Sylvester J. (Capt.), 2, 137
Farmville, Virginia, 5, 91, 92
Fauling, William N., 137
Faulk, Jared, 137
Faulkner, Isaac N., 113, 137
Favors, William W., 138
Ferrell, John D., 138
Field, Charles (Gen.), 71, 74, 87
Field's Division, 74, 75, 78, 80, 84, 87, 92
Fifth Corps, 75
Fifth South Carolina regiment, 79
First Corps, 87, 92
First Texas Regiment, 46
First Volunteer Regiment, 1
Fisher, H.L., 138
Fisher, Thomas, 138
Flanagan, William, 112
Flangue, John, 110, 138
Flanigan, William A., 138
Fleming, Absalom F., 138
Fleming, Leonard, 138
Fleming, Thomas, 138
Florence, LaFayette, 138
Florence, Peyton M., 112, 138
Fluker, R.H. (Cpl.), 111
Fluker, Robert H., 138
Fluker, William T. (Pvt.), 11, 111, 138
Flury, C.H., 114, 138
Flury, John Joseph (Cpl.), 113, 138
Flury, William A., 114, 138
Flynt, Henry H., 138
Flynt, James W., 138
Flynt, Samuel J. (Capt.), 111, 138
Forbes, H.W. (Capt.), 89, 90, 139
Ford, Jordan R., 139
Ford, Joshua A., 139
Fort Benning, 94
Fort Field, 82
Fort Gilmer, 5, 83, 84
Fort Gregg, 82,
Fort Harrison, 80, 81, 82, 84, 87
Fort Jackson, 1
Fort Johnson, 82, 83, 87
Fort Sanders, 69
Fort Sumter, 1
Fort Warren, 94
Fortson, Abner T., 139

Fortson, Blanton B., 139
Fortson, DeLancey A., 113, 139
Fortson, Elijah R., 113, 139
Fortson, John B., 113, 139
Fortson, John H., 139
Fortson, Moses E., 113, 139
Fortson, William, 139
Fortson, William (Sgt.), 113
Fortson, William E., 139
Fortson, William W., 139
Fowler, S.W., 139
Fraley, LaFayette I., 139
Franklin, 39
Franklin, Abraham, 139
Franklin, Henry, 139
Franklin, Manuel, 110, 140
Franklin, Samuel, 140
Franklin County, 1
Franks, Josephus, 140
Franks, William P., 140
Frazier's Farm, 13, 16
Frederick, Maryland, 21
Fredericksburg, 5, 32, 34
Freeman, Edward D., 109, 140
Freeman, William M., 140
Fuller, Milton, 140
Furgerson, Wilkes W., 112, 140

Gable, H.F., 140
Gaines, D., 140
Gaines, Francis, 113, 140
Gaines, James A., 140
Gaines, James A. Jr., 140
Gaines, Lindsay A., 140
Gaines, Livingston J. (Cpl.), 113, 140
Gaines, Lt Lindsay, 112
Gaines, Peter C., 113, 140
Gaines, Thomas S., 140
Gaines Mill, 12
Galloway, Richard B., 112, 140
Garner, Thomas J., 141
Garnett, James, 11, 12
Garnett's Farm, 5
Garret, James V., 141
Garrett, A.J., 141
Garrett, Herbert E., 141
Gary's cavalry, 80, 82, 83, 84, 87
Gates County, 39
Gaulding, William D., 141
Germanna Ford, 72
Getty, George W. (Gen.), 72

Gettysburg, 5, 43, 44, 45, 49, 50, 55, 61
Ghann, Thomas A., 111, 141
Gheesling, Virgil A., 111, 141
Gibson, George W., 141
Gilbert, M.S., 141
Gill, Isaac M., 109, 141
Gill, Johnathan, 109
Gill, Micajah A., 109, 141
Gill, William, 141
Gillespie, J.M., 141
Ginn, James H., 141
Ginn, Middleton G., 141
Gladden, S.G.W., 141
Glaze, Anderson, 141
Glaze, Houston, 141
Gloer, Isaac D., 141
Gloer, John S., 142
Golaspy, James W., 142
Goochland Artillery, 81
Goolsby, Gilbert, 142
Gordon, Georgia, 93
Gordonsville, Virginia, 16
Gothard, Henry C., 142
Graham, William P., 142
Granite Farm, 93
Grant, Ulysses (Gen.), 62, 69, 70, 72, 74, 75, 76, 77, 78, 80, 84, 87, 91, 92
Graves, George W., 142
Gray, Robert, 142
Green, John W., 109, 142
Green, William H., 142
Greencastle, Pennsylvania, 42, 43
Greenville, Tenn., 3
Greenway, William M., 142
Gregg, John (Gen.), 25, 80, 82, 84, 88
Gregg's Texas Brigade, 79
Gresham, J. Hulbert W., 142
Gresham, J.H.W., 112
Griffin, G.W., 142
Griffin, William N., 142
Grimes, Thomas, 142
Groveton, Virginia, 17
Grubbs, G.W., 142
Grubbs, W.M., 113, 142
Gruson, William E., 142
Gudey, W.T., 142
Guerrant, Lieutenant (CSA, "Goochland Artillery"), 81
Guest, J.P., 142
Guest, Spencer, 143
Guinea Station, Virginia, 34

Gullatt, Absalom, 143
Gullatt, Henderson, 143
Gullatt, Peter, 143
Gulley, J.W., 143
Gulley, James, 112
Gully, James M., 143

Hackney, Jesse M., 11, 143
Hadden, Chalmers C., 113, 143
Hagenbaugh, J., 143
Hagerstown, Maryland, 21, 22
Hagerstown Turnpike, 22
Hailey, George W., 143
Hailey, James, 143
Hall, G.W.,
Hall, W.M., 143
Hall, W.W., 143
Hall, William S., 143
Hallow, J., 143
Hamby, James W., 143
Hamby, John P., 143
Hamby, Levi T., 143
Hamby, Terrel T., 143
Hamilton, Charles, 144
Hammock, G.R., 144
Hammock, James M., 144
Hammock, William H., 144
Hammond, William H., 144
Hamser, D.H., 144
Hancock, Winfield (Gen.), 72, 74
Hancock, M.A., 144
Hancock County, 1, 93
Hanover Junction, 5, 75
Harbin, John M., 144
Harbor, Thomas H., 144
Harden, Robert T., 112, 144
Hardwick, William H., 144
Hardy, A.H., 34
Hardy, Aaron H. (Cpl.), 112, 144
Harland, J., 144
Harmon, F. C., 144
Harper, B., 144
Harper, Wilkins J., 144
Harper, William M., 144
Harper's Ferry, 21
Harris, A.F., 144
Harris, J.D., 144
Harris, J.H., 144
Harris, Jeptha A., 144
Harris, Samuel P., 145
Harris, T.W., 111, 145

Index

Harris, W.P., 145
Harris, William G., 145
Harrisburg, PA, 43
Harrison, E.A., 145
Harrison, John T., 145
Harrison, Montgomery, 145
Harrison, Thomas J., 145
Harrison, Virgil M., 145
Harrison's Landing, 16
Hart County, 1, 93
Hatsfield, A.J., 145
Haverell, Allen, 145
Hawes, Thomas D., 112, 145
Hawkins, A., 183
Hawkins, James F., 145
Hawkins, William, 183
Haygood, Atticus Green, 1, 145
Haynie, Robert B., 145
Haynie, Smith S., 145
Heard, George E., 145
Heard, Mark L., 110, 145
Heard, Robert M., 145
Hearnsberger, 36, 49
Hearnsberger, Adam, 145
Hearnsberger, John T., 146
Hearnsberger, Stephen S. Z. (Capt.), 12, 13, 146
Heckman, Charles (Gen.), 82
Hembree, Anthony D., 146
Hembree, James A., 110, 146
Henderson, James H., 146
Hendley, John W., 146
Hendrick, Charles N., 111, 146
Hendricks, Isaiah, 146
Hendricks, W. W., 146
Henley, James E., 146
Henry Hill, 17, 19
Herdin, W.R., 183
Herringdine, Joseph R. (Sgt.), 111, 146
Hester, Thomas J., 146
Higginbotham, Eli, 113, 146
Higginbotham, Nelson R., 146
Higginbotham, Willis H., 146
Higgins, C. James A., 146
Higgonbotham, Nelson, 112
High Bridge, 91
Hill, A.P. (General), 25, 43, 72
Hill, Kendrick, 110, 147
Hill, Wiley T., 147
Hill's Corps, 74
Hines, Joseph S., 147
Hinton, Jesse H., 147
Hinton, John T., 147
Hinton, Noah, 109, 147
Hodge, Richard, 147
Hoke, Robert F. (Gen.), 87
Hoke's Division, 84
Holbrook, Jesse T. (Sgt.), 110, 147
Holbrook, Nathan J., 110, 147
Holbrook, P.C., 110, 147
Holbrook, William Y., 147
Holland, B.F., 147
Holland, John T., 147
Hollingsworth, Warren, 113
Hollingsworth, Warren T., 147
Hollingsworth, William J., 147
Holmes, William R. (Lt. Col., commander GA 2nd Regiment), 25
Holmes, B.J., 183
Holmes, G.A., 147
Holsey, Marcus M., 147
Holtzclaw, Timothy, 147
Hood, John Bell (Gen.), 39, 40, 44, 50, 55, 56, 61, 62
Hood's Division, 32, 40, 44, 55
Hooker, Joseph (Gen.), 39, 43, 62
Hooks, Green L., 147
Hooks, H.M., 147
Hopkins, Martin V., 147
House, John W., 147
House, Leiston, 148
Howard, Col. (CSA commander Ala. Brigade), 78
Howell, C.A., 111, 148
Howell, James H., 148
Howell, Joseph, M., 148
Howell, Thomas J., 148
Hoyler, C., 183
Hubbard, John W., 148
Hubbard, T. P., 148
Hubbard, William D., 110, 148
Hudson, David (Capt.), 110, 148
Hudson, J. C., 148
Hudson, J. S., 148
Hudson, J.H., 148
Hudson, James M., 148
Hudson, John S., 148
Hudson, M. (Sgt.), 110
Hudson, T. J., 148
Hudson, William D., 148
Hulme, Easton LaFayette, 148
Hulme, G.W., 148

Hulme, J.D., 112
Hulme, John D., 110, 149
Hulme, John H., 149
Humphrey, James M., 149
Humphrey, N. M., 149
Hunbun, James, 149
Hungerford, Thomas, 149
Hunt, Elijah, 149
Hunt, Sion W.H., 149
Hunt, W.J.C., 149
Hyman, Abram, 149
Hyman, Henry, 149

Isbell, Robert G., 149
Ivey, John W., 149
Ivey, Myrick, 149

Jackson, 16, 17, 32
Jackson, Frederick,
Jackson, John W., 149
Jackson, Joseph, 113, 149
Jackson, Matthew G., 149
Jackson, Thomas H. (Capt.), 27, 36, 150
Jackson, Thomas J. "Stonewall" (Gen.), 12, 17, 74
Jackson, William H., 111, 150
James, Alvin A., 113, 150
James, John, 110, 150
James River, 77, 78, 79, 80
Jenkins, E.P., 150
Jenkins, Micah (Gen.), 62, 65, 74
Jennings, James A., 150
Jesse, Thomas H., 150
Johnson, C.C., 150
Johnson, F.W.S., 111, 150
Johnson, James H., 150
Johnson, James W., 150
Johnson, John J., 111, 150
Johnson, Joseph E. (Gen.), 56, 91
Johnson, M., 183
Johnson, Michael, 150
Johnson, Robert H., 150
Johnson, Tapley B., 150
Johnson, Theophilus J., 150
Johnson, William, 150
Johnston, Joseph (Gen.), 9, 11
Jones, Benjamin, Jr., 111, 150
Jones, D.R., 3, 17, 21
Jones, J.W., 151
Jones, J.W., Sr. (Sgt.), 112
Jones, James, 150
Jones, James, Jr., 112

Jones, James A., 150
Jones, James W., Jr., 150
Jones, John, 110
Jones, John (Sgt.), 111
Jones, John H., 151
Jones, John M., 151
Jones, John P., 151
Jones, John S., 151
Jones, Joshua H., 151
Jones, Martin, 151
Jones, Moses J., 151
Jones, R.W., 151
Jones, William L., 151
Jones Division, 3
Jordan, Aaron, 151
Junkin, James (Lt.), 109, 151
Justice, Preston, 151

Keels, J., 151
Kendall, Levi, 151
Kendall, William R., 109, 151
Kerlin, David S., 151
Kershaw, Joseph B. (Gen.), 56, 90
Kesler, Phillip J., 151
King, John H., 152
King, John M., 152
King, Rufus, 152
King, William B., 152
Kinnebrew, Edward N., 152
Kinnebrew, William H., 152
Kirkpatrick, John K., 152
Knight, Andrew,, 152
Knight, Downs, 110, 152
Knight, Marcus A., 152
Knox, Michael, 152
Knoxville, Tennessee, 2, 5, 69, 70

Laird, J.P., 152
Lamar, LaFayette, 152
Lamar, LaFayette (Capt.), 2
Lamar, Lavoiscia L., 152
Landers, B.L., 111, 152
Lane, John A., 152
Langston, Junius C., 152
Langston, Shannon A., 152
Lary, J.H. (Cpl.), 111
Lary, James H., 152
Lary, John, 153
Lary, Jonathan, 111
Latimer, G.R., 153
Latimer, Mark, 153
Latimer, T.W., 153

Index

Latimer, Thomas H., 153
Latimer, Thomas H. (Capt.), 2
Lauglin, John, 153
Law, Evander M. (Gen.), 45, 56, 78
Law's Brigade, 40, 42, 57, 62
Lawrence, J.R., 153
Layfield, John, 153
Leach, James W., 153
Leach, W. C., 153
Lebanon Church, VA, 9
Lee, Robert E. (General), 11, 12, 16, 21, 31, 32, 39, 40, 41, 43, 44, 50, 55, 61, 71, 72, 74, 75, 76, 77, 80, 82, 84, 87, 91, 92, 109
Leesburg, Virginia, 21
Lester, T., 183
Leuth, J.S., 153
Leverett, Elijah, 153
Leverett, Hardy, 153
Lewis, Hamlin, 153
Lincoln, 21, 32
Lincoln County, 1
Linder, John, 153
Linder, Lee, 153
Lindsey, Joseph S., 153
Lindsey, W., 153
Linn, Joseph C., 153
Little, Col. (commander, 11th GA Regt.), 25, 78, 79
Little, Frank L., 153
Little, J. Wilber F., 153
Little, Wilber, 111
Little Round Top, 44, 50
Local Defense Forces, 76, 82
Lockart, Asa G., 153
Loehr, George, 154
Loflin, James A., 154
Loftin, James B.A., 154
Lofton, B. H., 2
Lofton, Bedford H., 154
Lofton, James H., 154
Logan, Thomas (Col., commander Hampton's Legion, SC), 63, 64
Longstreet, James (Gen.), 16, 17, 19, 21, 31, 39, 44, 55, 56, 61, 62, 65, 69, 70, 71, 72, 74, 76, 88, 92
Longstreet's Corps, 16, 17, 21, 32, 36, 39, 40, 41, 44, 56, 61, 69, 70, 71, 72, 77, 91, 92
Lookout Creek, 62
Lookout Mountain, 61
Lookout Valley, 5, 62, 69

Lotheridge, John H., 154
Lovett, W.J., 154
Lovingood, George, 110
Lovingood, George W., 154
Lovingood, Samuel J., 154
Lovingood, William L., 154
Lovit, James A., 154
Lucas, William, 154
Lucroy, Jesse M., 154
Lumpkin, Samuel J., 154
Lunceford, Thomas W., 109, 154
Lunsford, William P., 154
Lyles, James, 154
Lynchburg, 92
Lynchburg Stage Road, 92
Lyons, B.F., 154

Macon, 94
Madden, J.T., 154
Mahoney, Micajah L., 154
Mailey, J.M., 154
Mailey, Joseph R., 155
Mailey, Martin V., 155
Mailey, W. D., 155
Malvern Hill, 5, 13, 16, 77
Manassas, Virginia, 2, 3, 5, 17, 19
Manassas Gap, 3
Manassas Railroad, 19, 41
Manchester, Virginia, 37
Marchman, William L., 155
Marcum Station, 41
Marcus, Madison (Capt.), 83, 88
Marcus, Madison A., 155
Marcus, Madison J., 155
Marshall, Daniel P., 155
Marther, E., 183
Martin, Benjamin T., 111, 155
Martin, Judge (Capt.), 81
Martin, Luther H., 155
Martin, Luther H. (Capt.), 2
Martin, W.B., 155
Martin, W.G., 155
Martin, William Q., 155
Martin, William T., 155
Maryland, 16, 21, 37, 42, 71
Mason, Alfred, 113, 155
Mason, J.D., 155
Mason, James J., 155
Mason, Thomas K., 155
Massey, P.B., 183
Mathews, James F., 155
Mathews, William H., 156

Matthews, Charles W. (Lt. Col., commander, 17th GA Regt.), 58
Matthews, A.C., 156
Matthews, George B., 156
Matthews, J.F., 156
Matthews, James F., 114
Mattox, Hosea B., 113, 156
Mattox, Nathan M., 156
Mattox, William H., 156
Mattox, Z.H. Clark, 156
Mauldin, Benjamin W., 110, 156
Mauldin, Isaac N., 156
Mauldin, James F., 156
Maxwell, James K., 156
Mayre's Heights, 33
McArther, J.S., 183
McCall, John P., 156
McCarty, John T., 156
McClanhan, J.W., 110
McClellan, George B. (Gen.), 5, 9, 12, 21, 25, 31, 32
McClellan, Thorntotine P., 156
McClendon, William E., 156
McClesky, John (Pvt.), 11
McCluskey, John, 156
McConnel, J.P., 183
McCook, B. Franklin, 156
McCook, Dawson, 157
McCord, Elisha A., 112, 157
McCord, James A. (Sgt.), 112, 157
McCord, John W., 157
McCormigh, S., 157
McCullum, A. Cyrus, 157
McDaniel, Elbert C., 157
McDaniel, Solomon G., 157
McDonald, John W., 157
McDougald, William M., 157
McFarland, D.S., 157
McFarland, James, 157
McFarland, Thomas A., 110, 157
McFarland, William, 157
McGregor, John A. (Capt., commander, Co. E, 17th GA Regt.), 26
McGregor, Adolphus, 157
McGregor, William L., 157
McIntosh, William M. (Col.), 1, 11, 12, 13, 157
McLanahan, J.W., 157
McLaw, Lafayette (Gen.), 47, 62, 69
McLaw's division, 55
McLendon, Isaac A., 157
McLewis, ___ (Capt.), 58

McMurray, Madison M., 158
McWhorter, Jesse, 158
Meade, George (Gen.), 43, 44, 72
Meadows, William T., 158
Mechanicsville, Virginia, 71
Medlock, George B., 158
Medlock, James E., 114, 158
Mibbard, W.P., 183
Michie, Junius, 158
Middlebrooks, George C., 158
Middlebrooks, Henry C., 109, 158
Middlebrooks, J.T., 158
Middleway, Virginia, 42
Miles, Nelson (Gen.), 92
Millican, William T. (Col.), 2, 12, 13, 20, 22, 26, 27, 32, 158
Missionary Ridge, 61
Mitchell, D.J., 158
Mitchell, Ephraim, 158
Mitchell, James A., 111, 158
Mitchell, James H., 158
Mitchell, Roland, 158
Mitchell, Wiley T., 110, 158
Mitchell, William E., 158
Mobley, Isaac M., 158
Monk, R. A., 158
Moody, D.M., 183
Moon, J.M., 110
Moon, John S., 158
Moon, Joseph M., 159
Moon, William H., 159
Moon, William P., 159
Moore, Albert, 159
Moore, Charles R., 159
Moore, Ebenezer I., 159
Moore, James A., 159
Moore, Lucius A., 159
Moore, R.F., 113, 159
Moore, Thomas P., 159
Moore, W.P., 111, 159
Moore, William M., 159
Moran, William B., 159
Morris, James F., 110, 159
Morris, Peter, 159
Morris Creek Station, 3
Morristown, 3, 70
Moulder, William J., 159
Mule Shoe, 75
Mullally, John T., 159
Mullikin, Felix L., 159
Mumford, Daniel R., 112, 159
Mumford, Robert D., 112, 159

Index

Murden, John M., 160
Murden, Mack H., 160
Murden, Redmon S., 160
Murrah, Benjamin, 160
Murrah, John W., 160
Murray, William T., 112, 160
Musgrove, Joseph E., 160
Myers, Aaron, 160

Napoleon's Old Guard, 38
Nash, Henry H., 160
Nash, J. B., 160
Nash, J. C., 160
Neel, Charles M., 114, 160
Neel, J.H., 160
Neel, William S., 160
Nelms, David L., 160
Nelms, Vandiver C., 112, 160
Nelson, George W., 160
Nelson, John W., 160
New Hope Church, 92
New Market, 5, 79, 80, 81, 83
New York regiments, 83
Newsom, G.B., 160
Nichols, George T., 160
Ninth USCT Regiment, 83
Norfolk, 10
Norman, Elijah B., 113, 161
Norman, George W., 161
Norman, Isaac W., 161
Norman, J.L., 110
Norman, James J., 161
Norman, John H., 112, 161
Norman, John L., 161
Norman, John S., 161
Norman, Peyton S., 161
Norman, Thomas B., 161
Norman, William L., 161
North Anna River, 75
North Carolina, 36, 39, 91
Norwood, Levi M., 161
Nunn, Uriah W., 161

Oak Grove, 12
Obarr, J. Hezekiah, 161
Obarr, Whitner, 161
Ogilvie, James S., 161
Oglesby, Jefferson C., 162
Oglethorpe Barracks, 1
Old Rock (Benning), 39, 71, 94
Oliver, J.D., 162
Oliver, John A., 162

Orange and Alexandria railroad, 72
Orange Court House, 9, 40
Orange Plank Road, 72
Orange-Fredericksburg Turnpike, 72
Ord, Edward O.C. (Gen.), 80, 81, 82
Ordinance of Secession, 38
Orrie, Louis, 162
Owens, Asher L., 162
Owens, Francis E., 162
Owens, William D., 162

Pace, George A. (Capt.), 13, 110, 162
Page, John O., 162
Pannell, Abraham, 162
Paris, Virginia, 41
Parker, James P., 162
Parker, Joseph H., 162
Parker, Mason E., 162
Parker, William T., 162
Parks, John K., 162
Parks, Lewis, 162
Parnell, A., 162
Parnell, John R., 162
Parrott, A.B., 162
Partridge, William J., 109, 163
Pascal, William Cobb, 163
Pascal, William O., 163
Pasnett, H.H., 163
Patterson, Wiley W., 163
Payne, Asa S., 163
Payne, James M., 163
Payne, John, 110
Payne, John B., 163
Payne, John W., 163
Peak, G. A., 163
Pearman, C.C., 163
Pearman, Weldon C., 163
Pearson, George W., 163
Peck, Josiah S., 163
Peeler, G.R., 163
Pegg, Leander M., 163
Pendley, J.H., 163
Peninsula Campaign, 9, 13, 16
Pennsylvania, 21, 43, 71
Pennsylvania regiments, 83
Pensacola, Florida, 1
Perrin, William B., 163
Perry, Herman H. (Capt.), 35, 58, 90
Perryman, J.A., 163
Petersburg, Virginia, 5, 55, 75, 76, 77, 78, 80, 87, 88, 91
Phillips House, 81

Pickens, John, 163
Pickett, George, 44
Piedmont pike, 41
Pierce, Lovick, Jr., (Lt.), 49, 109, 163
Pinkston, H.B., 114, 164
Pinkston, William, 111
Pinkston, William T., 164
Pledger, S.L., 113
Pledger, Simeon L., 164
Pledger, William P., 164
Plum Run Valley, 50
Point Lookout, Maryland, 93
Pond Mountain, 17
Pool, William R. (Capt.), 2, 164
Pope, 17
Portsmouth, 10
Potomac River, 21, 31, 42
Powers, John, 164
Prather, Thomas Z., 109, 164
Prescott, William H., 164
Prewitt, W.H., 164
Price, B.G., 183
Price, Laneston H., 164
Price's house, 12
Psalmonds, Thomas H. (Sgt.), 109, 164
Pullen, E. B., 164
Pullen, Elijah B., 164
Pullen, J.D., 164
Pullen, John M., 164
Pullen, John T., 164
Pullen, William G., 164
Pulliam, Francis M., 164
Pulliam, John, 165
Pulliam, Mathew E., 165
Pulliam, Nathan B., 165

Quinn, Leonidas W., 165
Quinn, William A. Jr., 165

Rachels, John L., 165
Racoon Ford, 16, 40
Rapidan River, 16, 17, 40, 50, 72
Rappahannock River, 9, 17, 32, 34, 39, 40
Ray, A. J., 165
Ray, James A., 165
Ray, John T., 165
Ray, William R., 114, 165
Redfiern, Andrew, 114
Redfiern, E.W., 114, 165
Redfiern, James, 114, 165
Redfiern, W. Andrew, 165
Reed, W.A.P., 165

Reese, Columbus, 165
Reeves, Jesse, 111, 165
Reid, Felix C. (Sgt.), 111, 165
Reid, Jabez M., 165
Reid, William W., 166
Remsen, James B. (Sgt.), 112, 166
Remsen, Rem, 112, 166
Remsen, Thomas H., 112, 166
Reynolds, David S., 166
Reynolds, James R., 111, 166
Reynolds, John, 166
Reynolds, William, 114
Reynolds, William James, 166
Rhodes, Greenberry B., 109, 166
Rhodes, Robert M., 166
Rhodes, Simeon, 166
Rhodes, William H., 166
Richardson, J.M., 166
Richmond, 5, 9, 10, 11, 12, 16, 32, 35, 36, 37, 39, 55, 71, 72, 75, 76, 77, 78, 79, 80, 81, 82, 84, 87, 89, 91, 92, 93
Richmond Enquirer, 78, 79
Ricketson, William S., 166
Rickett's Division (U.S.), 17
Rigsby, William, 166
Ringgold, Georgia, 56
Ritchie, A. C., 166
Roberson, J.A.P., 167
Roberson, William (Chaplain), 113
Roberson, William F., 167
Roberson, Wingfield, 167
Roberson, Wingfield (Lt.), 113
Roberts, Edward M., 110, 167
Roberts, J.B., 183
Roberts, T.E., 167
Roberts, William H., 167
Robertson, 62
Robertson, James (Gen.), 56, 57, 64
Robertson, G.C., 167
Rock brigade, 88
Rocker, Charles J., 167
Rocky Hill, 90
Roe, C.W.G., 167
Roe, Samuel L. (Cpl.), 78, 167
Roebuck, Robert C.C., 167
Rogers, J.C., 111, 167
Rogers, William, 183
Rohrersville, 22
Rose, A. J., 167
Rosecrans, William (Gen.), 55, 56, 61, 62, 69
Roster of Fifteenth Georgia, 183

Index

Roster of Paroles at Appomattox, 109
Roster of the 15th Georgia Infantry Regiment, 115
Round Top, 44
Rowland, G.M., 167
Rowland, W., 167
Rowland, W.H., 167
Rowland, William, 167
Rowzee, Theodore F. (Sgt.), 112, 167
Rucker, Alexander, 167
Ruff, James C., 167
Ruff, Martin, 110, 167
Rumbley, William R., 167
Ruskin, J.G., 168
Russell, David A., 109, 168

Sale, Hickerson M., 168
Sale, Thomas S., 168
Sammons, Benjamin F., 110, 168
Sands, S.W., 183
Sane, W., 183
Sasnett, H. H., 168
Sasnett, William Pembroke, 168
Saunders, S.D., 168
Savannah, 1
Sawyer, J., 183
Saylers Creek, 91
Scarborough, Frederick B., 168
Scarborough, William B., 168
Scott, Hartwell G., 168
Scott, J.A., 114, 168
Scott, Noah, 109, 168
Scott, Oscar, 114
Scott, Oscar D., 168
Scott, Winfield (General), 5
Seago, Eli M. (Lt. Col., commander, 10th GA Regt.), 58
Seals, Henry B., 168
Seals, William D., 168
Second Corps, 72
Second Georgia Regiment, 22, 23, 25, 35, 58, 82
Second Manassas, 19, 20, 93
Second Regiment, 22, 23, 25, 32, 56
Second Wisconsin Regiment, 36
Seidel, Charles W., 168
Seven Days Campaign, 12
Seventeenth Georgia regiment, 3, 17, 22, 25, 26, 32, 33, 38, 56, 58, 65, 79, 81, 82
Seventh Georgia Regiment, 13
Seventh USCT Regiment, 83

Sewell, Snencer, 168
Sewell, William F., 110, 169
Seymour, Marshall M., 169
Shannon, ____ (Major), 36, 58
Shannon, James D.,
Shannon, John H., 169
Shannon, John L., 169
Shannon, John M., 169
Shannon, Peter J. (Maj.), 19, 20, 32, 74, 109, 169
Shannon, Thomas E., 169
Shannon, William D., 169
Shannon, William J., 169
Sharp, A.D., 169
Sharp, J.H., 169
Sharp, Levi L., 169
Sharp, Thomas J., 169
Sharpsburg, 5, 20, 21, 22, 31, 35, 37
Shenandoah River, 42
Shenandoah Valley, 3, 12, 41
Sheperd, William S. (Lt. Col., commander 2nd GA Regt.), 58
Sheperdstown, 25
Sheridan, 92
Sherman, William T. (Gen.), 62, 70, 80, 88, 90, 91, 93
Sherman's army, 89, 94
Shirley, J.D., 169
Shirley, Joel M., 169
Shirley, William M., 169
Shoe, J.C., 62
Shoemodder, W., 170
Shumate, John D., 170
Simmons, Charles, E., 170
Simmons, J.C., 109
Simmons, William, 111
Simmons, William H., 170
Simmons. J. Clarence, 170
Simmons. Marcellus A., 170
Simpson, E.W., 170
Simpson, Edward, 170
Simpson, Leonard K, 170
Sims, James R., 170
Sims, John J., 170
Sims, William B., 170
Sink, W.A., 170
Skrine, Eugene A., 170
Slack, Luke R. (Cpl.), 109, 170
Slay, G. F., 170
Slay, James T., 170
Sligh, S., 58
Smith, A.J., 170

Smith, Andrew, 170
Smith, Daniel C., 170
Smith, Francis W., 171
Smith, Franklin, 171
Smith, G.W., 171
Smith, George, 171
Smith, Henley G., 171
Smith, Henry F., 171
Smith, I.T., 111, 171
Smith, I.W, 183
Smith, James W., 110, 171
Smith, John H., 171
Smith, John L., 171
Smith, Joseph T. (Capt.), 2, 171
Smith, T. B., 171
Smith, T. J. (Major), 13
Smith, Theophilus J. (Capt.), 2, 171
Smith, Thomas S., 111, 171
Smith, W.T., 110
Smith, William P., 171
Smith, William T., 171
Smith, William W., 171
Snellings, George W., 171
Snellings, Peter P., 172
Snellinos, William H., 172
Snicker's ford, 42
Snipes, W.W., 172
Snipes. L.G., 172
Sorrow, M.H., 172
Sorrow, McKenzie, 172
Sorrow, Stinson P., 172
Sorrow, Terrell T., 172
South Mountain, 21
Sparta, 89, 93
Spotsylvania, 5, 74, 75
Spratling, Henry (Sergeant), 109
Spratling, Henry E., 172
Spratling, Henry G., 172
Spratling, James M., 172
Spratling, Johnson M., 172
Spratling, William J., 172
Stafford, John, 172
Starr, Alfred N., 172
Starr, James, 172
Starrett, Benjamin F., 172
Starrett, William S., 172
Steadman, Levi, 172
Steed, Adoniram J., 112, 172
Stephens, Linton (Lt. Col.), 1, 172
Stephens. John A., 172
Stephenson, Alexander W., 172
Stephenson, David L., 173

Stephenson, Joseph W., 173
Stephenson, Newton W. (Cpl.), 112, 173
Stewart, G.M., 173
Stewart, Thomas J., 173
Stokes, J. S., 173
Stone, Jesse David, 173
Stone, Robert G., 114, 173
Stone, W.H., 173
Stone Bridge, 22
Story, Lewellyn, 173
Stovall, George M., 173
Stovall, J.B., 173
Stovall, J.C., 110, 173
Stovall, Job H., 173
Stovall, Josiah T., 173
Stratten, Alexander H., 173
Stribling, Francis H., 173
Stribling, Isaac N. (Sgt.), 109, 173
Stribling, J.M., 173
Stribling, Micajah L., 109, 173
Stribling, Thomas M., 174
Stuart, J.E.B. (General), 12, 16
Suffolk, Virginia, 10, 36, 39
Sullivan, James, 174
Supreme Court of Georgia, 38
Sutton, Moses G., 174
Sweetwater, Tennessee, 69
Swint, Edmund (Cpl.), 111, 174
Sykes, William A. Epps, 174

Taliaferro County, 1
Tate, Edmund B., Jr., 174
Tate, Enos R., 174
Tate, Jasper S. (Cpl.), 110, 174
Tate, W. T., 174
Tatum, William P., 112, 174
Taylor, Columbus W., 174
Taylor, J.J., 174
Taylor, James L., 174
Taylor, James M., 174
Taylor, John H.C., 174
Taylor, William C., 111, 174
Taylor, William T., 174
Taylor, Zachary B., 112, 174
Teague, John, 110, 175
Teasley, Alfred J., 113, 175
Tebow, John, 175
Tenent, William, 113
Tennent, Henry A., 175
Tennent, Orville T., 175
Tennent, William C., 175
Terry, James J., 175

Index

Terry, John W., 175
Terry, W.A.J., 175
Terry, William T., 175
Texans, 81, 83
Texas Brigade, 40, 46, 80, 81, 82, 84, 87
Third Corps, 72
Thirteenth New Jersey Regiment, 35
Thomas, Henry, 175
Thomas, Thomas W. (Col., commander 15th GA Regt.), 1, 3, 12, 175
Thomas, William A., 175
Thomas, William M., 175
Thomasson, James C., 175
Thomasson, John F., 175
Thomaston, Matthew D., 175
Thompson, Frederick T., 175
Thompson, J.M., 175
Thompson, James B. (Sgt.), 49
Thompson, John P., 175
Thornton, Mallory J., 175
Thoroughfare Gap, 5, 17, 20
Thrasher, Clark Tyrell, 176
Thrasher, H., 176
Thrasher, L. H., 176
Thrasher, T.J., 176
Thrasher, Tyrrel, 176
Tidewater Virginia, 9
Tilley, John (Lt.), 11
Tilley, John M., 176
Tollard, William A., 176
Tolly, H., 176
Toombs, Robert (Gen.), 1, 11, 12, 13, 16, 19, 20, 22, 24, 25, 26, 27, 31, 34, 35, 37, 38, 71, 94
Toombs Brigade, 3, 9, 16, 17, 21, 22, 33
Treadwell, Terry, 176
Trout, J.M., 176
Turman, George E., 176
Turman. Thomas M., 176
Twentieth Regiment, 3, 20, 22, 23, 24, 26, 32, 33, 56, 57, 58, 79, 82, 83

U.S. Army Airborne and Ranger Schools, 94
U.S. Army Infantry Center, 94
Union cavalry, 16, 43, 87, 88
Union colored troops, 81
Union I Corps, 22
Union II Corps, 22
Union prisoners, 93
Union prisons, 71
Union XII Corps, 22

Unionists, 42
University of Georgia, 38
University of Virginia, 3
Upperville, 41
Ussery, H., 176

Valley Forge, 3
Valley of Death, 50
Varina Road, 80
Vasser, George L., 176
Vaughn, A.W., 176
Vaughn, James P., 176
Vaughn, Joshua, 176
Vaughn, Peter D., 176
Vaughn, Samuel, 176
Veal, J.M., 176
Veazey, Prior G., 111, 177
Vest, Alfred W., 177
VI Corps, 92
Vickery, Charles E., 177
Vickery, James Percy (Sgt.), 113, 177
Vicksburg, 40

Waddell, James D (Col., commander 2nd GA Regt.), 58
Wade, J.A.C., 177
Wade, W.G., 177
Wagner, Joseph, 177
Walker, L., 177
Wall, John T., 177
Waller, Benjamin, 177
Waller, George L., 177
Waller, William A., 111, 177
Walseman, William, 112, 177
Walters, B.W.,
Walters, Dean W., 177
Walters, Franklin, 177
Walters, Henry Freeman, 177
Walters, J.G., 177
Walters, John F., 178
Walters, Joseph Charles, 178
Walters, W. R. (Lt.), 78
Walters, William R., 178
Wanslev, William J., 178
Ward, Thomas, 178
Ware, Robert, 4, 50, 93
Ware, Robert Andrews, 178
Ware, Thomas L. (Sgt.), 2, 3, 4, 10, 11, 16, 34, 36, 39, 40, 41, 42, 43, 44, 49, 50, 93, 178
Ware, William S., 112, 178
Warren, Gouverneur K. (Gen.), 75

Warren, Epps, 178
Warren, H.G., 178
Warren, Thomas J., 111, 178
Warrenton, Va., 32, 183
Warthen, David D. (Sgt.), 113, 178
Warthen, George W., 178
Warthen, William T., 178
Washington, A., 178
Washington, Georgia, 31, 94
Watkins, John R., 178
Wauhatchie, Tennessee, 62, 65
Weaver, Henry C., 178
Webb, Andrew J., 112, 178
Webb, John C., 179
Webb, Martin, 113, 179
Welban, Elijah J., 179
Wells, Jeremiah S., 179
Wells, William, 179
West, A.A., 179
West, William H., 179
West Point, 31
West Point, Virginia, 10
West Point (ship), 9
Westbrook, Samuel D., 179
Westbrook. Thomas S., 179
Wharton, T.R., 179
Wheatley, Ezra, 179
Wheatley, Greenberry, 179
Wheatley, Leonard P., 109, 179
Wheatley, O., 179
Wheatley, Timothy, 179
Wheelis, David M., 179
Wheland, John, 114, 179
White, Alexander, 179
White, Alfred, 183
White, Archibald L., 179
White, George, 111, 180
White, J., 180
White, Luke H., 180
White, M.D., 180
White, N.A., 180
White, T., 180
White, Tinsley R., 113, 180
White, William B., 180
Wilderness, 5, 72, 79
Wiley, Samuel H. (Pvt.), 2, 4, 88, 89, 93, 111, 180
Wiley, Sylvanus G., 180
Wilkes County, 1

Wilkins, F. M., 180
Wilkins, Judas L., 180
Williams, George T., 109, 180
Williams, J., 180
Williams, William W., 180
Williams, Y., 183
Williamsburg Road, 10
Williamson, T.J., 183
Williamsport, 22, 25, 42
Willingham, John C., 180
Willis, Alice, 36
Willis, Anna, 36
Willis, Ennis, 109, 180
Willis, J.H., 180, 183
Willis, James H., 180
Willis, Richard M.M., 180
Willis, Thomas B., 181
Willis, William J., 181
Willis, William W., 181
Wilson, Benjamin C., 181
Winchester, 31
Winchester pike, 41
Windle, S.N., 183
Wofford's Brigade, 90
Wood, J., 183
Wood, William R., 181
Woodruff, James W., 109, 111, 181
Wright, Ambrose (Gen., brigade commander Anderson's Div.), 20
Wright, A., 181
Wright, Francis M., 181
Wright, James, 181
Wright, John T., 181
Wright, Joseph B., 114, 181
Wright, S. B. H., 181
Wright, T.G., 113, 181
Wvnn, Samuel, 181

XVIII Corps, 82

Yarborough, J.J., 181
Yates, Elisha, 181
Yorktown, 9, 10, 11, 37
Youngblood, C.J., 183
Yow, Thomas Anderson, 182

Zachary, David, 65

ABOUT THE AUTHOR

J. DAVID DAMERON JR. was born in Washington D.C. and raised in Virginia. He holds advanced degrees in History and Education and he is an alumnus of Campbell University, the University of North Carolina and Troy State University. He is also a graduate of the U.S. Army, John F. Kennedy Special Warfare School, where he specialized in Unconventional Warfare. He is a combat veteran and served in the Special Forces. With twenty-four years of federal service, Dave now works as a civilian research specialist in the Concepts and Analysis Division of the U.S. Army Infantry Center, Fort Benning, Georgia. Dave serves on several museum history advisory committees and he has authored several articles as well as non-fiction history books, which include *A History and Roster of the Fifteenth Georgia, General Henry Lewis Benning, King's Mountain: The Defeat of the Loyalists*, and a forthcoming biography of Horace King. He is a member of the Veterans of Foreign Wars, the American Legion, the Special Forces "Decade" Association, and the Organization of American Historians. Dave is married to the former Pamela Gail Brown of Kingsport, Tennessee, and they have two children, Kevin and Christina.

www.ingramcontent.com/pod-product-compliance
Lightning Source LLC
Chambersburg PA
CBHW050142170426
43197CB00011B/1930